W9-CFM-279

# CliffsTestPrep™

## LSAT®

## 5TH EDITION

*by*

*Peter Z Orton, PhD*

*Contributing Authors*

Rajiv Rimal, PhD

Thomas P. Wolfe, PhD

Rich Michaels, MA

Howard Horwitz, MA

Wiley Publishing, Inc.

## About the Author

Dr. Peter Z Orton (BA, Princeton; M Ed, Harvard; PhD, Stanford) is a former lecturer, instructor, and developer of test preparation programs at universities, colleges, and law schools. His materials have been used in LSAT preparation programs for more than 15 years. Dr. Orton has written and directed four films on test preparation distributed nationally through Churchill Films.

## Author's Acknowledgments

The author would like to thank his original Cliffs editor, Michele Spence, for her fine editing. He would also like to thank Hungry Minds editor Kathleen Dobie for her careful attention to the production process. Thanks are also extended to Dr. Ken Held, Dean of La Verne College of Law, for permission to use excerpts from the school's Law Reviews.

The author would also like to thank his parents, Williams and Esta Orton, for their support and love through the years.

## Publisher's Acknowledgments

### Editorial

**Project Editor:** Kathleen A. Dobie

**Acquisitions Editor:** Gregory W. Tubach

**Copy Editor:** Corey Dalton

**Technical Editor:** Michele Spence

### Production

**Proofreader:** Joel K. Draper

Wiley Indianapolis Composition Services

**CliffsTestPrep™ LSAT® 5th Edition**

Published by:
**Wiley Publishing, Inc.**
909 Third Avenue
New York, NY 10022
www.wiley.com

Copyright © 2001 Peter Z Orton.

Published by Wiley Publishing, Inc., New York, NY
Published simultaneously in Canada

Library of Congress Control Number: 2001024793

ISBN: 0-7645-6395-5

Printed in the United States of America

10 9 8 7 6 5

**Note:** If you purchased this book without a cover, you should be aware that this book is stolen property. It was reported as "unsold and destroyed" to the publisher, and neither the author nor the publisher has received any payment for this "stripped book."

LIMIT OF LIABILITY/DISCLAIMER OF WARRANTY: THE PUBLISHER AND AUTHOR HAVE USED THEIR BEST EFFORTS IN PREPARING THIS BOOK. THE PUBLISHER AND AUTHOR MAKE NO REPRESENTATIONS OR WARRANTIES WITH RESPECT TO THE ACCURACY OR COMPLETENESS OF THE CONTENTS OF THIS BOOK AND SPECIFICALLY DISCLAIM ANY IMPLIED WARRANTIES OF MERCHANTABILITY OR FITNESS FOR A PARTICULAR PURPOSE. THERE ARE NO WARRANTIES WHICH EXTEND BEYOND THE DESCRIPTIONS CONTAINED IN THIS PARAGRAPH. NO WARRANTY MAY BE CREATED OR EXTENDED BY SALES REPRESENTATIVES OR WRITTEN SALES MATERIALS. THE ACCURACY AND COMPLETENESS OF THE INFORMATION PROVIDED HEREIN AND THE OPINIONS STATED HEREIN ARE NOT GUARANTEED OR WARRANTED TO PRODUCE ANY PARTICULAR RESULTS, AND THE ADVICE AND STRATEGIES CONTAINED HEREIN MAY NOT BE SUITABLE FOR EVERY INDIVIDUAL. NEITHER THE PUBLISHER NOR AUTHOR SHALL BE LIABLE FOR ANY LOSS OF PROFIT OR ANY OTHER COMMERCIAL DAMAGES, INCLUDING BUT NOT LIMITED TO SPECIAL, INCIDENTAL, CONSEQUENTIAL, OR OTHER DAMAGES.

Note: This book is intended to offer general information on the LSAT. The author and publisher are not engaged in rendering legal, tax, accounting, investment, real estate, or similar professional services. Although legal, tax, accounting, investment, real estate, and similar issues addressed by this book have been checked with sources believed to be reliable, some material may be affected by changes in the laws and/or interpretation of laws since the manuscript in this book was completed. Therefore, the accuracy and completeness of the information provided herein and the opinions that have been generated are not guaranteed or warranted to produce particular results, and the strategies outlined in this book may not be suitable for every individual. If legal, accounting, tax, investment, real estate, or other expert advice is needed or appropriate, the reader is strongly encouraged to obtain the services of a professional expert.

**Trademarks:** Wiley, the Wiley Publishing logo, Cliffs, CliffsNotes, CliffsAP, CliffsComplete, CliffsTestPrep, CliffsQuickReview, CliffsNote-a-Day, and all related logos and trade dress are registered trademarks or trademarks of Wiley Publishing, Inc., in the United States and other countries. All other trademarks are the property of their respective owners. Wiley Publishing, Inc. is not associated with any product or vendor mentioned in this book.

For general information on our other products and services or to obtain technical support, please contact our Customer Care Department within the U.S. at 800-762-2974, outside the U.S. at 317-572-3993, or fax 317-572-4002.

Wiley also published its books in a variety of electronic formats. Some content that appears in print may not be available in electronic books.

# Table of Contents

## PART I: INTRODUCTION

## PART II: ANALYSIS OF EXAM AREAS

# PART III: THREE FULL-LENGTH PRACTICE TESTS

# Preface

**Your LSAT score can make the difference! And thorough preparation helps you do your best!**

This LSAT study guide is direct, precise, and easy to use. The comprehensive test preparation program can be carefully completed in a reasonable time and provides everything you need to do your best on the LSAT. The strategies and materials presented in this guide have been researched, tested, and evaluated in actual LSAT preparation classes.

This guide also features the PATTERNED PLAN OF ATTACK for each section, focusing on

1. The ability tested
2. The basic skills necessary
3. Understanding directions
4. Analysis of directions
5. Suggested approach with samples
6. Practice-review-analyze-practice

This LSAT study guide includes three complete LSAT practice exams—similar to the actual LSAT in question types and time allotments—with answers and in-depth explanations.

*CliffsTestPrep LSAT* was written to give you maximum return on your investment of study time. Follow the study guide checklist and work through this book systematically. It will give you the edge to do your best.

# Study Guide Checklist

❑ 1. Read the LSAT Information Bulleting and Sample Test included in your Registration Packet.

❑ 2. Become familiar with the Test Format, page 3.

❑ 3. Familiarize yourself with the with the answers to Questions Commonly Asked about the LSAT, page 4.

❑ 4. Learn the techniques of Two Successful Overall Approaches, page 5.

❑ 5. Carefully read Part II: Analysis of Exam Areas, beginning on page 7.

❑ 6. Strictly observing time allotments, take Practice Test 1, section by section (review answers after each section), beginning on page 111.

❑ 7. Check your answers and analyze your results, beginning on page 161.

❑ 8. Fill out the Tally Sheet for Problems Missed to pinpoint your mistakes, page 162.

❑ 9. While referring to each item of Practice Test 1, study ALL the Answers and Complete Explanations, beginning on page 163.

❑ 10. Review as necessary the Analysis of Exam Areas, beginning on page 7.

❑ 11. Strictly observing time allotments, take Practice Test 2, section by section (review answers after each section), beginning on page 179.

❑ 12. Check your answers and analyze your results, beginning on page 227.

❑ 13. Fill out the Tally Sheet for Problems Missed to pinpoint your mistakes, page 228.

❑ 14. While referring to each item of Practice Test 2, study ALL the Answers and Complete Explanations, beginning on page 229.

❑ 15. Take Practice Test 3 (beginning on page 243) in its entirety and at one sitting, following time allotments carefully. Follow with a review of all test answers, beginning on page 295.

❑ 16. Carefully reread Part II: Analysis of Exam Areas, beginning on page 7.

❑ 17. Go over Final Preparation, page 308.

# PART I

# INTRODUCTION

# Introduction

| Format of the LSAT Exam | | | |
|---|---|---|---|
| **Section** | **Subject Area (Order Will Vary)** | **Time** | **Number of Questions** |
| I | Reading Comprehension | 35 minutes | 26–28 |
| II | Analytical Reasoning | 35 minutes | 22–24 |
| III | Logical Reasoning | 35 minutes | 24–26 |
| IV | Logical Reasoning | 35 minutes | 24–26 |
| V | Experimental | 35 minutes | varies |
| | Essay | 30 minutes | |

**Total time: 205 minutes (which includes 1/2 hour for writing the essay)**

**Approximately 125 questions (96–104 questions count toward your score)**

Important Note: The order in which the sections appear and the number of questions in each section will vary because there are several forms of the LSAT. *The experimental section may appear at any point in the test* and will probably repeat one of the common sections. The experimental section does not count toward your score.

## General Description

The LSAT consists of 175 minutes of multiple-choice questions plus a 30-minute unscored essay. All multiple-choice questions are of equal value. The test is scored from 120 to 180. The sections are

- Reading Comprehension—You will answer questions about reading passages. No legal or special knowledge is necessary and referring back to the passage is permitted.

- Analytical Reasoning—You will derive information and deduce spatial and other relationships from groups of conditions or statements.

- Logical Reasoning—You will derive logical conclusions and relationships from a variety of situations and passages.

- Essay—You will write an essay on a topic provided. The essay will not be graded, but a copy will be sent with your test score to your prospective law schools.

These sections and the essay question will require no specific knowledge from any specialized course or courses. They purport to measure your reading, reasoning, and analytical skills. Remember, no formal background in law is required or necessary.

# Questions Commonly Asked About the Exam

**Q: Who administers the LSAT?**

**A:** The Law School Admission Test is administered by Law School Admission Services, Inc. If you wish any information not covered in this book, write to Law School Admission Services, Box 2000, Newton, PA, 18940.

**Q: Can I take the LSAT more than once?**

**A:** You may repeat the LSAT, but it can only be taken three times in a two-year period. Also, be advised that your prospective law school(s) will receive all your scores, along with the average of those scores.

**Q: What materials may I bring to the LSAT?**

**A:** Bring your admission ticket/identification card, positive identification (with picture, descriptive information, and so forth), a watch, three or four sharpened Number 2 pencils, and a good eraser. A pen for writing the essay will be provided at the exam. You may not bring scratch paper or books. You may plan your essay using the scratch paper provided and rely on the space provided in the test booklet for scratch work during the objective test.

**Q: If necessary, may I cancel my score?**

**A:** Yes. You may cancel your score by notifying the test center supervisor on the day of the test or by sending a mailgram to LSAS within five days of the test date. Your LSAT score report will note that you have canceled a score and have seen the test questions.

**Q: Should I guess on the LSAT?**

**A:** Yes. There is no penalty for guessing on the LSAT. Before taking a wild guess, remember that eliminating one or more of the choices increases your chances of choosing the right answer.

**Q: How should I prepare for the LSAT?**

**A:** Because knowledge of particular subject matter is not necessary for the LSAT, the mastery of test-taking strategies will contribute most successfully to a good score. Courses involving critical thinking, reading comprehension, writing, and simple logic can also be helpful.

**Q: When is the LSAT administered?**

**A:** The LSAT is administered four times during the school year, in October, December, February, and June. Three of these administrations will probably occur on Saturday mornings, beginning at 8:30 a.m., and one administration may occur on a Monday afternoon (usually the June administration).

**Q: Where is the LSAT administered?**

**A:** The LSAT is administered at a number of colleges and universities worldwide. A list of testing centers is included in the LSAT/LSDAS Registration Packet, published by LSAS.

**Q: How and when should I register?**

**A:** Complete registration materials are included in the LSAT/LSAC Registration Packet, available free at the Office of Testing at your university or from most law schools. There are three ways to register: online, by telephone, by mail. The Registration/Information Packet carefully explains each method. You should register at least five weeks prior to the exam date.

**Q: What is LSDAS?**

**A:** The Law School Data Assembly Service collects the necessary information for your application to law school, arranges it into the standardized format preferred by many law schools, and mails it upon the applicant's request. Registration material for the LSDAS is provided in the LSAT/LSDAS Registration Packet.

# Taking the LSAT: Two Successful Overall Approaches

Many who take the LSAT don't get their best score because they spend too much time dwelling on hard questions, leaving insufficient time to answer the easy questions they can get right. Don't let this happen to you. Use the following system to mark your answer sheet:

## I. The "Plus-Minus" Strategy

1. Answer easy questions immediately.

2. Place a "+" in your question booklet next to problems that seem solvable but are too time consuming; mark a guess on your answer sheet and go on to the next question.

3. Place a "–" in your question booklet next to any problem that seems impossible. Then take a guess on your answer sheet and move on.

Act quickly. Don't waste time deciding whether a problem is a "+" or "–". And always record an answer on your answer sheet before you move on to the next question, even if you're just guessing.

After working all the problems you can do immediately, go back and work your "+" problems. If you finish them, try your "–" problems (sometimes when you come back to a problem that seemed impossible, you will suddenly realize how to solve it).

Your question booklet should look something like this after you finish working the easy questions:

    1.

+2.

    3.

–4.

+5.

**Remember:** You do not have to erase the pluses and minuses you made on your *question booklet*. And be sure to fill in all your answer spaces—if necessary, with a guess. Because there is no penalty for wrong answers, leaving an answer space blank makes no sense. And, of course, remember that you may work in only one section of the test at a time.

## II. The Elimination Strategy

Take advantage of being allowed to mark in the testing booklet. As you eliminate an incorrect answer choice from consideration, mark it out in your question booklet as in the following example:

(A̶)

?(B)

(C̶)

(D̶)

?(E)

Notice that some choices that aren't crossed out are marked with question marks, signifying that they are possible answers. This technique will help you avoid reconsidering those choices you have already eliminated and will help you narrow down your possible answers.

These marks in your *testing booklet* need not be erased.

# PART II

# ANALYSIS OF EXAM AREAS

# Introduction to Reading Comprehension

You're allowed 35 minutes to complete the Reading Comprehension section, which typically contains four passages and 26 to 28 questions.

## Ability Tested

This section tests your ability to understand, interpret, and analyze reading passages on a variety of topics.

## Basic Skills Necessary

Readers who can quickly grasp a passage's main ideas, supporting points, and author's perspective do well on this section.

## Directions

Each passage in this section is followed by questions based only on what is *stated* or *implied* in the passage. Choose the best answer to each question, realizing that the correct answer may not necessarily always be a "perfect" answer, but merely the *best* of the five choices given. You may refer back to the passage if necessary.

## Analysis

1. Answer all the questions for one passage before moving on to the next passage. If you don't know an answer, don't waste time: Take an educated guess. Don't leave blanks.

2. Use only the information stated or implied in a passage. Do not consider "outside" information (information not indicated by the passage) even if it seems more accurate than the given information.

3. For most questions, you will need to consider *all* the choices before marking your answer. For example, choice (C) may appear to be the correct answer to a question. However, continuing to read the choices for that question may reveal that (E) is an even better choice.

4. For questions requiring a definitive fact or specific detail stated in the passage, reading *all* the choices may not be necessary. These "specific fact" questions are not common, however.

5. Don't get stuck on any particular word in the passage that may be unfamiliar to you. Use the context of that phrase or sentence to help you clarify that word. If you still cannot discern a word's meaning, simply mark it, but keep the flow of your reading going.

# Suggested Approach with Sample Passages

1. *Skim?* Some candidates have found that skimming the questions (but never the answer choices!) *before* reading the passage helps them know what to look for when reading the passage. Others maintain that the questions are of such a general nature that skimming questions beforehand isn't particularly helpful and, in fact, wastes valuable time. In this regard, you should use these practice materials to discover which approach is effective for *you.*

2. Read the passage, marking important points, essential ideas, names, definitions, and so forth. Mark just a few *key items* per paragraph, being careful not to overmark. Marking key points helps you stay focused on the task at hand and also "organizes" the passage should you need to refer to it later when considering the questions.

3. Circle the "heart" of each question (... *best title,* ... *author's purpose,* ... *which must be true?,* and so forth) to help you avoid careless mistakes in misreading what is actually being asked.

4. Use the "elimination strategy" of crossing out obviously incorrect choices (thus avoiding having to reconsider them) to help you save valuable time.

5. Determine quickly that a particular passage is difficult to understand. If it is, you may wish to leave it for last (that is, the final passage you'll read in that section). Even if you leave a passage and its questions to do last, fill in guesses for the questions, just in case you don't have time to return to them.

## Sample Passages

### Sample 1

For most of recorded history, the law treated children and adults alike, and so they were subjected to the same procedures and punishments. It was not until recently that a separate system was established to handle juvenile defendants. Early reformers believed that in handling juvenile offenders, society should not be concerned with whether the child was guilty
(5) or innocent, but rather with rehabilitating him. The underlying philosophy of the juvenile justice system was this: Because the child brought within the system is essentially good, he should be treated—not as a criminal—but as a neglected child who needs care and guidance. Therefore, a criminal proceeding was considered inappropriate.

This basic philosophy is present in each state's juvenile justice system. Although the sys-
(10) tems vary from state to state, they all operate under the premise that the emphasis should be on the offender rather than the offense, on rehabilitation rather than punishment.

In juvenile proceedings, formality and strict rules of procedure have given way to informality and flexibility. In the process, constitutional protections generally accorded an adult offender were not applied to proceedings involving a minor. As a result, the juvenile justice
(15) system has been criticized because the treatment ordered for the child was often harsher and more arbitrary than that for an adult. For example, not only was the juvenile denied the appellate recourse available to an adult offender, but also he or she often never received the promised protection and rehabilitation.

(20)      In 1967, the Supreme Court began enumerating what rights should be applied to juvenile proceedings. Among those procedural protections the Court recognized were adequate notice of charges, representation by counsel or by appointed counsel, privilege against self-incrimination, and opportunity to confront and cross-examine witnesses. In 1970, proof beyond a reasonable doubt was required when the youth had been charged with an act which would be a crime if committed by an adult.

(25)      While incorporating safeguards into juvenile proceedings, the Court did not ignore the basic approach of the juvenile justice system. It was careful not to unduly inhibit the informality, flexibility, or speed of the proceedings. In order to do so, the need for constitutional safeguards was often balanced against the need for fair and speedy treatment of the minor.

     In a later case, in 1974, a seventeen-year-old was charged with conduct which if com-
(30) mitted by an adult would have constituted robbery. At the adjudicatory hearing, based on the testimony of two prosecution witnesses and of the defendant, the juvenile court found the allegations to be true, and at a subsequent hearing adjudged him to be unfit for treatment as a juvenile and ordered that he be tried as an adult. This, the Court found, violated the Double Jeopardy Clause of the Fifth Amendment, in that evidence was introduced at the
(35) adjudicatory hearing to determine if the juvenile committed the act charged before a determination was made whether to transfer him to the criminal court to be tried as an adult.

     Allowing a transfer does satisfy the need for flexibility as, in some instances, the youngster will most likely not benefit from the specialized guidance and treatment provided in the juvenile justice system. But such a determination must be made before evidence is heard on
(40) the merits. The Court, while realizing that mandating a transfer decision before an adjudicatory hearing does impose an additional burden on the juvenile justice system, concluded that rather than inhibiting the flexibility and informality of juvenile proceedings, likelihood of better treatment of the youth will be increased.

     These Supreme Court cases concerning juveniles have raised issues of due process per-
(45) taining to the adjudication stage of the proceedings. However, it is still unclear what rights attach at the initial detention stage. In this area, where constitutional safeguards have yet to be defined, state law still controls.

## Questions

**1.** The passage is concerned primarily with

    **A.** the juvenile justice system in the United States.

    **B.** the rehabilitation rather than the punishment of juveniles.

    **C.** the needs of juvenile defendants in criminal proceedings.

    **D.** the constitutional safeguards of juvenile defendants.

    **E.** constitutional protections and juvenile proceedings.

**2.** In the United States, the juvenile justice system is based upon the unproven assumption that

   **A.** children are good rather than evil.

   **B.** hearings should be informal and speedy.

   **C.** misbehavior should be punished.

   **D.** the laws of evidence cannot be applied to minors.

   **E.** children, like adults, should not be subject to double jeopardy.

**3.** It can be argued that, at one time, a juvenile offender was at a greater disadvantage than an adult for all of the following reasons EXCEPT:

   **A.** He or she may be denied protections an adult would automatically receive.

   **B.** The chief concern of the juvenile court is the offender rather than the offense.

   **C.** The offender may not be protected against self-incrimination.

   **D.** He or she may not have been represented by counsel.

   **E.** A juvenile may never have had the opportunity to appeal a decision.

**4.** We can infer from the passage that before 1970, in a juvenile hearing, a charge that would be criminal in an adult court

   **A.** would be transferred to trial in an adult criminal court.

   **B.** could not be transferred to trial in an adult criminal court.

   **C.** would not have required proof beyond a reasonable doubt.

   **D.** would not be brought to trail speedily.

   **E.** would be tried without the informality used in a juvenile court.

**5.** In lines 29-36, the author cites the case of 1974 in order to

   **A.** demonstrate the need for flexibility in the juvenile courts.

   **B.** cite an example of juvenile rights properly protected.

   **C.** support the case for increased protection of juvenile rights in state courts.

   **D.** cite an example of the failure to incorporate safeguards in the judicial system.

   **E.** demonstrate the need for fair and speedy trials of minors.

**6.** We can infer that compared to their rights at adjudication hearings, the rights of juveniles at the time of their arrest are

    **A.** very nearly the same.

    **B.** different from state to state.

    **C.** clearly defined.

    **D.** seldom threatened.

    **E.** similar to those of adults.

**7.** The author of the passage probably regards the present juvenile legal procedures as

    **A.** unfair to the juveniles.

    **B.** unfair to adults.

    **C.** improved but with ;more to be done.

    **D.** fair to both juveniles and adults.

    **E.** ideal.

## Marked Passage

The marked passage could look like this:

    For most of recorded history, the law treated children and adults alike, and so they were subjected to the same procedures and punishments. It was not until recently that a separate system was established to handle juvenile defendants. Early reformers believed that in handling juvenile offenders, society should not be concerned with whether the child was guilty

(5)  or innocent, but rather with rehabilitating him. The underlying philosophy of the juvenile justice system was this: Because the child brought within the system is essentially good, he should be treated—not as a criminal—but as a neglected child who needs care and guidance. Therefore, a criminal proceeding was considered inappropriate.

    This basic philosophy is present in each state's juvenile justice system. Although the sys-

(10) tems vary from state to state, they all operate under the premise that the emphasis should be on the offender rather than the offense, on rehabilitation rather than punishment.

    In juvenile proceedings, formality and strict rules of procedure have given way to informality and flexibility. In the process, constitutional protections generally accorded an adult offender were not applied to proceedings involving a minor. As a result, the juvenile

(15) justice system has been criticized because the treatment ordered for the child was often harsher and more arbitrary than that for an adult. For example, not only was the juvenile denied the appellate recourse available to an adult offender, but also he or she often never received the promised protection and rehabilitation.

    In 1967, the Supreme Court began enumerating what rights should be applied to juvenile

(20) proceedings. Among those procedural protections the Court recognized were adequate notice of charges, representation by counsel or by appointed counsel, privilege against self-incrimination, and opportunity to confront and cross-examine witnesses. In 1970, proof

beyond a reasonable doubt was required when the youth had been charged with an act which would be a crime if committed by an adult.

(25)    While incorporating safeguards into juvenile proceedings, the Court did not ignore the basic approach of the juvenile justice system. It was careful not to unduly inhibit the informality, flexibility, or speed of the proceedings. In order to do so, the need for constitutional safeguards was often balanced against the need for fair and speedy treatment of the minor.

In a later case, in 1974, a seventeen-year-old was charged with conduct which if commit-
(30)    ted by an adult would have constituted robbery. At the adjudicatory hearing, based on the testimony of two prosecution witnesses and of the defendant, the juvenile court    found the allegations to be true, and at a subsequent hearing adjudged him to be unfit for treatment as a juvenile and ordered that he be tried as an adult. This, the Court found, violated the Double Jeopardy Clause of the Fifth Amendment, in that evidence was introduced at the adjudica-
(35)    tory hearing to determine if the juvenile committed the act charged before a determination was made whether to transfer him to the criminal court to be tried as an adult.

Allowing a transfer does satisfy the need for flexibility as, in some instances, the youngster will most likely not benefit from the specialized guidance and treatment provided in the juvenile justice system. But such a determination must be made before evidence is heard on
(40)    the merits. The Court, while realizing that mandating a transfer decision before an adjudicatory hearing does impose an additional burden on the juvenile justice system, concluded that rather than inhibiting the flexibility and informality of juvenile proceedings, likelihood of better treatment of the youth will be increased.

These Supreme Court cases concerning juveniles have raised issues of due process per-
(45)    taining to the adjudication stage of the proceedings. However, it is still unclear what rights attach at the initial detention stage. In this area, where constitutional safeguards have yet to be defined, state law still controls.

## Marked Questions and Answers

> **1.** The passage is concerned primarily with
>
> A.   the juvenile justice system in the United States.
>
> B.   the rehabilitation rather than the punishment of juveniles.
>
> C.   the needs of juvenile defendants in criminal proceedings.
>
> D.   the constitutional safeguards of juvenile defendants.
>
> E.   constitutional protections and juvenile proceedings.

**Answer E.** Although all five of the choices are plausible, the focus of the passage is on juvenile justice proceedings and some Supreme Court decisions guaranteeing constitutional protections to the defendants.

2. In the United States, the juvenile justice system is based upon the unproven assumption that

    A. children are good rather than evil.

    B. hearings should be informal and speedy.

    C. misbehavior should be punished.

    D. the laws of evidence cannot be applied to minors.

    E. children, like adults, should not be subject to double jeopardy.

**Answer A.** The first paragraph of the passage asserts that the underlying philosophy of the juvenile system is that the *child brought within the system is essentially good.* The system supports informal and speedy hearings (choice B) but cannot be said to be based upon them as an assumption.

3. It can be argued that, at one time, a juvenile offender was at a greater disadvantage than an adult for all of the following reasons EXCEPT:

    A. He or she may be denied protections an adult would automatically receive.

    B. The chief concern of the juvenile court is the offender rather than the offense.

    C. The offender may not be protected against self-incrimination.

    D. He or she may not have been represented by counsel.

    E. A juvenile may never have had the opportunity to appeal a decision.

**Answer B.** Although the statement of choice B is true (paragraph 2), it would not necessarily support the argument. All of the other four choices are genuine disadvantages that might once have existed.

4. We can infer from the passage that before 1970, in a juvenile hearing, a charge that would be criminal in an adult court

    A. would be transferred to trial in an adult criminal court.

    B. could not be transferred to trial in an adult criminal court.

    C. would not have required proof beyond a reasonable doubt.

    D. would not be brought to trail speedily.

    E. would be tried without the informality used in a juvenile court.

**Answer C.** Because the passage specifically points out the requirement of proof beyond a reasonable doubt in 1970 and the paragraph is listing the gradual increase in juvenile rights, we can assume that this protection may not have existed before 1970.

**5.** In lines 29-36, the author cites the case of 1974 in order to

    **A.** demonstrate the need for flexibility in the juvenile courts.

    **B.** cite an example of juvenile rights properly protected.

    **C.** support the case for increased protection of juvenile rights in state courts.

    **D.** cite an example of the failure to incorporate safeguards in the judicial system.

    **E.** demonstrate the need for fair and speedy trials of minors.

**Answer B.** The case cited describes the higher court's reversal of the juvenile court's decision and is an example of juveniles being given the same protection an adult could expect.

**6.** We can infer that compared to their rights at adjudication hearings, the rights of juveniles at the time of their arrest are

    **A.** very nearly the same.

    **B.** different from state to state.

    **C.** clearly defined.

    **D.** seldom threatened.

    **E.** similar to those of adults.

**Answer B.** According to the final paragraph, the constitutional safeguards at this time are yet to be defined and are determined by state laws.

**7.** The author of the passage probably regards the present juvenile legal procedures as

    **A.** unfair to the juveniles.

    **B.** unfair to adults.

    **C.** improved but with more to be done.

    **D.** fair to both juveniles and adults.

    **E.** ideal.

**Answer C.** Given the question, the adults are irrelevant. Although much of the passage is approving, it is clear that the author believes more can be done to protect juveniles' rights.

# Sample 2

As you read the following passage, focus on what the author is really saying or what point the author is trying to make. Also pay attention to how the passage is put together—the structure.

Woodrow Wilson won his first office in 1910 when he was elected governor of New Jersey. Two years later, he was elected president in one of the most rapid political rises in our history. For a while, Wilson had practiced law but found it both boring and unprofitable; then he became a political scientist and finally president of Princeton University. He
(5) did an outstanding job at Princeton, but when he was asked by the Democratic boss of New Jersey, Jim Smith, to run for governor, Wilson readily accepted because his position at Princeton was becoming untenable.

Until 1910, Wilson seemed to be a conservative Democrat in the Grover Cleveland tradition. He had denounced Bryan in 1896 and had voted for the national Democratic candidate
(10) who supported gold. In fact, when the Democratic machine first pushed Wilson's nomination in 1912, the young New Jersey progressives wanted no part of him. Wilson later assured them that he would champion the progressive cause, and so they decided to work for his election. It is easy to accuse Wilson of political expediency, but it is entirely possible that by 1912 he had changed his views as had countless other Americans. While governor of
(15) New Jersey, he carried out his election pledges by enacting an impressive list of reforms.

Wilson secured the Democratic nomination on the 46th ballot. In the campaign, Wilson emerged as the middle-of-the-road candidate—between the conservative William H. Taft and the more radical Theodore Roosevelt. Wilson called his program the New Freedom, which he said was the restoration of free competition as it had existed before the growth of
(20) the trusts. In contrast, Theodore Roosevelt was advocating a New Nationalism, which seemed to call for massive federal intervention in the economic life of the nation. Wilson felt that the trusts should be destroyed, but he made a distinction between a trust and legitimately successful big business. Theodore Roosevelt, on the other hand, accepted the trusts as inevitable but said that the government should regulate them by establishing a new regu-
(25) latory agency.

Always look for the main point of the passage. There are many ways to ask about the main point of a passage: What is the main idea? What is the best title? What is the author's purpose?

---

**1.** The author's main purpose in writing this passage is to

   **A.** Argue that Wilson is one of the great U.S. presidents.

   **B.** Survey the difference between Wilson, Taft, and Roosevelt.

   **C.** Explain Wilson's concept of the New Freedom.

   **D.** Discuss some major events of Wilson's career.

   **E.** Suggest reasons that Wilson's presidency may have started World War I.

---

**Answer D.** Choices A and E are irrelevant to the information in the passage, and choices B and C mention secondary purposes rather than the primary one.

Some information is not directly stated in the passage but can be gleaned by reading between the lines. This implied information can be valuable in answering some questions, such as the following.

---

**2.** The author implies which of the following about the New Jersey progressives?

   **A.** They did not support Wilson after he was governor.

   **B.** They were not conservative Democrats.

   **C.** They were more interested in political expediency than in political causes or reforms.

   **D.** Along with Wilson, they were supporters of Bryan in 1896.

   **E.** They particularly admired Wilson's experience as president of Princeton University.

---

**Answer B.** In the second paragraph, Wilson's decision to champion the progressive cause after 1912 is contrasted with his earlier career, when he seemed to be a conservative Democrat. Thus, you may conclude that the progressives, whom Wilson finally joined, were not conservative Democrats as Wilson was earlier in his career. Choices A and D contradict information in the paragraph, while choices C and E are not suggested by any information given in the passage.

Watch for important conclusions or information that might support a conclusion.

---

**3.** The passage supports which of the following conclusions about the progress of Wilson's political career?

   **A.** Few politicians have progressed so rapidly toward the attainment of higher office.

   **B.** Failures late in his career caused him to be regarded as a president who regressed instead of progressed.

   **C.** Wilson encountered little opposition once he determined to seek the presidency.

   **D.** The League of Nations marked the end of Wilson's reputation as a strong leader.

   **E.** Wilson's political allies were Bryan and Taft.

---

**Answer A.** The second sentence in the first paragraph explicitly states that Wilson "was elected president in one of the most rapid political rises in our history."

Understand the meaning and possible reason for using certain words or phrases in the passage, and take advantage of the line numbers given.

**4.** In the statement "Wilson readily accepted because his position at Princeton was becoming untenable" (lines 6-7), the meaning of "untenable" is probably which of the following?

   **A.** Unlikely to last for years

   **B.** Filled with considerably less tension

   **C.** Difficult to maintain or continue

   **D.** Filled with achievement that would appeal to voters

   **E.** Something he did not have a tenacious desire to continue

**Answer C.** On any reading comprehension test, keep alert to the positive and negative connotations of words and phrases in each passage as well as in the questions themselves. In the case of *untenable,* the prefix *un-* suggests that the word has a negative connotation. The context in which the word occurs does as well. Wilson *left* his position at Princeton; therefore, you may conclude that the position was somehow unappealing. Only two of the answer choices, C and E, provide a negative definition. Although choice E may attract your attention because *tenacious* looks similar to *tenable,* the correct choice is C, which is the conventional definition of *untenable.*

Your answer choice must be supported by information either stated or implied in the passage. Eliminate those choices that the passage does not support.

**5.** According to the passage, which of the following was probably true about the presidential campaign of 1912?

   **A.** Woodrow Wilson won the election by an overwhelming majority.

   **B.** The inexperience of Theodore Roosevelt accounted for his radical position.

   **C.** Wilson was unable to attract two thirds of the votes but won anyway.

   **D.** There were three nominated candidates for the presidency.

   **E.** Wilson's New Freedom did not represent Democratic interests.

**Answer D.** Choices A, B, and C contain information that the passage does not address. You may eliminate them as irrelevant. Choice E contradicts the fact that Wilson was a Democratic candidate. The discussion of Taft and Roosevelt as the candidates who finally ran against Wilson for the presidency supports choice D.

# Practice Reading Comprehension Passages and Questions

*Questions 1 through 7 are based on the following passage.*

The custom of patrilineal succession began in medieval England as a response to its social and legal system whereby "the inheritance of property
(5) was often contingent upon an heir's retention of the surname associated with that property." In more recent times and as divorce became more prevalent in our society, the question of a child's sur-
(10) name continued to be of paramount importance, not so much in the context of determining rights to property inheritance, but rather in deciding whether a child of divorced parents should have
(15) the mother's or the father's name or a combination of the two. The traditional rule followed by the courts in the past has been that, even where the mother has been awarded custody of the chil-
(20) dren, the father had a "primary right or protectable interest in having the minor children bear his name." Courts have been reluctant to depart from the common law tradition of patrilineal succes-
(25) sion, emphasizing in their decisions the need for continuing parent-child relationships. The typical rationale is that "the link between a father and child in circumstances such as these is uncertain
(30) at best, and a change of name could further weaken, if not sever, such a bond." The arguments for adhering to the traditional rule are many, but the primary two seem to be that the rule pro-
(35) vides a certain method of administrative record keeping and that "identification with the paternal surname may give a healthy sense of family as well as ethnic and religious identity and also maintain
(40) [the child's] rightful link with an absent or noncustodial father."

In a divorce, the parties involved frequently do battle over many issues with a primary issue pivoting around the chil-
(45) dren. Under the common law, these questions have often been resolved using sex-discriminatory presumptions wherein the mother would be awarded custody and the father ordered to pay
(50) support in exchange for which the children would retain his surname.

These presumptions, while reflecting society's views in the past, have often failed to take into consideration what
(55) was best for the child's welfare. In an attempt to correct this situation, the courts and many state legislatures have developed a standard whereby the best interests of the child have become the
(60) controlling consideration in determining custody and support and, more recently, in deciding what the child's surname should be.

In a 1980 landmark case, the
(65) California Supreme Court, in appraising the rights of both parents, held, "Henceforth, as in parental custody disputes, the sole consideration when parents contest a surname shall be the
(70) child's best interest. Expressions to the contrary [in previous cases] are disproved." The Court then delineated the following factors which were to be considered in applying the best interests
(75) standard: the length of time that the child had used a surname, the preservation and the development of the child's relationship with each parent, and the difficulties, harassment, or embarrass-
(80) ment that the child may experience from bearing the present or proposed surname.

1. All of the following statements can be used to explain why the question of parental surname is more often raised now than in the past EXCEPT:

   A. The bias in favor of men was greater in the past.

   B. In the past, there were fewer divorces.

   C. In the past, property rights were more important.

   D. In the past, a change of surname might lead to loss of property.

   E. Women had fewer legal rights in the past.

2. The argument that a child of divorced parents by keeping the parental name may be given a "healthy sense of family" (line 38), "ethnic and religious identity" (lines 38-39), and a "rightful link with an absent . . . father" (line 40) is based upon all of the following doubtful assumptions EXCEPT:

   A. Ethnic identity is determined by the father.

   B. Religious identity is determined by the father.

   C. Record keeping systems cannot handle changes of names.

   D. A father's name gives a sense of family.

   E. A link to an absent father should be maintained.

3. Which one of the following arguments can be used to support one of the most used reasons for children's retention of the father's name—preservation of the parent-child relationship?

   A. Either parent will maintain contact regardless of the child's last name.

   B. A system capable of dealing with name changes of divorced mothers ought to be able to deal as well with children's name changes.

   C. A bureaucratic convenience should not be set above preserving the parent-child relationship.

   D. A father is less likely to maintain contact with a child whose name differs from his own.

   E. A mother is less likely to maintain contact with a child whose name differs from her own.

4. When the passage refers to awarding custody of the children to the mother and requiring child support from the father with retaining of his name as the result of "sex-discriminatory presumptions" (line 47), it alludes to the belief of all the following EXCEPT:

   A. Child raising is the province of the female.

   B. Wage earning is the province of the male.

   C. The male family name has precedence over the female.

   D. Trading the use of the father's name for child support is acceptable.

   E. Women can earn more than men.

**5.** Which of the following does the author of the passage apparently favor as the surname of a child of divorcing parents?

   **A.** Whichever name serves the child's best interest

   **B.** The surname of the father

   **C.** The surname of the mother

   **D.** The hyphenated surnames of both parents

   **E.** Whichever name serves the best interest of the custodial parent

**6.** According to the passage, which of the following means have been used to change the criteria by which a child's surname is determined?

   **A.** The action of the courts and the passage of state laws

   **B.** The passage of federal laws

   **C.** A Constitutional amendment

   **D.** A ruling by the U.S. Supreme Court

   **E.** The governor's intervention

**7.** In applying the best interest standard, all of the following might be considered EXCEPT:

   **A.** the length of time the parents have been married.

   **B.** any embarrassment the name might cause.

   **C.** the length of time the surname has been used by the child.

   **D.** the preservation of the child's relationship with the custodial parent.

   **E.** the preservation of the child's relationship with the noncustodial parent.

*Questions 8 through 14 are based on the following passage.*

In seventeenth-century England, the government's interest in the religious upbringing of children outweighed that of the parents. This interest reached its
(5) peak in 1699 when a "Papist" who attempted to educate children was found guilty of a crime punishable by perpetual imprisonment. By the nineteenth century, England's attitudes and laws
(10) had changed. It became settled law that the father's authority to guide and govern the education of his children "is not to be abrogated or abridged without the most coercive reason."
(15) In the United States, problems concerning the religious education of children have received different treatment due to the protection given religious liberty under our constitution. Such prob-
(20) lems cannot be solved by favoring one religion over another. From the beginning, the courts have been hesitant to intrude into matters involving religious disputes and have followed a "hands-
(25) off" approach. A majority of these cases involved custody disputes between parents of different faiths. While a few of these cases acknowledged it was the child's welfare and best interest that was
(30) of paramount importance and thus gave some weight to the child's religious preference, their decisions were actually based on a preference between the parents' religions. In fact, the courts' atti-
(35) tude towards the religious education of the child was that it should be strictly a matter of parental choice. This doctrine of parental authority has been repeatedly affirmed and upheld.
(40) In 1900, the Louisiana Supreme Court held that a minor of 17 years of age did not have the legal right to leave her mother's house without consent to enter a nuns' convent. The court never

(45) entertained the possibility that this young woman had an independent right to pursue her religious beliefs or education independent of her mother. In the same year, the courts held that an act re- (50) quiring parents to send their children to a public school "unreasonably interferes with the liberty of parents and guardians to direct the upbringing and education of children under their control." Another (55) case, while upholding the right of the state to intervene when the religious upbringing involved dangers to the child's health and well-being, also recognized the parents' right to guide their chil- (60) dren's religious education.

The doctrine of parental authority was reaffirmed by the United States Supreme Court in a 1972 case in which Amish parents refused to continue their chil- (65) dren's education beyond the elementary school level. They believed that a high school education would expose the children to worldly ways and thus threaten their salvation. In upholding the exemp- (70) tion of the Amish from Wisconsin's compulsory education laws, the court cited "a charter of rights of parents to direct the religious upbringing of their children" and stated further that the "pri- (75) mary role of the parents in the upbringing of their children is now established beyond debate as an enduring American tradition."

This decision and others like it lead (80) one to conclude that, at minimum, there is a very strong presumption favoring parental control or, at most, the parents have a constitutionally based right to control the religious education of their (85) children. However, recognition of the parents' independent, constitutional right over the child's religious training has had profound and far-reaching effect. Such

(90) recognition has essentially removed the system of laws concerning the regulation and protection of children and substituted in its place a system of parental regulation. To the extent that a parent's constitutional right to control exists, the (95) child's independent rights to exercise choice do not exist. Consequently, the expansion of one requires the reduction of the other.

**8.** Which of the following titles best summarizes the content of the passage?

A. Religious Rights: New Developments of the Laws

B. The Traditional and Current Religious Rights of Minors

C. The Rights of Minors from the Seventeenth Century to the Present

D. The Rights of Parents Versus the Rights of Children

E. The First Amendment and the Religious Rights of Minors

**9.** In England in 1880, the Roman Catholic father of a child born of a Baptist mother would probably have been legally allowed to do all of the following EXCEPT:

A. ignore the child's religious education.

B. bring up the child as a Roman Catholic.

C. bring up the child as a Baptist.

D. make sure that the child was brought up very religiously.

E. abrogate his authority without reason.

**10.** Where the American courts have acted in disputes involving religion and a child, the decision has chiefly been determined by a

   **A.** concern for the best interest of the child.

   **B.** preference for the religion of one of the parents.

   **C.** concern for the welfare of the mother of the child.

   **D.** concern not to favor one religion over another.

   **E.** preference for a more established religion.

**11.** The second of the cases cited in lines 48-54 suggests that, in cases involving the upbringing and education of minors,

   **A.** parents alone have power.

   **B.** children enjoy some religious autonomy.

   **C.** a guardian has the same legal status as a parent.

   **D.** the central concern is the child's well-being.

   **E.** the court recognized that minors' rights differ from parents' in certain narrowly defined areas.

**12.** Judging from the later cases cited in the passage, we can infer that a modern court deciding a case like that in Louisiana in 1900 (lines 40-48) would

   **A.** agree with the decision made in 1900.

   **B.** regard the case as beyond the jurisdiction of the courts.

   **C.** make its decision on the basis of the threat to the minor's health.

   **D.** uphold the young woman's right to choose for herself.

   **E.** make its decision on the basis of the threat to the minor's well-being.

**13.** A legal decision supporting the religious preference of a father over that of a mother might be defended plausibly by arguing that

   **A.** a father has the right to educate his children in any religion he chooses.

   **B.** a father does not have the right to choose the religion of his children.

   **C.** a father's religious preference may be supported constitutionally as long as one religion is not preferred.

   **D.** the courts are reluctant to intervene in cases involving children's religious rights.

   **E.** the courts are reluctant to intervene in cases involving the conflict of two different religions.

**14.** The passage argues that in the United States, the religious rights of minors

   **A.** are the same as those of adults.

   **B.** have steadily declined in the last eighty years.

   **C.** have steadily expanded in the last eighty years.

   **D.** will increase only when parental rights are reduced.

   **E.** are well protected by the First Amendment.

*Questions 15 through 20 are based on the following passage.*

Let us take the terms "subjective" and "objective" and see if we can make up our minds what we mean by them in a statement like this: "Philosophers and
(5) artists are subjective; scientists, objective." First, the two terms make up a semantic pair. The one has no meaning without the other. We may define each by antonym with the other. We may de-
(10) fine them by synonym by translating the last syllable and say that "subjective" pertains to a subject and "objective" pertains to an object. By operation analysis we may say that subjects perceive or
(15) conceive objects in the process of knowing. The word "knowing" reminds us that we are talking about the central nervous system and should waste no time in examining our terms for their sensory,
(20) affective, and logical components. The terms are primarily logical. What, then, is the basic logical relation that establishes whatever meaning they have? What goes on in the world when a poet
(25) is being subjective, and how does it differ from what goes on when a scientist is being objective?

When the poet sings "Drink to me only with thine eyes," he is responding
(30) immediately or in retrospect to an object, his beloved, outside himself; but he is fundamentally concerned with the sensations and emotions which that object stimulates in him; and whether the
(35) object justifies his praise in the opinion of others, or indeed whether there actually is such an object, is quite irrelevant to his purpose, which is the weaving of a beautiful pattern of sound and imagery
(40) into a richly affective concept of feminine loveliness. This is to be subjective.

Now the scientist is primarily concerned with the identity and continuity of the external object that stimulates his

(45) response. It need not seem absurd to locate the Eiffel Tower, or Everest, or the Grand Canyon, for that matter, in the mind because it is so perfectly obvious that they can exist as the Eiffel Tower,
(50) Everest, or the Grand Canyon nowhere else. Perhaps we can move a little closer to our definition of "objective" by suggesting a distinction between an object and thing. Let us define object as the ex-
(55) ternal cause of a thing. Whether objects "exist" is obviously not discussable, for the word "object" as used here must necessarily stand not for a thing but for a hypothesis. There is, for example, no
(60) way of telling whether objects are singular or plural, whether one should say the stimulus of the Eiffel Tower experience or the stimuli of the Eiffel Tower experience. If then, it is impossible even for
(65) the scientist to escape the essential subjectivity of his sensations, generalizations, and deductions, what do we mean by calling him objective?

**15.** Which of the following is NOT a semantic pair?

A. chaos/order

B. fact/fiction

C. sitting/standing

D. light/darkness

E. virtue/vice

**16.** Which of the following pairs best exemplifies the subjective/objective opposition as defined by the passage?

A. art/philosophy

B. knower/known

C. object/thing

D. stimulus/stimuli

E. emotion/sensation

**17.** The passages refers to "Drink to me only with thine eyes" (lines 28-29) primarily to

    **A.** suggest the affective powers of sound and imagery.

    **B.** exemplify the objective.

    **C.** exemplify the subjective.

    **D.** demonstrate how art can bestow universal significance on an object.

    **E.** illustrate the difference between literal and metaphorical language.

**18.** Given the content of the first and second paragraphs, the reader expects that the third paragraph will

    **A.** explain how the scientist is objective.

    **B.** define the identity and conformity of external objects.

    **C.** analyze what it is to be subjective.

    **D.** discriminate between an object and a thing.

    **E.** explore the implications of objectivity.

**19.** According to the passage, "objectivity" depends on the assumption that

    **A.** discrete objects exist external to the mind.

    **B.** one's vocation in life should be logical.

    **C.** subjectivity is a cognitive weakness.

    **D.** science is a viable discipline.

    **E.** the Eiffel Tower is a singular stimulus, not a diffuse experience.

**20.** Faced with this statement, "What you see is just in your head," the author of the passage would be likely to

    **A.** disagree strongly.

    **B.** agree that the statement is probably true.

    **C.** argue against the appropriateness of the word "just".

    **D.** assume that the person making the statement is not a scientist.

    **E.** argue that what is seen cannot be located outside or inside the mind.

*Questions 21 through 27 are based on the following passage.*

    During the Middle Ages in Europe, animation, the fusion of the soul into the fetus, was believed to occur sometime between conception and birth. Life from
(5) that point was deemed begun. Roman Catholic physicians, on one end of the spectrum, concluded that animation probably occurred at conception, while the Jewish emphasis, at the other end,
(10) required live birth. The secular community reflected a similar variation in views.

    During this time the English common law made a distinction between abortion
(15) in early pregnancy and abortion in later pregnancy. Sir Edward Coke determined that abortion was murder only if the fetus (1) was quickened (movement in utero experienced by the pregnant
(20) woman), (2) was born alive, (3) survived for a period, (4) then died. If the quickened fetus died in utero and was stillborn, the offense was probably something less than what we call a mis-
(25) demeanor and was then called misprision. An abortion before quickening was not a crime at all. The clear result was that for a woman under common law

(and the abortionist), abortion was pro-
(30) tected under the law in those prequick-
ening weeks.

As common law, criminal law reflected the quickening requirement; an
execution would be postponed only if a
(35) woman was found to be quick with
child. Civil law similarly developed a
forty-week period during which a pre-
sumptive heir could be displaced by live
issue and which continues to be a basis
(40) for the Rule against Perpetuities.

In this country, the common law was
adopted by all the states (except
Louisiana) and was in effect when the
Ninth Amendment was adopted.
(45) "English and American women enjoyed
a common-law liberty to terminate at
will an unwanted pregnancy from the
reign of Edward III to that of George III.
This common-law liberty endured, in
(50) England from 1327 to 1803 and in
America from 1607 to 1830." The first
antiabortion statute in the United States
was passed in 1821 in Connecticut.
Connecticut, however, continued the
(55) distinction between quickened and nonquickened fetuses. Illinois in 1827 was
the first state to abolish this distinction.
In 1830, the New York legislature became the first to recognize the exception
(60) of the woman's life being endangered
from a continued pregnancy. The clear
implication is that until abrogated by
statute, the common law continued to
protect the liberty that women (and
(65) those who performed abortions) had enjoyed since the fourteenth century.

Slowly, over the years, exceptions, in
addition to the woman's life being endangered, began to appear. The drafting
(70) of the Model Penal Code in 1960–61 resulted in additional exceptions: (a)
where there was a risk that the unborn
child would be deformed and (b) where
the pregnancy resulted from rape or
(75) incest.

The legislative intent behind the state
statutes abrogating the common law was
to protect the life of the woman (however paternalistically) from the danger
(80) surrounding the unsophisticated medical
techniques, not to protect the fetus/em-
bryo. Nether did legislators attempt to
include any religious or moral concern
for the embryo/fetus.

(85) The ensuing years brought improved
medical conditions, lessening the need
for protective legislation, which culminated in the Roe decision. Cessante ra-
tione legis, cessat et ipsa lex: When the
(90) reasoning for the law ceases, the law
itself ceases.

21. Given their views on animation, we can
infer that Jewish theologians in the
fourteenth century

   A.  had no objection to abortion early
       in the pregnancy.

   B.  disapproved of abortion at any
       time.

   C.  agreed with Catholic theologians
       about abortion.

   D.  believed that the father rather than
       the mother should determine
       whether or not an abortion should
       be performed.

   E.  believed that the mother rather than
       the father should determine
       whether or not an abortion should
       be performed.

22. A woman in Connecticut in 1825 who
    had an abortion before the fetus
    quickened would

   A.  not be guilty of a crime if her life
       were in danger because of the
       pregnancy.

   B.  not be guilty of a crime if there
       were a risk that the child would be
       born deformed.

C.  not be guilty of a crime if the pregnancy resulted from rape or incest.

D.  not be guilty of a crime.

E.  be guilty of a crime.

23. In the eighteenth century, the execution of a pregnant woman sentenced to death for a crime would be delayed if the

A.  woman was in an early stage of pregnancy.

B.  woman had minor children wholly dependent upon her.

C.  legal father of the unborn child requested a delay.

D.  woman was in the sixth month of her pregnancy.

E.  unborn child had begun to move.

24. In lines 78-79, the parenthetical phrase "however paternalistically" can best be paraphrased as:

A.  nevertheless in a fatherly manner.

B.  no matter how overprotectively.

C.  on the other hand, in a manner that is fatherly.

D.  fatherly and protectively.

E.  yet as fatherly as possible.

25. The author reviews the abortion laws of the Middle Ages through the nineteenth century in order to

A.  call attention to the errors of the past.

B.  prove that a woman's right to an abortion is protected by the Ninth Amendment.

C.  show that the laws protecting the life of the fetus have no long legal precedent.

D.  suggest that a woman's claim to abortion rights arose only in the twentieth century.

E.  contrast the laws of Connecticut with those of New York.

26. In the last sentence of the passage, "when the reasoning for the law ceases, the law itself ceases," the phrase "reasoning for the law" refers to

A.  protecting the health of the unborn.

B.  protecting the health of the mother.

C.  religious consideration of the mother.

D.  religious consideration of the child.

E.  moral consideration of both the mother and the child.

27. From reading this passage, one can infer that the author

A.  is strongly opposed to abortion at any time.

B.  opposes abortion under most circumstances.

C.  has no discernible bias either for or against abortion.

D.  supports the Court's decision in Roe.

E.  sees strong arguments on both sides of the abortion rights question.

# Answers for Reading Comprehension Practice Questions

1. **C.** There is no reason to assume property rights were more or less important in the past. The other four statements can be used to explain the greater frequency in raising this question.

2. **C.** The issue of record keeping has no relevance to the argument presented in the question.

3. **D.** Choices A, B, C, and E would all undermine the idea of the necessity of children's retention of the father's name. In addition, choices B and C have to do with bureaucratic process, not the preservation of the parent-child relationship. Only choice D supports retention of the father's name.

4. **E.** "Women can earn more than men" is not a "sex-discriminatory presumption."

5. **A.** The author appears to support the standard based upon the child's best interest.

6. **A.** The passage refers to state laws and to the courts.

7. **A.** The last paragraph of the passage cites all of these except the length of time the parents have been married, which may well be irrelevant to the welfare of the child.

8. **B.** The passage is specifically concerned with the religious rights of minors, not with the more general rights of minors. Since two of the five paragraphs deal with the past, choice B is preferable to choice A.

9. **E.** According to the first paragraph, by the nineteenth century the father's authority was of paramount importance, so he could legally do choices A, B, C, or D. Choice E is correct. The father's authority "is not to be abrogated or abridged without the most coercive reason."

10. **B.** The second paragraph asserts that the decisions were actually based on a preference between the parents' religions.

11. **C.** The decision refers to the liberty of parents and guardians.

12. **A.** The cases cited in the passage repeatedly uphold the parental authority in cases of minors' religious rights.

13. **C.** The constitutional concern is that one religion not be preferred above another. The First Amendment is not concerned with gender preferences.

14. **D.** The passage concludes with the assertion that the expansion of a child's rights requires the reduction of the parents'.

15. **C.** In lines 7-8, the passage says that in a semantic pair "the one [term] has no meaning without the other." In short, semantic pairs are pairs of direct opposites. Only choice C is not such a pair.

16. **B.** The first paragraph says, "subjects perceive or conceive objects in the process of knowing." The pair that may best be substituted in that is knower and known.

17. **C.** The passage uses "Drink to me only with thine eyes" to show that the poet is fundamentally concerned with sensations and emotions. The quotation is an example of the subjective. In fact, the author finishes the paragraph by saying, "This it is to be subjective."

**18. A.** Since the passage begins with the idea that the artist is subjective and the scientist objective, and the second paragraph deals with the subjectivity of the artist, you suspect the third paragraph to be about the objectivity of the scientist.

**19. A.** The author tells us that scientists, defined as objective, are "primarily concerned with the identity and continuity of the external object that stimulates [their] response." That is, to be objective one must believe that the world is a collection of stable objects, each of which always looks the same. Choice E is a single example consistent with this assumption, but is not itself broad enough to support the question of objectivity in general. Choice D is also too broad to be the best answer. Choice C is not an assumption allowed by the passage.

**20. C.** The author concludes by saying that "it is impossible even for the scientist to escape the essential subjectivity of his sensations, generalizations, and deductions." Since everything is subjective, since different people each see the same thing a bit differently, one is seeming to devalue this case by saying that "what you see is just in your head." In your head is not an unimportant place; according to the passage, it is the only place.

**21. A.** Since the Jewish theologians of the Middle Ages believed that life began at birth rather than at conception, we can infer they would not object to abortion early in the pregnancy before the child was "alive."

**22. D.** The Connecticut antiabortion law of 1821 retained the distinction between quickened and nonquickened fetuses, so there would be no crime in this case.

**23. E.** An execution would be postponed only if a woman was found to be quick with child.

**24. B.** In this context, however is an adverb meaning no matter how, not a conjunction. The author apparently approves of the concern with protecting the woman's life even if the society that does so is inclined to be paternalistic to women.

**25. C.** The point of the passage is to show that there is far more legal precedent for protecting the abortion rights of women than is generally known. The argument is that the reaffirmation of these rights in the Roe decision restores to women rights that had been theirs until the mid nineteenth century.

**26. B.** The passage argues that many abortion laws were adopted to protect the health of the mother, not that of the unborn. Thus, with better medical conditions, the laws are needed no longer.

**27. D.** The argument of the passage is that women have always had abortion rights, that laws to protect their health are no longer needed, and thus the decision to restore these rights, in Roe, is a sensible one.

# A PATTERNED PLAN OF ATTACK
## *Reading Comprehension*

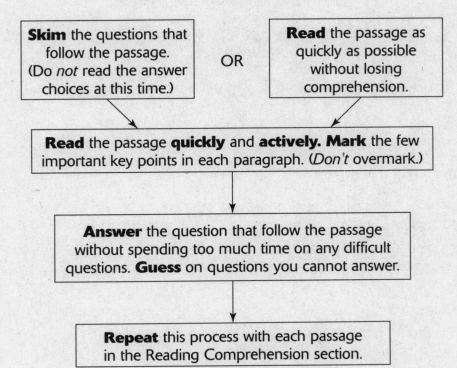

**Skim** the questions that follow the passage. (Do *not* read the answer choices at this time.)

OR

**Read** the passage as quickly as possible without losing comprehension.

**Read** the passage **quickly** and **actively. Mark** the few important key points in each paragraph. (*Don't* overmark.)

**Answer** the question that follow the passage without spending too much time on any difficult questions. **Guess** on questions you cannot answer.

**Repeat** this process with each passage in the Reading Comprehension section.

# Introduction to Analytical Reasoning

The Analytical Reasoning section lasts 35 minutes and typically contains 22 to 24 questions.

## Ability Tested

This section tests your ability to discern the relationships embodied in a set of conditions and to derive information from the conditions.

## Basic Skills Necessary

The ability to organize abstract relationships in order to solve a "puzzle" is important here; students familiar with several ways of displaying such relationships are likely to do well.

## Directions

You will be presented several sets of conditions. A group of questions follows each set of conditions. Choose the best answer to each question, drawing a rough diagram of the conditions when necessary.

## Analysis

1. For this section, you are looking for the *correct* answer. Once you encounter a satisfactory answer, do not read and analyze other answer choices; mark as your answer choice the first correct answer you arrive at.

2. Displaying information—sketching diagrams and charts of the conditions—is invaluable; not doing so significantly increases the difficulty of the problems.

## Suggested Approach with Samples

### Location Diagram (Simple)

Some Analytical Reasoning problems require that you organize information into a simple location diagram to more easily answer the questions. These problems deal with persons or items in certain positions, or places on the maps, or objects in a line, and so forth.

# Sample Set

Eight adults—A, B, C, D, E, F, G, and H—are seated around the perimeter of a square table. The following conditions are true about their seating:

An equal number of adults sits on each side of the table.

A woman is always seated next to a man.

Half of the adults are women.

A woman is always seated between two men.

## Questions

**1.** All of the following must be true EXCEPT:

  **A.** A man is always seated directly across from a woman.

  **B.** A man is seated between two women.

  **C.** Two men never sit in adjacent seats.

  **D.** People of the same sex sit directly across from each other.

  **E.** Two adjacent seats always contain one man and one woman.

**2.** Which of the conditions repeats information that may be inferred from the initial facts or previous conditions?

  **A.** The first condition

  **B.** The second condition

  **C.** The third condition

  **D.** The fourth condition

  **E.** None of the conditions

**3.** If a man changes places with a woman to his right, which of the following must now be true?

  **A.** One side of the table will seat just men.

  **B.** One side of the table will seat just women.

  **C.** At least two sides of the table will seat a man and a woman.

  **D.** Two sides of the table will seat just men.

  **E.** All sides of the table will seat a man and a woman.

## Explanation

To set up the diagram, simply draw the format (in this case, a square table with two seats on each side) and fill in the seats accordingly. There are two possible setups for this example:

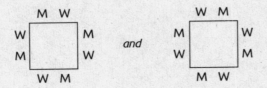

## Answers

After you set up the location diagram, you can answer questions 1 and 3 very easily simply by referring to your chart:

1. **D.**

2. **E.** None of the statements repeats information. Note that the last condition eliminates this possible setup:

3. **C.** Choice E could possibly be true, depending upon which of the original seating plans you use, but choice C is true of the alterations of both original seating charts and hence "must be true."

# Location Diagram (Complex)

Some Analytical Reasoning questions require drawing a more complex location diagram. These more complex diagrams may have variables within their structures or may even be incomplete—that is, you may not be able to completely fill in the entire diagram.

# Sample Set

Six people are standing in a straight line to get tickets to a concert. Each person is wearing a hat that is either blue, red, yellow, or green. Each person is wearing a coat that is either red, brown, black, or blue. The clothing worn by people in the line must meet the following restrictions:

The same colors may not be worn by people standing next to each other.

No one can wear a hat and coat that are the same color.

The third person in line is wearing a yellow hat and a brown coat.

The first person in line is wearing a red hat and a blue coat.

The sixth person in line is wearing a red coat.

## Questions

---

**1.** The second person in line must be wearing which of the following?

    **A.** A yellow hat

    **B.** A green hat

    **C.** A red coat

    **D.** A blue coat

    **E.** A red hat

---

**2.** What color coat must the second person in line be wearing?

    **A.** Red

    **B.** Brown

    **C.** Black

    **D.** Blue

    **E.** Either blue or red

---

**3.** If the fifth person wears a blue coat with a yellow hat, then the sixth person's hat must be which one of the following?

    **A.** Red

    **B.** Yellow

    **C.** Green

    **D.** Red or yellow

    **E.** Red or green

---

## Explanation

To set up the diagram, first draw the format:

| | 1 | 2 | 3 | 4 | 5 | 6 |
|---|---|---|---|---|---|---|
| Hat (R, Blu, Y, G) | R | | Y | | | |
| Coat (R, Br, Bla, Blu) | Blu | | Br | | R | |

Then fill in the information that you can quickly derive:

|  | 1 | 2 | 3 | 4 | 5 | 6 |
|------|-----|-----|-----|---|---|---|
| Hat | R | G | Y | | | |
| Coat | Blu | Bla | Br | | | R |

Notice that you can derive positions for two colors for the hat and coat. You can't complete anything else, so, at this point, you should proceed to the questions.

## Answers

1. B.
2. C.
3. C.

Notice that question 3 is an "if" question (it begins with the word *if*). Therefore, you may use your location diagram to help answer the question, but information given in this question should *not* be *permanently* entered into the diagram, as *it refers to this question only*.

# Connection Chart

Another type of Analytical Reasoning problem requires the construction of a connection chart. A connection chart is a very simple diagram showing the relationship among numerous items. For instance:

# Sample Set 1

Tom has been given six numbers—1, 2, 3, 4, 5, and 6—to make a decal. The numbers are in different sizes and only certain sizes look good together. Tom will not combine sizes that will not look good together. The following statements about the appearance and arrangement of the numbers are true:

The 2 will not look good with the 6.

The 1 will look good with the 3 or the 4 but not with both together.

Tom must use the 1 or the 2, or both.

Tom may use only three symbols on the decal.

## Questions

**1.** If 3 and 6 are chosen, then

    **A.** 1 must be chosen.

    **B.** 2 must be chosen.

    **C.** 4 must be chosen.

    **D.** 5 must be chosen.

    **E.** none must be chosen.

**2.** If 4 and 5 are chosen, then

    **A.** 3 may be chosen.

    **B.** 6 may be chosen.

    **C.** 2 must be chosen.

    **D.** 1 may be chosen.

    **E.** 2 cannot be chosen.

**3.** If 6 is chosen, but 5 isn't chosen, which of the following may also be chosen?

    **A.** 1 and 2

    **B.** 1 and 4

    **C.** 3 and 4

    **D.** 2 and 3

    **E.** 2 and 4

## Explanation

A connection diagram should be as simple as possible. For the sample question, the following diagram may be drawn:

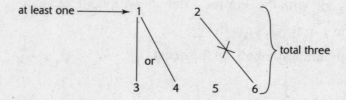

Notice that lines indicate which numbers will go together, but a line marked with an "x" indicates numbers that won't look good together. Also notice the positioning of the numbers (1 and 2 on top) shows that either or both from that row *must* be chosen.

## Answers

Now that the chart has been drawn, the questions are easily answered:

**1.** A.

**2.** D.

**3.** B.

## Sample Set 2

A department store plans five one-day sales for the next year, one of which will be the yearly clearance sale. Each sale can be held either on a weekday during one week (Monday through Friday) or on the Sunday of a holiday weekend (Memorial Day Sunday, Easter Sunday, Labor Day Sunday, or Christmas Sunday). If exactly two sales are planned for Sundays, one of those must be the yearly clearance sale; if exactly two sales are planned for weekdays, one of those must be the yearly clearance sale. In addition, the director of sales issues the following conditions:

If a sales event is planned for Monday, a sales event must also be planned for Easter Sunday.

A sales event must be planned for Thursday if a sales event is planned for Tuesday.

Planning a sales event for Wednesday also requires planning a sales event for Friday.

Planning a sales event for Friday also requires planning a sales event for Wednesday.

No sales event schedule may include both Friday and Memorial Day Sunday.

No more than three Sundays may be chosen for sales events; no more than three weekdays may be chosen for sales events.

## Questions

**1.** Which of the following schedules of sales events does NOT violate the sales director's conditions?

A. Wednesday, Friday, Memorial Day Sunday, Easter Sunday, Christmas Sunday

B. Wednesday, Thursday, Friday, Easter Sunday, Christmas Sunday

C. Monday, Memorial Day Sunday, Easter Sunday, Labor Day Sunday, Christmas Sunday

D. Monday, Wednesday, Thursday, Memorial Day Sunday, Easter Sunday

E. Monday, Tuesday, Easter Sunday, Labor Day Sunday, Christmas Sunday

**2.** Suppose the annual clearance sale is scheduled for a Monday. Which one of the following days must also be on the sales event schedule?

    **A.** Christmas Sunday

    **B.** Labor Day Sunday

    **C.** Memorial Day Sunday

    **D.** Thursday

    **E.** Tuesday

**3.** If the sales director decides not to schedule a sales event on either Monday or Thursday, which of the following is possible?

    **A.** The annual clearance sale is held on Christmas.

    **B.** The annual clearance sale is held on Easter Sunday.

    **C.** The annual clearance sale is held on Wednesday.

    **D.** A sale is held on Memorial Day Sunday.

    **E.** A sale is held on Tuesday.

**4.** If a sales event is planned for Monday, which of the following days could NOT be the yearly clearance sale?

    **A.** Christmas Sunday

    **B.** Easter Sunday

    **C.** Memorial Day Sunday

    **D.** Thursday

    **E.** Tuesday

**5.** Which of the following are acceptable as three of the five days for sales events?

    **A.** Tuesday, Wednesday, Friday

    **B.** Tuesday, Wednesday, Thursday

    **C.** Monday, Wednesday, Friday

    **D.** Monday, Tuesday, Friday

    **E.** Monday, Tuesday, Wednesday

**6.** Suppose the yearly clearance sale is held on Friday. If so, on which of the following days must a sales event be planned?

**A.** Labor Day Sunday

**B.** Memorial Day Sunday

**C.** Thursday

**D.** Tuesday

**E.** Monday

## Answers

From the conditions, you can draw the following chart:

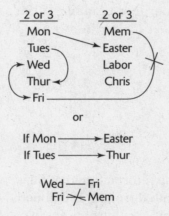

1. **B.** Eliminating the incorrect choices may be the most effective way to answer this question. The fifth condition eliminates choice A; the last condition eliminates choice C; the third condition eliminates choice D; and the second condition eliminates choice E.

2. **D.** If the annual clearance sale is Monday, then only one other weekday can be chosen to make a total of two weekdays. This eliminates either Wednesday or Friday since choosing one requires the other to be chosen. It also eliminates Tuesday, since choosing Tuesday requires Thursday to be chosen. This leaves Thursday as the other weekday.

3. **C.** If Monday or Thursday are not planned for sales events, then Tuesday will not be planned either because choosing Tuesday requires also choosing Thursday. This leaves exactly Wednesday and Friday as the two weekdays chosen. The annual clearance sale will thus be on either Wednesday or Friday and so cannot be on a holiday Sunday.

4. **E.** This question states that if a sales event is planned for Monday, which day could NOT be the yearly clearance sale. So this question starts with having one weekday chosen (Monday). According to the conditions, if a sales event is planned for Tuesday, then one must also be planned for Thursday. Since the yearly clearance sale will be one of the *two* weekdays or *two* Sundays, Tuesday cannot be the clearance sale since it would be one of *three* weekdays (Monday, Tuesday, Thursday).

5. **C.** Perhaps the most effective way of answering this question is to eliminate the incorrect choices. Remember, no more than three weekdays can be chosen. Choices A and D are each incorrect because choosing Tuesday requires also choosing Thursday. Choices B and E are each incorrect because choosing Wednesday requires also choosing Friday. Choice C will work along with Easter Sunday and either Labor Day Sunday or Christmas Sunday.

6. **A.** If Friday is the yearly clearance sale, then a sales event is planned for exactly two weekdays, and the other weekday must be Wednesday (see the fourth condition). Since the fifth condition rules out sales events on both Friday and Memorial Day Sunday, the other three sales days must be Easter Sunday, Christmas Sunday and Labor Day Sunday (the last of which is answer choice A).

# Comparison Charts

Another type of Analytical Reasoning problem gives information that can be organized into comparisons or very simple equations. For example, "Tom's weight is twice his sister Susan's weight; Arnold's weight is three times his son Tom's weight." Your simple equations would then be:

$$T = 2S$$

and

$$A = 3T$$

You can see that if you are given the information that Susan weighs 30 pounds, then you know that Tom weighs 60 pounds and Arnold weighs 180 pounds. Most of these types of relationships require common sense reasoning and the ability to see and make comparisons.

# Sample Set

A group of nuclear scientists have been working with six nuclear particles—Alpha B, Alpha Q, Alpha Z, Beta M, Beta O, and Beta V. These nuclear particles are to be used in a linear accelerator, and only the following is known about their relative speeds:

Alpha Q is the same speed as Beta M.

Alpha B is 600 miles per hour faster than Beta Q.

Alpha Z is twice as fast as Alpha Q.

None of the Beta particles is faster than any of the Alpha particles.

Alpha B is 400 miles per hour faster than Beta M.

Beta V is 300 miles per hour slower than Beta O.

No two Alpha particles are the same speed.

No two Beta particles are the same speed.

## Questions

**1.** Which of the following must be true?

  **A.**  Beta O is faster than Beta V.

  **B.**  Alpha Z is faster than Alpha B.

  **C.**  Beta V is faster than Beta M.

  **D.**  Alpha Z is the same speed as Alpha Q.

  **E.**  Beta V is faster than Beta O.

**2.** Which of the following may be faster than Alpha Z?

  **A.**  Alpha Q

  **B.**  Alpha B

  **C.**  Beta O

  **D.**  Beta M

  **E.**  Beta V

**3.** If Beta M travels at 2,000 miles per hour,

  **A.**  Alpha Q travels at 2,400 miles per hour.

  **B.**  Alpha Z travels at 4,000 miles per hour.

  **C.**  Alpha B travels at 2,600 miles per hour.

  **D.**  Beta O travels at 2,200 miles per hour.

  **E.**  Beta V travels at 2,100 miles per hour.

**4.** If Alpha Q travels at 3,000 miles per hour, which of the following must be FALSE?

  **A.**  Alpha B travels at 3,600 miles per hour.

  **B.**  Alpha Q is slower than Alpha Z.

  **C.**  Alpha Z is faster than Alpha B.

  **D.**  Alpha Z travels at 6,000 miles per hour.

  **E.**  Beta M travels at 3,000 miles per hour.

**5.** If Beta O travels at 2,300 miles per hour, all the following must be true EXCEPT:

   **A.** Beta V travels at 2,000 miles per hour.

   **B.** Alpha B travels at 2,900 miles per hour.

   **C.** Beta M travels at 2,500 miles per hour.

   **D.** Alpha Z travels at 5,000 miles per hour.

   **E.** Alpha Q travels at 2,700 miles per hour.

**6.** Assume that the scientists remove Alpha Q and decide to test another particle, Alpha D, and Alpha D is faster than Alpha B but slower than Alpha Z. If all the original information is still true, which of the following is the order of particles from fastest to slowest?

   **A.** Alpha Z, Alpha D, Alpha B, Beta M, Beta O, Beta V

   **B.** Alpha B, Alpha Z, Alpha D, Beta M, Beta O, Beta V

   **C.** Alpha Z, Alpha D, Alpha B, Beta O, Beta M, Beta V

   **D.** Alpha Z, Alpha D, Beta O, Alpha B, Beta V, Beta M

   **E.** Alpha Z, Beta M, Alpha D, Alpha B, Beta O, Beta V

## Answers

From the information given, the following relationships (equations) can be drawn:

$$Aq = Bm$$
$$Ab = Bo + 600$$
$$Az = 2Aq$$
$$Ab = Bm + 400$$
$$Bv = Bo - 300$$

and the chart

$$\left.\begin{array}{l} Ab \\ Az \end{array}\right\} ? \quad \leftarrow Faster$$

$$Aq \text{---} Bm \quad \leftarrow Same$$
$$Bo$$
$$Bv \quad \leftarrow Slower$$

**1. A.** Since Beta V is 300 miles per hour slower than Beta O, Beta O must be faster than Beta V. We cannot be sure of the relationship between Alpha Z and Alpha B, so B is not necessarily true. Choices C, D, and E are each false.

**2. B.** Alpha Z is faster than all the Betas; hence C, D, and E are incorrect. Alpha Z is faster than Alpha Q, so A is incorrect. Since no definitive relationship may be drawn between Alpha B and Alpha Z, B is the correct response.

**3. B.** Because Beta M travels at 2,000 mph, and Alpha Q is the same speed as Beta M, then Alpha Q's speed is also 2,000 mph. Since Alpha Z is twice as fast as Alpha Q, Alpha Z must travel at 4,000 mph.

Or, if Beta M travels at 2,000 mph, you can plug into the relationships (equations as follows):

$$Aq = Bm$$
$$Aq = 2,000$$

Now,

$$Az = 2Aq$$
$$Az = 2 \text{ times } 2,000 = 4,000$$

4. **A.** Only A must be false. If Alpha Q travels at 3,000 mph, Alpha Z must travel at 6,000 mph. Also, if Alpha Q travels at 3,000 mph, Beta M travels at 3,000 mph. Using the statement that Alpha B travels 400 mph faster than Beta M, Alpha B therefore travels at 3,400 mph. So C is not false. Choice B is not false, because we are given that Alpha Z travels twice as fast as Alpha Q. Only A is false. From the above, we see that Alpha B travels at 3,400 mph, not 3,600 mph.

5. **E.** If Beta O travels at 2,300 mph, according to the second statement, Alpha B travels at 2,900 mph. Using the fifth statement, Beta M must travel 2,500 mph. Therefore, from the first statement, Alpha Q's speed is also 2,500 mph, not 2,700 mph.

6. **A.** From the conditional information given in the question, the order of the faster Alpha particles (from fast to slow) is Alpha Z, then Alpha D, then Alpha B. Using the second and fifth statements, we know that Alpha B is 600 miles per hour faster than Beta O, but only 400 miles faster than Beta M. Therefore, Beta M must be faster than Beta O (by 200 mph). And from the sixth statement, Beta V is slower than Beta O. Therefore, the order of the remaining Beta particles, from fast to slow, is Beta M, then Beta O, then Beta V.

# Maps

Being able to draw a simple map using compass directions may be required on this section of the test. Know how to differentiate the positions of the compass, including such directions as northeast, due south, directly west, and so forth. For example, "A is north of B" is not the same as "A is due north of B." ("Due" means "directly.")

# Sample Set

Seven groups of campers (A, B, C, D, E, F, and G) embark on a hiking expedition into the Sierra Madres. At the first sign of nightfall, the campers set up campsites around a well, as follows:

Campsite A is due south of the well.

Campsite B is due east of campsite A and due south of campsite C.

Campsite G is west of the well.

Campsite F is south of the well.

Campsite D is east of campsite C.

Campsite E is directly northeast of the well.

## Questions

**1.** How many campsites could be south of the well?

   **A.** 2

   **B.** 3

   **C.** 4

   **D.** 5

   **E.** 6

**2.** How many campsites must be east of the well?

   **A.** 1

   **B.** 2

   **C.** 3

   **D.** 4

   **E.** 5

**3.** All of the following could be true EXCEPT:

   **A.** Campsite C is north of campsite E.

   **B.** Campsite A is south of campsite D.

   **C.** Campsite B is east of campsite F.

   **D.** Campsite G is north of campsite F.

   **E.** Campsite B is east of campsite D.

**4.** Which of the following must be true?

   **A.** Campsite D is west of campsite A.

   **B.** Campsite E is north of campsite B.

   **C.** Campsite G is south of campsite A.

   **D.** Campsite A is east of campsite B.

   **E.** Campsite C is south of campsite B.

**5.** Which of the following is a possible order of campsites a traveler could encounter while traveling due east from campsite F?

**A.** GABD

**B.** ABE

**C.** GECD

**D.** GBCD

**E.** GABE

**6.** What is the maximum number of campsites that a camper could encounter traveling directly southwest from campsite E?

**A.** 1

**B.** 2

**C.** 3

**D.** 4

**E.** 5

**7.** If a new group of settlers form campsite H, and campsite H is north of campsite F and west of campsite C, then which of the following must be true?

**A.** Campsite H is north of campsite G and west of campsite D.

**B.** Campsite H is south of campsite E and east of campsite C.

**C.** Campsite B is south of campsite H and north of campsite F.

**D.** Campsite D is east of campsite H and east of campsite A.

**E.** Campsite G is west of campsite H and south of campsite F.

## Answers

From the information given, a diagram may be drawn:

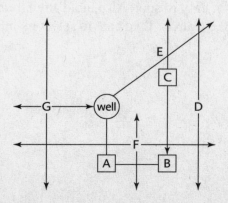

1. **E.** All the campsites *except E* could be south of the well, because E is *north*east of the well.

2. **D.** From the diagram, only campsites B, C, D, and E *must* be east of the well.

3. **E.** Since campsite B is due south of campsite C, and campsite D is east of campsite C, campsite D must also be east of campsite B. Therefore, E cannot be true.

4. **B.** Campsite B is due east of A and therefore south of the well. Since E is northeast of the well, E must be north of B. So choice B must be true. G, west of the well, has great range north or south. So C is not necessarily true. All the other statements are false.

5. **A.** Traveling *due* east from F (which is south of the well), a traveler would never encounter campsite E, which is northeast of the well. Therefore, choices B, C, and E may be eliminated. Nor would a traveler going due east encounter both B and C as these two campsites are located in a directly north-south fashion. Only choice A is possible: campsite G, then A, then B, then D.

6. **D.** Traveling directly southwest from E, one could encounter D, C, G, and F.

7. **D.** If campsite H is west of campsite C, then campsite D will not only be east of campsite A, but also east of campsite H. None of the other choices necessarily have to be true.

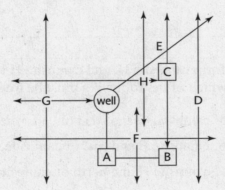

# Group Displays

A very common type of diagram is the simple group, or grouping, display in which you group items by similarities and differences. Always write out or abbreviate the group headings, don't just use a letter because you might confuse a letter with one of the items in a group. Also, underlining the group heading makes it easy to spot. Also, note any limitations on a group (for example, "Only two boys can be on the team"). Take care to select members from the proper group.

# Sample Set

Three flags (1, 2, and 3) are to be designed using nine colors: red, orange, yellow, green, blue, indigo, violet, black, and white. The design of the flags must not violate any of the following conditions:

Each flag must contain exactly three or exactly four colors.

Each color must be used.

With the exception of white, each color can be used in only one flag.

White must be used in all flags.

If flag 1 contains violet, flag 3 must contain both red and orange.

Flag 1 must contain indigo.

Flag 2 may not contain green or red.

Blue may not be used in the same flag with green or orange.

## Questions

1. Which of the following color designs does NOT violate the conditions?

   A.   1: indigo, orange, white
        2: black, green, yellow, white
        3: violet, blue, red, white

   B.   1: indigo, blue, green, white
        2: violet, orange, white
        3: black, yellow, red, white

   C.   1: indigo, white
        2: black, violet, blue, white
        3: green, orange, red, white

   D.   1: violet, indigo, red, white
        2: black, blue, yellow, white
        3: green, orange, white

   E.   1: black, violet, indigo, white
        2: blue, yellow, white
        3: green, orange, red, white

**2.** If flag 1 is composed of four colors, two of which are black and yellow, which of the following must be true?

    **A.** Flag 2 contains orange.

    **B.** Flag 1 contains green.

    **C.** Flag 2 contains blue.

    **D.** Flag 3 contains indigo.

    **E.** Flag 3 contains violet.

**3.** If flag 1 is composed of four colors, two of which are violet and green, which of the following is possible?

    **A.** Flag 2 contains orange and white.

    **B.** Flag 2 contains yellow and white.

    **C.** Flag 3 contains blue and white.

    **D.** Flag 2 contains indigo and white.

    **E.** Flag 1 contains indigo and black.

**4.** Which of the following are three possible colors for flag 1 if it is composed of exactly four colors?

    **A.** Red, white, and blue

    **B.** Blue, white, and orange

    **C.** Blue, white, and green

    **D.** Violet, white, and red

    **E.** Violet, white, and orange

**5.** If red, white, and blue are used together in one flag, which of the following must be FALSE?

    **A.** Flag 2 contains orange.

    **B.** Flag 3 contains yellow.

    **C.** Flag 3 contains green.

    **D.** Flag 1 contains violet.

    **E.** Flag 1 contains black.

**6.** Which trio of colors can Flag 2 include?

  **A.** Red, white, and blue

  **B.** Blue, white, and orange

  **C.** Indigo, white, and yellow

  **D.** Violet, white, and orange

  **E.** Black, white, and green

## Answers

From the facts and conditions, you can sketch the following display.

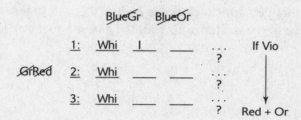

1. **E.** Perhaps the most effective way of addressing the question is to eliminate the choices that violate each condition. Immediately, you can eliminate choice C because flag 1 contains only two colors. Choice A is incorrect because flag 2 contains green, which violates the seventh condition. Choice B is incorrect because it violates the condition that blue may not be used with green. Choice D can be eliminated because flag 1 contains violet, but flag 3 does not contain both red and orange, as the fifth condition requires. Choice E conforms to all the conditions.

2. **C.** If flag 1 contains black and yellow and two other colors, white and indigo are the two others (see the fourth and sixth conditions). From the seventh condition, we now know that flag 3 must contain green and red. Since blue may not be used in the same flag with green (eighth condition), blue must therefore be in flag 2.

3. **B.** If two of the colors of flag 1 are violet and green, then the other two colors of flag 1 must be white and indigo (see the fourth and sixth conditions). From the seventh condition, we now know that flag 3 must contain red. From the fifth condition, we also now know that flag 3 contains orange. So flag 3 is red, orange, white, and either yellow or black. This leaves flag 2 to be composed of white and blue and possibly yellow and/or black. Choice B is the only choice that is possible.

4. **A.** From the fifth condition, we can eliminate choices D and E: if flag 1 contains violet, then both red and orange must be in flag 3, not also in flag 1. From the eighth condition, we can eliminate choices B and C because blue may not be used with either green or orange. That leaves choice A as the only remaining possibility.

**5. D.** If flag 1 were to contain violet as choice D states, then flag 3 must contain both red and orange (see the fifth condition). The question stem tells us that red and blue are used together in one flag. So that would put blue and orange together—which violates the eighth condition. Therefore, choice D, flag 1 contains violet, must be false. A tough one!

**6. D.** An effective way of attacking this question is to work from the conditions to eliminate the choices that violate the conditions. The seventh condition eliminates choices A and E. The eighth condition eliminates choice B. The sixth condition eliminates choice C. This leaves choice D as the only choice possible.

# Schedule Diagrams

Some Analytical Reasoning problems require that you organize information into a simple time, date, or day schedule in order to answer the questions more easily. These questions deal with persons, items, or events that can appear or occur only at certain times, days, or dates. Pay special attention to when these persons, items, or events *cannot* appear or occur. This will help you limit the possibilities.

# Sample Set

Two self-contained teams (Alpha and Beta) work simultaneously in a factory, each team constructing the same vehicle composed of five separate sections: J, K, M, Q, and Z. However, each team may assemble in whatever order they choose, as long as they follow these restrictions:

Each section takes exactly one workday to assemble.

Both teams start Monday morning and end on Friday afternoon.

Because of tool limitations, both teams may not be assembling the same section on the same day.

The Beta team must assemble section Z on Thursday.

On Monday, only sections M, Q, and Z are available for assembly.

On Tuesday, only sections J and Z are available for assembly.

On Wednesday, only sections K, M, Q, and Z are available for assembly.

On Thursday, only sections K, M, and Z are available for assembly.

On Friday, all sections are available for assembly.

## Questions

**1.** Which of the following sections must the Alpha team assemble on Friday?

    **A.** J

    **B.** K

    **C.** M

    **D.** Q

    **E.** Z

**2.** Which of the following statements must be true?

    **A.** Alpha assembles section Q on Monday.

    **B.** Alpha assembles section Z on Tuesday.

    **C.** Alpha assembles section M on Wednesday.

    **D.** Beta assembles section M on Monday.

    **E.** Beta assembles section K on Wednesday.

**3.** Which of the following could be true?

    **A.** On Monday, Alpha does not assemble section M or Q.

    **B.** On Monday, Beta does not assemble section M or Q.

    **C.** On Wednesday, Beta does not assemble section K, M, or Q.

    **D.** On Wednesday, Alpha does not assemble section M or Q.

    **E.** On Thursday, Alpha does not assemble section K or M.

**4.** If Alpha assembles section Q on Monday, which of the following must be true?

    **A.** Alpha assembles section M on Friday.

    **B.** Alpha assembles section K on Wednesday.

    **C.** Beta assembles section M on Monday.

    **D.** Beta assembles section K on Wednesday.

    **E.** Beta assembles section Q on Wednesday.

5. Which of the following pairs of statements could be true?

   A. Alpha assembles section M on Thursday; Beta assembles section M on Wednesday.

   B. Alpha assembles section Q on Wednesday; Beta assembles section M on Monday.

   C. Alpha assembles section M on Wednesday; Beta assembles section M on Monday.

   D. Alpha assembles section Q on Wednesday; Alpha assembles section M on Thursday.

   E. Alpha assembles section M on Monday; Beta assembles section Q on Wednesday.

6. If Beta assembles section Q on Friday, which of the following statements CANNOT be true?

   A. Beta assembles section K on Wednesday.

   B. Beta assembles section M on Monday.

   C. Alpha assembles section K on Thursday.

   D. Alpha assembles section Q on Wednesday.

   E. Alpha assembles section Q on Monday.

## Answers

The following schedule diagram can be drawn for questions 1 through 6.

|  | M, Q, Z Mon | J, Z Tues | K, M, Q, Z Wed | K, M, Z Thur |
|---|---|---|---|---|
| Alpha |  | Z |  |  |
| Beta |  | J |  | Z |

1. **A.** Since Beta assembles section Z on Thursday, Beta must assemble section J on Tuesday because it is the only other available section besides Z on that day. Since section J is not available on Monday, Wednesday, or Thursday, Alpha must assemble section J on Friday.

2. **B.** Since Beta assembles section Z on Thursday, Alpha must assemble section Z on Tuesday because it is the only available section besides J on that day.

3. **D.** On Wednesday only sections K, M, Q, and Z are available for assembling. Since Alpha assembles section Z on Tuesday, only sections K, M, and Q remain possible to be assembled by Alpha on Wednesday. Therefore, Alpha could assemble section K on Wednesday.

4. **C.** If Alpha assembles section Q on Monday, this leaves only sections Z and M available for Beta to assemble on Monday. Since from the facts we are told that Beta is assembling section Z on Thursday, that leaves section M for Beta to assemble on Monday.

**5. C.** Choice A cannot be true: If Alpha and Beta each assemble section M on Thursday and Wednesday respectively, that leaves only section Q for both teams to assemble on Monday, which is not permitted. Choice B leaves no section for Alpha to assemble on Monday. Choice D does not allow Alpha to assemble all five sections because K is not available for assembly on Monday. Choice E is not possible because it does not allow Beta a new section to assemble on Monday. Only choice C is possible.

**6. D.** If Beta assembles section Q on Friday, then it must assemble section M on Monday. Therefore Alpha must assemble section Q on Monday, which means Alpha cannot assemble section Q on Wednesday.

# Elimination Chart

One type of Analytical Reasoning problem presents information that excludes or eliminates other possibilities. For instance, four people receiving four different grades or five animals belonging to five different owners—as soon as one item is placed, it narrows the placement of the other items.

## Sample Set

Two men (Ben and Arnold) and two women (Lydia and Dolly) have four different professions: dancer, magician, violinist, and salesperson, but not respectively. A game show contestant is trying to match the people with their professions. He is given the following information:

> Ben is not the dancer.
>
> The violinist is a woman.
>
> The dancer is not a woman.
>
> Dolly is the magician.

## Questions

**1.** From the information given, the contestant can deduce that Lydia must be the

    **A.** magician.

    **B.** dancer.

    **C.** violinist.

    **D.** salesperson.

    **E.** Cannot be determined

**2.** If the two men switch professions, which of the following must be true?

    **A.** Ben will be the salesperson.

    **B.** Arnold will be the dancer.

    **C.** Arnold will be the violinist.

    **D.** Arnold will be the magician.

    **E.** Arnold will be the salesperson.

## Explanation

Set up your diagram; realize that as soon as you place an item, you can then eliminate it every-where else in the grid. The grids presented here are fairly formal, and you may not need to draw such elaborate grids. In many cases, you can arrive at the correct answer by using varia-tions of these techniques in a less formal, simpler diagram or, in some cases, even mentally. Mark what you know is *not* true as well as what you know to be true. For instance, first set up your diagram as follows:

|        | Magician | Violinist | Dancer | Salesperson |
|--------|----------|-----------|--------|-------------|
| Ben    |          |           |        |             |
| Arnold |          |           |        |             |
| Lydia  |          |           |        |             |
| Dolly  |          |           |        |             |

Now notice that the first information statement allows you to eliminate Ben as the dancer:

|        | Magician | Violinist | Dancer | Salesperson |
|--------|----------|-----------|--------|-------------|
| Ben    |          |           | —      |             |
| Arnold |          |           |        |             |
| Lydia  |          |           |        |             |
| Dolly  |          |           |        |             |

The second information statement eliminates both of the men from being the violinist:

|  | Magician | Violinist | Dancer | Salesperson |
|---|---|---|---|---|
| Ben |  | — | — |  |
| Arnold |  | — |  |  |
| Lydia |  |  |  |  |
| Dolly |  |  |  |  |

The third information statement tells you the dancer is not a woman:

|  | Magician | Violinist | Dancer | Salesperson |
|---|---|---|---|---|
| Ben |  | — | — |  |
| Arnold |  | — |  |  |
| Lydia |  |  | — |  |
| Dolly |  |  | — |  |

Thus, you now know that the dancer must be Arnold. You should now eliminate magician and salesperson as possibilities for Arnold:

|  | Magician | Violinist | Dancer | Salesperson |
|---|---|---|---|---|
| Ben |  | — | — |  |
| Arnold | — | — | ✔ | — |
| Lydia |  |  | — |  |
| Dolly |  |  | — |  |

The fourth information statement says that Dolly is the magician:

| | Magician | Violinist | Dancer | Salesperson |
|---|---|---|---|---|
| Ben | — | — | — | |
| Arnold | — | — | ✔ | — |
| Lydia | — | | — | |
| Dolly | ✔ | — | — | — |

You can now see that Ben must be the salesperson, and Lydia must, therefore, be the violinist.

## Answers

1. **C.** The violinist is Lydia.

2. **E.** From the statements, you can derive that Ben is the salesperson. If, according to this question, the two men switch professions, then Arnold will be the salesperson.

# Information Display

Some Analytical Reasoning problems won't fit into a neat diagram. Therefore, it may be helpful to simply list or display the information gathered from the conditions in as simple a way as possible. For instance:

# Sample Set

Tina's Doberman has a litter of six puppies. Each of the puppies is a solid color. The puppies have the following characteristics:

Exactly three puppies have floppy ears.

Only two of the puppies are brown.

Exactly five of the puppies are female.

## Questions

**1.** Which of the following must be true?

    **A.**  At least two of the females have floppy ears.

    **B.**  Three of the females have floppy ears.

    **C.**  One of the brown puppies has floppy ears.

    **D.**  All of the females have brown eyes.

    **E.**  Exactly two of the females have brown eyes.

**2.** Which of the following must be true?

    **A.**  Two of the females are brown.

    **B.**  All of the females have floppy ears.

    **C.**  All of the brown puppies are females.

    **D.**  One of the females is brown with floppy ears.

    **E.**  One of the females is brown.

## Explanation

This particular problem does not fit into either a location, a connection, or an elimination diagram, but displaying the facts in a simple diagram may be helpful:

### 6 Puppies

| | | |
|---|---|---|
| *Ears:* | 3 floppy | 3 not floppy |
| *Color:* | 2 brown | 4 not brown |
| *Sex:* | 5 females | 1 male |

## Answers

**1. A.** Since five of the puppies are female, the sixth puppy (male) could have floppy ears, which would leave two of the females to have floppy ears.

**2. E.** Since five of the six puppies are female, and since there are two brown puppies, at least one female must be brown.

# Practice Analytical Reasoning Questions

*Questions 1 through 6 are based on the following information.*

A film festival committee is scheduling seven films to be screened, one per evening, during a weeklong film festival. Three films—A, B, and C—were directed by Alfred Hitchcock. Three films—D, E, and F—were directed by Steven Spielberg. One film—G—was directed by a novice director. The festival screenings begin on a Monday evening and end on the following Sunday evening. The festival schedule must follow these conditions:

> Hitchcock's B film may not be screened on Monday or Saturday or immediately before or immediately after Spielberg's F film.

> The novice director's film must not precede any of the other films.

> Hitchcock's A film must not be screened after Spielberg's E film.

> All three films by the same director may not be screened consecutively.

1. Which of the following is an acceptable schedule for the film festival, from Monday to Sunday?

   A. F, D, B, E, C, A, G

   B. D, B, C, F, A, E, G

   C. C, B, F, A, E, D, G

   D. A, D, F, C, E, G, B

   E. A, B, D, E, F, C, G

2. If Hitchcock's C and A films are screened Monday and Friday, respectively, which of the following must be true?

   A. Hitchcock's B is screened just after Spielberg's D.

   B. Spielberg's F is screened just after Hitchcock's C.

   C. Hitchcock's A is screened just after Hitchcock's B.

   D. Spielberg's F is screened on Thursday.

   E. Spielberg's D is screened on Wednesday.

3. If Spielberg's F is screened on Wednesday, which of the following must be true?

   A. E is screened on Thursday.

   B. C is screened on Thursday.

   C. D is screened on Saturday.

   D. B is screened on Friday.

   E. A is screened on Monday.

4. If three consecutive screenings are E, D, and C, respectively, then which of the following is possible?

   A. E immediately follows F.

   B. F immediately follows C.

   C. B immediately follows C.

   D. F immediately follows A.

   E. E immediately follows A.

**5.** If C is screened on Wednesday, which of the following may NOT be screened on Thursday?

   **A.** F

   **B.** E

   **C.** D

   **D.** B

   **E.** A

**6.** If films E and F are screened Wednesday and Thursday, respectively, then which of the following must be true?

   **A.** D is screened on Monday.

   **B.** C is screened on Monday.

   **C.** C is screened on Friday.

   **D.** B is screened on Friday.

   **E.** A is screened on Tuesday.

*Questions 7 through 12 are based on the following information.*

Eight children each performed one solo at a musical recital consisting of eight solos. Two girls (Nancy and Patty) each played clarinet; two girls (Judith and Ronnie) each played the violin; three girls (Xina, Sally, and Fran) each played drums; the boy (Arnold) played the trumpet. The following are true about the recital:

   None of the girls' solos was followed by a boy's solo.

   Sally performed after Xina.

   Patty performed after Nancy.

   Except for the trumpet, each solo must be either preceded or followed by a solo of the same instrument.

   A violin solo was performed neither third nor last.

**7.** Which of the following is possible?

   **A.** Nancy performed fifth.

   **B.** Nancy performed fourth.

   **C.** Nancy performed third.

   **D.** Xina performed eighth.

   **E.** Xina performed third.

**8.** All of the following are possible sequences for the third, fourth, and fifth spots, respectively, EXCEPT:

   **A.** Patty, Ronnie, Judith

   **B.** Xina, Sally, Ronnie

   **C.** Xina, Sally, Judith

   **D.** Xina, Fran, Judith

   **E.** Fran, Sally, Ronnie

**9.** Which of the following statements violates the conditions?

   **A.** Patty performed fourth.

   **B.** Patty performed third.

   **C.** Nancy performed second.

   **D.** Fran performed third.

   **E.** Fran performed second.

**10.** Which of the following statements is possible if Fran's solo immediately followed Sally's solo?

   **A.** Patty performed eighth.

   **B.** Patty performed fourth.

   **C.** Patty performed seventh.

   **D.** Xina performed third.

   **E.** Xina performed fourth.

**11.** Xina could have performed in all of the following spots EXCEPT:

A. Second

B. Third

C. Fourth

D. Sixth

E. Seventh

**12.** If Xina performed either immediately before or immediately after either Ronnie or Judith, which of the following is NOT possible?

A. Fran performed after Sally.

B. Patty performed before Ronnie.

C. Xina performed after Judith.

D. Fran performed before Sally.

E. Fran performed before Patty.

*Questions 13 through 18 are based on the following information.*

A magician has nearly perfected a series of tricks employing four different animals—a dove, a rabbit, a gerbil, and a snake—and either one or two magic boxes. When the magician places two of the four animals in the magic box, they both disappear and another of one of the two other animals magically appears in the box, as follows:

The snake and gerbil disappear and another dove appears.

The snake and dove disappear and another gerbil appears.

The dove and gerbil disappear and another snake appears.

The snake and rabbit disappear and another gerbil appears.

The gerbil and rabbit disappear and another dove appears.

However, when the dove and the rabbit are placed together in the box, only the dove disappears, leaving the original rabbit in the box.

**13.** If the magician starts with the four different animals and places a pair in each of two boxes, which of the following could be the animals magically appearing in both boxes?

A. A snake and a snake

B. A dove and a dove

C. A dove and a snake

D. A dove and a rabbit

E. A gerbil and a rabbit

**14.** Suppose the magician starts with the four different animals on the table, and after the magician performs one trick, the rabbit is gone. Which of the following animals could be left?

A. Gerbil, gerbil, snake

B. Dove, snake, snake

C. Dove, snake, gerbil

D. Gerbil, gerbil, dove

E. Dove, gerbil, dove

**15.** If the magician starts with the four different animals, and after the magician performs one trick, exactly one dove is among the remaining three animals, which of the following must be the other two animals remaining?

A. One snake and one rabbit

B. One gerbil and one rabbit

C. Two rabbits

D. Two snakes

E. Two gerbils

16. If the magician performs one trick, which of the following is possible for the three animals remaining?

    A. Two snakes and a gerbil

    B. Two gerbils and a rabbit

    C. Two doves and a gerbil

    D. Two snakes and a dove

    E. A rabbit, a dove, and a snake

17. If after performing one trick no snake is among the resulting three animals, the pair of animals placed in the magic box must have been

    A. the snake with another animal.

    B. the dove with another animal.

    C. the dove with the snake.

    D. the rabbit with the snake.

    E. the rabbit with the dove.

18. If two pairs of animals are placed one pair in each of two magic boxes, and a snake appears in exactly one of the boxes, then the animal in the other box must be

    A. a rabbit.

    B. a gerbil.

    C. a dove.

    D. the result of using a dove and a snake.

    E. the result of using a rabbit and a dove.

*Questions 19 through 24 are based on the following information.*

A college tennis squad is selecting four sets of doubles pairs to compete in a national tournament. At least one member of each pair must be an upperclassman. The upperclassmen are AB, CQ, DP, WI, LX, and MA. The underclassmen are OZ, SA, FF, ZN, and VE. No player may be paired more than once or with more than one partner. In addition:

  DP cannot be paired with OZ.

  ZN and LX are injured and will play only if a healthy teammate is disqualified.

  FF will be paired only with CQ or WI.

  AB will not be paired with MA, OZ, or VE.

19. Which of the following is an acceptable set of partners for one of the pairs?

    A. SA and VE

    B. OZ and FF

    C. DP and MA

    D. AB and VE

    E. AB and OZ

20. Which of the following healthy underclassmen may play with AB?

    A. VE

    B. FF

    C. SA

    D. OZ

    E. WI

**21.** Suppose AB has been paired with a teammate. If SA is already paired with WI, and FF has been chosen to play with someone other than AB, who of the following choices can be paired with AB?

   **A.** MA

   **B.** OZ

   **C.** VE

   **D.** CQ

   **E.** DP

**22.** Suppose all the healthy underclassmen are paired. If CQ is not paired with OZ, FF, or VE, then SA's partner must be either

   **A.** AB or CQ.

   **B.** AB or MA.

   **C.** CQ or MA.

   **D.** DP or WI.

   **E.** DP or MA.

**23.** If pairs consist of only healthy players and CQ is not assigned to a team, then DP must be paired with

   **A.** AB.

   **B.** WI.

   **C.** MA.

   **D.** FF.

   **E.** VE.

**24.** Suppose MA, CQ, and SA are disqualified. With whom does OZ play?

   **A.** WI

   **B.** LX

   **C.** DP

   **D.** ZN

   **E.** VE

# Answers for Analytical Reasoning Practice Questions

From the facts and conditions, the following chart can be drawn for questions 1 through 6:

Hitch: A, B, C
Spiel: D, E, F
Novice: G

| ~~B~~ | | | | | ~~B~~ | N |
|------|------|-----|------|-----|-----|-----|
| Mon | Tues | Wed | Thur | Fri | Sat | Sun |

BF
FB
E…A
ABC in any order
DEF in any order

**1. B.** Perhaps the most effective way of working through this question is by using the conditions and eliminating those choices that violate the conditions. Choice A violates the third condition, that A must not be screened after E. Choice C violates the third condition: B and F are consecutive. Choice D violates the second condition: G precedes another film. And choice E has all three Spielberg films consecutive, which violates the last condition. Choice B is the only schedule that does not violate any conditions.

2. **E.** If C and A are screened Monday and Friday, then E must be screened on Saturday:

| Mon | Tue | Wed | Thur | Fri | Sat | Sun |
|-----|-----|-----|------|-----|-----|-----|
| C   |     |     |      | A   | E   | G   |

Since B may not be immediately before or immediately after F (first condition), the remaining film, D, must separate B and F. So D must be screened on Wednesday, leaving B and F to be screened on Tuesday and Thursday.

3. **D.** If F is screened on Wednesday, then B must be screened on Friday because from the first condition we know that B cannot be screened on Monday or Saturday or immediately before or immediately after F. (You should already have placed G in the final Sunday spot.)

4. **B.** Choice A. puts F just before EDC: FEDC. The third condition says A must come somewhere before E: . . . A . . . FEDC . . . G. But film B cannot be screened on Monday or Saturday and cannot be immediately before film F. So we have nowhere legal to put B; so this choice is not possible. Choice C says B follows C; so that gives. . . . EDCB . . . G. The third condition says A must come before E: . . . A . . . EDCB . . . G. Now, where to put F. Because F and B cannot be consecutive, F will have to go either before or after A, which would mean B is screened on Saturday, which violates a condition. So choice C is out. Choice D gives . . . AF . . . EDC . . . G because, from the conditions, A must not be screened after E. Now where does B live? Since B cannot be screened on Monday or Saturday or immediately after F, this choice also will not conform to the conditions. Choice E gives . . . AEDC . . . G. Since B cannot be screened on Monday or Saturday or immediately before or after F, this choice as well will violate the conditions. Only choice B is possible: ABEDCFG.

5. **E.** If C is screened on Wednesday and A is screened on Thursday, where can B go? The first condition says B cannot be screened on Monday or Saturday, and the fourth condition does not allow films A. B, and C to be shown consecutively.

| Mon | Tue | Wed | Thur | Fri | Sat | Sun |
|-----|-----|-----|------|-----|-----|-----|
|     |     | C   | A    |     |     | G   |

6. **C.** If E and F are screened on Wednesday and Thursday, then B must be screened on Tuesday (see the first condition).

| Mon | Tue | Wed | Thur | Fri | Sat | Sun |
|-----|-----|-----|------|-----|-----|-----|
|     | B   | E   | F    |     |     | G   |

That puts A in the Monday slot (see the third condition). Films C and D remain. Film D cannot be placed in the Friday slot, because this would put all three Spielberg films together. So we have:

| Mon | Tue | Wed | Thur | Fri | Sat | Sun |
|-----|-----|-----|------|-----|-----|-----|
| A   | B   | E   | F    | C   | D   | G   |

So C is screened on Friday.

From the facts and conditions, the following chart can be drawn for questions 7 through 12:

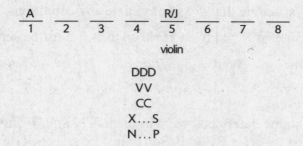

Because none of the girls' solos was followed by a boy's solo, Arnold must have performed first. Because *each solo must either be preceded or followed by a solo of the same instrument,* the solos of each type of instrument were performed consecutively. Because *a violin solo was not performed third or last,* a violin solo could also not have been performed second or seventh because this would leave one spot (either second or eighth) that would not accommodate a pair or trio of similar instrument solos. So, because the two consecutive violin solos could have been performed only in the forth, fifth, or sixth spots, the fifth spot must have been a violin solo.

**7. E.** Choice A is not possible: Nancy (clarinet) could not have performed fifth because fifth was a violin solo. A clarinet solo could also not have been performed fourth (choice B) because this would place the other clarinet solo third, leaving the second spot an open space. Choice C is not possible because if Nancy were to have performed third, the other clarinet solo (Patty) must have been performed second, which is not permitted by the third condition. And Xina could not have performed eighth (choice D) because Sally performed after Xina (second condition).

**8. D.** Only choice D is not possible because this sequence in the third, fourth, and fifth spots would cause Sally, the remaining drum solo, to take the second spot, which violates the second condition. All of the other choices are possible without violating any conditions.

**9. A.** If Patty were in the fourth, then the other clarinet solo (Nancy) must be in the third spot (see the third condition). This would leave the second spot open.

**10. A.** If Fran's drum solo immediately followed Sally's drum solo, then Xina's drum solo must have immediately preceded Sally's drum solo (see the second condition); so XSF. Therefore, the three drum solos were either in the second, third, and fourth spots or in the sixth, seventh, and eighth spots. So Xina could not have performed third or fourth. Because Patty was after Nancy (see the second condition) and there must be room for the other violin solo, Patty could not have performed fourth or seventh. This leaves just choice A, which is possible.

**11. C.** Xina, one of three drum solos, could not have performed fourth because the second condition requires Sally to perform after Xina.

**12. E.** If Xina performed *adjacent* to either Ronnie or Judith, then Xina must have performed sixth in order for Sally to perform after her (see the second condition). Fran (the third drum solo) must then have been either seventh or eighth, which means that Fran could not have performed before clarinetist Patty, who would have been second or third.

From the information given, the following chart can be made for questions 13 through 18:

$$S + G = D$$

$$S + D = G$$

$$D + G = S$$

$$S + R = G$$

$$G + R = D$$

$$D + R = R$$

13. **D.** By placing the rabbit and the dove in one box, and the snake and the gerbil in the other box, the resulting animals will be a rabbit and a dove.

14. **D.** If a rabbit has disappeared, one of two pairs would have been placed in the box, either the rabbit and the gerbil ($R + G = D$) or the rabbit and the snake ($R + S = G$). Choice D is the latter of these possibilities, losing the rabbit and snake and gaining another gerbil.

15. **E.** If exactly one dove is among the remaining three animals, then neither the original dove disappeared nor a second dove appeared. The only two animals that could have been placed in the box to achieve this result are the rabbit and the snake ($R + S = G$). Thus, the three animals remaining are the dove and two gerbils.

16. **B.** Of the choices, only two gerbils and a rabbit are possible for the three remaining animals. That will occur if the dove and the snake are placed in the box ($D + S = G$).

17. **A.** Placing the snake in the box with any other animal results in the snake's disappearing.

18. **B.** The only way of getting a snake is by placing a dove and gerbil together ($D + G = S$). That means the other box must contain a rabbit and a snake, which produces a gerbil.

From the facts you could make the following diagram for questions 19 through 24:

| Upper | Under |
|-------|-------|
| AB | OZ |
| CQ | SA |
| DP | FF |
| WI | VE |
| MA | |
| LX ←—injured—→ ZN | |

DP ⇸ OZ
AB ⇸ OZ
AB ⇸ MA
AB ⇸ VE

19. **C.** Choice A contains no upperclassmen. Choice B has FF without either CQ or WI. Choices D and E have AB paired with VE and OZ, respectively, which is prohibited by the facts. Only choice C is an acceptable set.

**20. C.** Choices A and D are directly prohibited by the facts. Choice B must play with CQ or WI, not AB. Choice E is not an underclassman. Only C is an underclassman who may play with AB.

**21. E.** From the facts, AB cannot play with MA, OZ, or VE, which eliminates choices A, B, and C. Since WI is already playing with SA, that leaves CQ to play with FF, which eliminates choice D. The only remaining player available in the choices to pair with AB is DP.

**22. A.** If all healthy underclassmen are paired, their four partners must each be an upperclassman. If CQ is not paired with OZ, FF, or VE, then FF must be paired with WI. That leaves only MA left to pair with OZ. VE must thus be paired with DP. That leaves SA with either AB or CQ.

**23. E.** If CQ is not assigned to a team, then each team consists of one upperclassman and one underclassman, and FF must play with WI. Therefore, AB must play with SA, which means OZ must play with MA, leaving VE to play with DP.

**24. B.** If MA, CQ, and SA are disqualified, so ZN and LX, although hobbled, must play to fill out the teams. That means FF and WI are paired as a team. Since AB cannot play with VE or OZ, AB must play with the ailing ZN as another team, and DP must play with VE. So OZ plays with the other injured player, LX.

# A PATTERNED PLAN OF ATTACK
## Analytical Reasoning

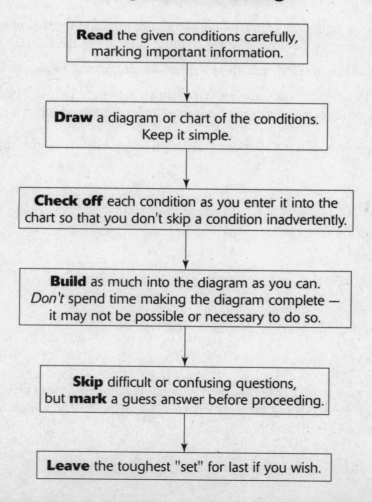

**Read** the given conditions carefully, marking important information.

**Draw** a diagram or chart of the conditions. Keep it simple.

**Check off** each condition as you enter it into the chart so that you don't skip a condition inadvertently.

**Build** as much into the diagram as you can. *Don't* spend time making the diagram complete — it may not be possible or necessary to do so.

**Skip** difficult or confusing questions, but **mark** a guess answer before proceeding.

**Leave** the toughest "set" for last if you wish.

The Logical Reasoning section lasts 35 minutes and typically contains 24 to 26 questions.

## Ability Tested

This section tests your ability to analyze and evaluate short passages or statements drawn from a variety of sources and presented in a variety of modes.

## Basic Skills Necessary

Candidates who can read critically and understand the reasoning in an argument tend to do well in this section. The ability to eliminate irrelevant information is also important.

## Directions

In the Logical Reasoning section, you're presented with brief passages or statements and are required to evaluate their reasoning. In each case, select the best answer choice, even though more than one choice may offer a possible answer. You should eliminate choices that are unreasonable or incompatible with common-sense standards.

## Analysis

1. Use only information given or implied in a passage. Do not consider outside information, even if it seems more accurate than the given information.

2. Note the stress on choosing the BEST answer; the testmakers strongly imply that there may be more than one good answer.

3. No special expertise in logic is necessary; do not arrive at your answer choice through the use of formal logical principles; rely on common sense.

## Suggested Approach with Samples

In most cases, the question will have the following structure: brief reading passage—question—answer choices. It may be helpful to read the question first (don't read the answer choices, however!) so that you have an idea of what to look for as you read the passage. After reading the passage, reread the question and assess the answer choices. If the question itself is long and involved, prereading the question may not be time effective. Practice will help you determine when prereading the question will be helpful to you.

# Preread the Question

Prereading the question allows you to read the passage with a *focus*. In this case, you are looking for the author's point; recognizing the concluding sentence as the author's point is valuable here.

# Sample Passage

Whatever else might be said about American elections, they are quite unlike Russian elections in that Americans make choices. And one choice they can make in this free country is to stay home.

---

Q. What is the author's point in the above passage?

    **A.** Americans who do decide to vote make more choices than those who do not.

    **B.** American elections embody many negative aspects, most of which are not embodied by Soviet elections.

    **C.** Choosing not to vote is the prerogative of a free citizen.

    **D.** All citizens vote in every Soviet election.

    **E.** Most American voters are not well informed enough to vote wisely.

---

# Read the Passage

Keep the question in mind when reading a passage, and also note the major issue and supporting evidence in the passage. Determine what the passage is about in general. In the preceding passage, the general topic is "free choice." Evidence supporting the issue of free choice is (1) the fact that Americans make choices when they vote and (2) the fact that Americans may make the choice not to vote.

# Eliminate Irrelevant Answer Choices

When considering the multiple choices, immediately eliminate those items that are (1) irrelevant to the question and/or the major issue of the passage and (2) not addressed in the passage.

Consider the preceding passage. The author's point is necessarily connected with the major issue of the passage—in this case, free choice. The author stresses the free choice *not to vote*, by way of making the point. You may eliminate all choices that do not address the free choice not to vote: A is irrelevant because it addresses the number of choices rather than the freedom of choice. B raises issues scarcely addressed in the passage—that is, the negative aspects of elections. D doesn't address the issue of choosing not to vote; although it notes that all Soviet citizens must vote, it neglects the main point—that Americans don't have to. E is irrelevant to the issue of free choice, stressing instead voter information. The best choice is C, which addresses the major issue, free choice, and also the author's specific point, the free choice not to vote.

# Categorize the Question

Most of the Logical Reasoning questions fall into a small number of categories or types. Immediately recognizing the type of question can be extremely helpful. While there may be occasional overlap, typically seven different types of Logical Reasoning questions occur on the LSAT. Since the Logical Reasoning questions comprise about 50% of your entire exam score, understanding the seven basic types of questions is essential. Knowing and anticipating the basic question types can help you simplify what may otherwise appear to be a long, involved question.

A brief analysis of these seven Logical Reasoning question types follows:

## Main Point/Conclusion

Recognizing the main issue can help you answer this type of question. You may be asked to identify the main point, main idea, or conclusion expressed in the passage. Or, more commonly, the passage may leave the point unstated, and the question may ask you to draw a logical connection.

Some of the ways this question type may be expressed are

- In the passage above, the author argues that . . .
- Which of the following statements best expresses the author's central point in the passage above?
- Based on the above passage, the author concludes . . .
- Which of the following best expresses the main point of the passage above?
- The author's argument is best expressed as . . .
- Which of the following best expresses the point the author is attempting to make?
- Which of the following is most probably the point to which the author's statements lead?
- If the author's point is a logically relevant inference that can be drawn from the premises in the passage, which of the following statements expresses that point?
- The author concludes that . . .
- Which of the following is supported by the passage above?
- The author's purpose in the passage above is to . . .

# Assumption

An assumption of an argument or statement is an unstated notion or foundation upon which the argument rests. For instance, consider this statement:

Legislative action is necessary in order to improve the quality of air in our community.

The brief statement above contains at least two unstated assumptions. First, it assumes that present air conditions are unsatisfactory, or are becoming so, and need to be improved. The statement also assumes that such proposed legislative action can be effective in resolving the air problem. (If it could not be effective, why would the author suggest such action?)

Some of the ways this question type may be expressed are

- Which of the following is an assumption that supports the conclusion in the passage above?
- The argument above logically depends on which of the following assumptions?
- In the argument above, the author assumes that . . .
- Which of the following assumptions underlies the passage above?
- Which of the following is an assumption necessary to the author's argument?
- A necessary part of the author's argument is the assumption that . . .?
- In drawing conclusions, the author relies on which of the following assumptions?
- Which of the following is the best formulation of the principle presupposed in the reasoning above?

# Inference

The process of *inferring*—logically proceeding from one statement or judgment to the next—will be required for this question type. For example:

In the last national election, 40% of the voters were male.

From the above statement, you can logically infer that a majority of voters (60%, in fact) were female. Note how this inference logically follows from the original statement. Be careful, however, to select the most direct answer choice on the LSAT. It would *not* be effective to continue your line of inference, such as *40% of voters were male; therefore 60% were female; therefore women have more political clout; therefore women's issues get higher priority from voters; therefore* . . . The correct answer is typically the most direct inference.

Some of the ways this question type may be expressed are

- Which of the following inferences can most reliably be drawn from the passage above?
- Which of the following can be inferred from the above passage?
- All of the following may logically be inferred from the passage above EXCEPT: . . .

- Which of the following can be validly inferred from facts or premises expressed above?
- Based on the passage, the author implies that . . .

## Effect of Additional Information on the Argument

This question type begins with a passage presenting an argument and then follows with a question asking you to select the choice that either *strengthens* or *weakens* that argument. For example:

The number of bear sightings in the United States during 2001 has risen dramatically. Therefore, the population of bears must be increasing.

Q. Which of the following, if true, weakens the argument above?

A. Increased home development in 1990 has resulted in many new communities being built on the edge of national forests.

Notice how this choice weakens the argument that increased bear sightings are necessarily a result of growing bear populations. Choice A instead indicates that the increased bear sightings may be a result of more people living closer to existing bear populations and thus weakens the argument.

The many varied wordings of this question type can be confusing and troubling. However, they are basically of two kinds: (1) Which strengthens the argument? or (2) Which weakens the argument?

Some of the ways this question type may be expressed are

- Which of the following contradicts the argument made in the passage above? *(weakens)*
- Which of the following would be a valid objection to the argument above? *(weakens)*
- Which of the following statements, if true, strengthens the argument above? *(strengthens)*
- Which of the following would provide the most support for the conclusion above? *(strengthens)*
- Which of the following, if true, would most effectively challenge the conclusion above? *(weakens)*
- Which of the following, if true, would constitute evidence that the conclusion is incorrect? *(weakens)*
- Which of the following additional information would challenge the author's conclusion? *(weakens)*
- Which of the following supports the conclusion in the passage above? *(strengthens)*
- Which of the following, if true, would undermine the conclusion of the argument? *(weakens)*
- The author's conclusion would be seriously weakened if it were proven that . . . *(weakens)*
- Which of the following is a serious drawback to the procedure suggested in the passage? *(weakens)*

- A logical critique of the argument above would most likely emphasize . . . *(weakens)*

- A proponent of the opposite point of view can most directly counter the author's argument by pointing out that . . . *(weakens)*

- Which of the following would call into question the validity of the author's conclusion? *(weakens)*

- Which of the following, if true, would confirm the author's conclusion? *(strengthens)*

- The implied conclusion would be more reasonable if which of the following were true? *(strengthens)*

# Method of Argument

This question type requires you to understand the author's method of persuasion (however faulty it may appear to be). It may even ask you to find a similar method in the choices. For example:

Since all men are mortal, and Susan is a mortal, Susan must be a man.

> Q. Which of the following arguments parallels the reasoning in the passage above?
>
> **A.** All skyscrapers in New York City are tall. Since Mr. Arnold is tall, Mr. Arnold must be a skyscraper in New York City.

In the example above, A exactly parallels the (faulty) reasoning in the passage.

Although some questions of this type may require you to find parallel reasoning, others may simply ask you to describe the reasoning process contained in the passage. Such a question and answer choice can go like this:

> Q. In the passage above, the author does which of the following?
>
> **A.** Presents a conclusion without adequately supporting it
>
> **B.** Presents a generalization to argue for a specific result
>
> **C.** Provides a scientific explanation for a nonscientific phenomenon
>
> **D.** Argues from an analogy to support a questionable premise
>
> **E.** Contradicts the premise with conditional information

Notice that the validity of the passage is not in question; you're asked to evaluate the process the author uses.

Some of the ways this question type may be expressed are:

- Which of the following supports its conclusion in the same way as the argument above?

- The author makes her point primarily by . . .

- Which one of the following is logically most similar to the argument above?

- Which of the following is structurally most like the passage above?

- In which of the following exists a logical flaw similar to the logical flaw in the passage above?

- The author would be following the same line of reasoning as that in the passage by . . .

- The author of the passage uses which of the following methods of persuasion?

- The argument above exhibits the same principles of inference as which of the following arguments?

## Conclusion/Deduction/Necessarily Follows

This question type requires you to draw a conclusion or make a deduction based upon the passage. The essential requirement is to select the answer choice that not merely *could* follow, but that *must necessarily* follow from the reasoning in the passage. In other words, several answer choices will be logically feasible, but you are to choose the one option that not only is possible, but *must* follow. For example, consider this passage:

The state unicameral of Nebraska has recently passed an anti-pollution bill aimed at reducing auto emissions. When the bill becomes law on January 1st of next year, it will no longer be legal for automobiles built after 1976 to be sold in Nebraska without anti-emission devices in working condition. A biannual inspection program is also part of the bill and will strictly enforce the automotive anti-emission requirements. Similar programs in fourteen other states have shown that such restrictions can significantly reduce carbon emissions in the atmosphere.

> Q. Which of the following can be logically deduced from the passage above?
>
> A. Auto-emission pollution in Nebraska will be eliminated.
>
> B. Auto-emission pollution in Nebraska will be reduced in the coming years.
>
> C. Auto-emission pollution significantly threatens the health of Nebraskans.
>
> D. Auto-emission pollution in Nebraska will be addressed through a legislative action.
>
> E. Auto emissions are the primary cause of pollution in Nebraska.

Choice D is the correct response: It is the only choice that must necessarily follow from the information given. Note that while choice B is possible, the specific bill passed by the Nebraska legislature may not be effective or may not be well enforced. The only certainty is that the bill (whether it will be effective or not) addresses the problem. Its ultimate outcome (reduction of pollution or not) is still in doubt.

Some of the ways this question type may be expressed are

- If the passage above is true, which of the following is also true?

- Following the logic in the passage above, which of the following may be deduced?

- From the passage above, which of the following can be reasonably concluded?

- According to the passage above, which of the following conclusions can be logically drawn?

- Based on the passage above, which of the following statements necessarily follows?

- Which of the following conclusions can be reasonably attributed to the author of the argument above?

- Given the passage above to be true, which of the following must therefore also be true?

For this question type demanding "near certainty" (not just what is possible), remember to look for one of the following key words or phrases: *what can be deduced; what can be concluded; what necessarily follows; what therefore is also true; must also be true.* Remember that the controlling idea is *"must."*

## Flaws

This question type asks the reader to detect errors in logic or reasoning in an argument or a process. For example:

To determine how many sophomores at his college enjoy ice skating, a researcher stood near the exit of the college skating rink and asked every passing sophomore. He found that 96% of those questioned enjoy ice skating and therefore concluded that approximately 96% of the entire sophomore class enjoy ice skating.

> Q. The student's research may be faulty because
>
> A. Due to the location where the questioner gathered his data, the sample may not have been representative of the entire sophomore class.

Some of the ways this question may be expressed are

- Which of the following inconsistencies seriously undermines the author's conclusion?

- Which of the following could constitute a reasonable explanation of the paradox presented above?

- Which of the following is an inherent flaw in the argument above?

- In which of the following is there a logical flaw similar to that in the passage above? (*Note:* Overlapping type with parallel reasoning.)

- Which of the following expresses an inconsistency contained in the argument above?

- The reasoning in the passage above is flawed because . . .

- The author's statement is weak because . . .

- The argument as expressed by the author is problematic because . . .

- The conclusion above is unsound because the author does not consider . . .

- Henry's response to Alice shows that he has interpreted Alice's remark to mean . . . (In this case, Henry has misinterpreted Alice, and you need to determine what his error is, based upon his response.)

## Other Possibilities

One or two miscellaneous question types not detailed in the general categories above may occur on your test. For example, you may find a "sentence continuation" question *(Select the most appropriate sentence to complete this passage.)*, a "passage relevance" question *(Which of the following data would be most helpful in evaluating the argument above?)*, and so forth. The listing of seven general types is not meant to indicate that no other question types may appear on your LSAT. However, the seven general categories previously detailed are the most commonly occurring Logical Reasoning question types and therefore are worth your careful attention.

# Glossary of Important Terms

Although the Logical Reasoning sections of the LSAT do not require knowledge of formal logic, an understanding of certain key words is important. The following terms appear occasionally on LSATs. You may wish to be familiar with their meanings.

**ambiguous**—Unclear.

**analogy, analogous**—Comparision based on a resemblance between elements otherwise unlike. For example, comparing an industrious person to an ant.

**arbitrary**—Occurring seemingly by chance or at random.

**assumption**—An unstated premise necessary for a logical conclusion.

**cause**—Condition that produces an effect.

**circumstantial evidence**—Evidence that tends to prove a fact by proving other events or circumstances, thus affording a basis for a reasonable inference to the fact at issue.

**counterargument, rebuttal, refutation**—Argument against a certain position.

**critique**—Critical evaluation or criticism.

**deduce**—What must logically follow. Not what is possible, feasible, or probable, but what *must* be true based on the passage.

**dictum**—Authoritative opinion or principle.

**documented evidence**—Substantiated support using authentic, objective information.

**effect**—Resulting condition produced by a cause.

**generalization**—Statement or principle that has broader application than to a particular or specific condition, yet encompasses the specific.

**inconsistent**—Contradictory.

**necessary**—Condition required for a particular result, though not necessarily sufficient. For example, being female is a necessary condition for a human being in order to give birth; however, it is not sufficient to ensure that giving birth will occur. (The lack of a necessary condition assures the lack of the result.)

**plausible**—Believable.

**premise**—Proposition taken for granted or assumed to be true as the basis of an argument.

**presupposition**—Assumption. To suppose beforehand. To require as an antecedent in logic.

**proponents**—Those in favor.

**proposition**—Point to be discussed or maintained in an argument.

**sufficient**—Condition whose existence assures the existence of another condition. For example, in some states, passing the bar is sufficient in order to practice law.

**unsubstantiated**—Unproven.

# Practice Logical Reasoning Questions

The strategies reviewed in this introduction are further explained and illustrated in the answers and explanations that follow the practice questions in this section and each practice test. To summarize:

- Preread questions when appropriate.
- Focus on the major issue and supporting evidence.
- Eliminate answer choices that are irrelevant.
- Note the type of question asked.

1. It is no wonder that most big cities have an increase in homeless people. As a result of middle- and high-income people's renovating and settling in the low-rent areas of cities, property values have skyrocketed beyond the means of those who once lived there. If the city could decrease rent levels to previous levels, then the problem of homelessness would be virtually eliminated.

Which of the following, if true, would most seriously weaken the claim that low-income housing solves the problem of homelessness?

A. Homelessness was a problem before low-rent areas became gentrified.

B. Homeless people are eager to find affordable housing.

C. The renovation of the low-rent areas has created more jobs and therefore more income for low-income city inhabitants.

D. Some homeless people cannot afford to pay for low-income housing.

E. Jobs and training are already available to the homeless through county job service programs.

2. Making an explosive device with dry ice is simple. Because dry ice expands as it changes from a solid to a gaseous state, the only challenge is to enclose the dry ice in an impermeable container. As the dry ice evaporates, pressure builds inside the container, which explodes with amazing force. Because people who make dry-ice bombs have been know to injure themselves and others, U.S. federal law prohibits the sale of dry ice to minors.

If all of the statements in this paragraph are true, a logical inference would be that

A. dry ice is not currently sold in the United States.

B. dry ice evaporates into carbon dioxide gas.

C. children in the United States are unable to make dry-ice bombs.

D. a permeable container would not make an effective dry-ice bomb.

E. outside the United States, more children than adults are injured by dry-ice accidents.

3. Ethologists, people who study animal behavior, have traditionally divided an organism's actions into two categories: learned behavior (based on experience) and instinctive behavior (based on genotype). Some current scholars reject this distinction, claiming that all behavior is a predictable interaction of genetic and environmental factors.

Which of the following statements, if true, supports the claim of these current scholars?

A. All organisms with identical genotypes and identical experience sometimes respond differently in different situations.

B. All organisms with different genotypes and identical experience always respond identically in identical situations.

C. All organisms with similar genotypes and similar experience always respond differently in identical situations.

D. All organisms with identical genotypes and identical experience always respond identically in identical situations.

E. All organisms with identical genotypes and different experience always respond identically in identical situations.

4. Reading is a complex physical and psychological process. Most theorists claim that people read in two ways. The first way, which usually precedes the second, is reading letter by letter. Using this process, readers process each letter individually and then mentally combine the letters to produce a word. The second way, typically used by more experienced readers, is reading on the basis of word shapes. Using this process, readers learn to recognize specific word shapes and do not need to look at each individual letter. Of course, advanced readers will use both of the processes, depending on the familiarity of the word shape.

Which of the following statements can be inferred from the passage above?

A. Advanced readers have given up reading letter by letter.

B. "Whole language reading," which is reading by word shapes, should be taught in elementary schools.

C. Beginning readers often find reading letter by letter more difficult than reading by word shape.

D. Skillful readers rely equally on the word-shape and letter-by-letter reading methods.

E. The more unfamiliar a word is, the more likely it is that a reader will read letter by letter.

**5.** A DINK (dual income, no kids) household is trying to plan vacations with each other to both Belize and France for a week in each place. The husband can leave work in the second and third weeks of March but can't take two weeks off in a row. The wife can take two weeks off in a row but can't leave work until the third week in March. The husband is willing to travel alone to Belize but not to France. And they both agree that Belize should never be visited before France.

Given the above scenario, we can conclude all of the following EXCEPT:

**A.** The wife will not travel to France.

**B.** The husband will not travel to Belize.

**C.** The couple will not have two weeks of vacation together.

**D.** The couple will not take separate vacations.

**E.** Each will be able to take only one week of vacation.

**6.** Computer scientist: All twelve of these programs have an exceptionally high error rate. Each of these programs enlists a similar algorithm, the "knuckler routine." If I rewrite the computer program in order to circumvent the knuckler routine, the error rate should drop dramatically for the problematic programs.

Which of the following, if true, would most seriously weaken the scientist's conclusion?

**A.** The errors in the programs were of five distinct classes.

**B.** Some other programs without the knuckler routine had high error rates.

**C.** The errors occurred most often just after the program made a call to the knuckler routine.

**D.** No computer programmer is able to write algorithms that are always efficient and error free.

**E.** An algorithm identical to the knuckler routine was known to be present in a similar program that worked flawlessly.

**7.** Our cars are the best automobiles on the road today. This is true because their economical fuel systems have done wonders to help diminish the use of fossil fuels and slow the increase of pollution in our world.

All of the following exhibit flawed reasoning similar to that of the argument above EXCEPT:

**A.** Our cereal is the best on the market because it is higher in fiber than competing brands.

**B.** The Skyranger is the most dangerous toy on sale for five-year-olds because the warning against toxicity if swallowed is not printed clearly.

**C.** Maverick chewing tobacco is the best brand available in a four-ounce container because Maverick is sold in tin boxes, while other brands are packaged in plastic.

**D.** Broccoli is better for your health than any other vegetable because it is high in vitamins A and C, folic acid, and eight other valuable nutrients.

**E.** A. G. Swanson Brokerage's is the most highly recommended entertainment security because its new movie, *Colosseum,* is sure to be a blockbuster.

**81**

8. Eden is a metaphor for a time of paradise and perfection

   Xavier: "Eden was."
   Yolanda: "Eden is."
   Zed: "Eden will be."

   Which of the following CANNOT be inferred from the statements above?

   A. Zed is optimistic about the future.

   B. Xavier, Yolanda, and Zed may disagree about some things.

   C. Yolanda views the present positively.

   D. Yolanda and Xavier completely disagree.

   E. Xavier has positive feelings about the past.

9. A series of studies showed that the people of Denmark and the people of Greenland have vastly different rates of cancer. The reason for this difference is that Greenlanders eat large amounts of cold-water fish, while Danes rarely do. These fish contain a polyunsaturated fatty acid thought to inhibit cancers. Therefore, if the Danes were to eat more cold-water fish, they would reduce their risk for cancer.

   All of the following statements, if true, would strengthen the above conclusion EXCEPT:

   A. Greenlanders who ate cold-water fish sparingly had cancer rates nearly the same as the Danes.

   B. Per capita, Danes and Greenlanders use tobacco with equal frequency.

   C. The polyunsaturated fatty acid from cold-water fish has been shown to reduce cancers in laboratory animals.

   D. Danes and Greenlanders live in similar climates, but unlike the Greenlanders, the Danes live chiefly in urban areas.

   E. The government-sponsored medical plans in Denmark and Greenland are among the best in the Northern Hemisphere.

10. Businessman: The only airline I will fly is Eagle Air because they have never had an accident in their entire three years of operation.

    The argument above logically depends on which of the following assumptions?

    A. Eagle Air flies to all of the cities that I wish to visit.

    B. Eagle Air's safety record is the result of the meticulous maintenance of its fleet by highly qualified engineers.

    C. Eagle Air's record of service sufficiently predicts continual safety for future flights.

    D. The intense stresses experienced by airplanes in flight eventually causes component failure, which may lead to disastrous results.

    E. Other airlines with a similar number of flights have had one or more crashes in the last three years.

11. To apply for a job at a certain semiconductor plant in Boise, Idaho, a person must either have a bachelor's degree in engineering or an associate's degree in a science-related field. To be hired for an entry-level position, applicants with an associate's degree must also have at least five years of work experience. An applicant with similar work experience as well as a bachelor's degree in engineering is considered overqualified for entry-level work and can be hired only in a management position.

If the above statements are true, which of the following must also be true?

A. A new entry-level employee with five years of work experience will not hold a bachelor's degree in engineering.

B. The plant in Boise receives more applications from people with associate's degrees than from people with bachelor's degrees.

C. Work experience is more sought after than education.

D. Some applicants with associate's degrees are hired at management level.

E. If management positions are not available, an applicant with a bachelor's degree and work experience may be hired at entry level.

*Questions 12 and 13 are based on the following passage.*

Carnivore: Meat is high in protein. We need to eat meat protein to help our muscles grow.

Vegetarian: Your muscles don't need meat in order to grow. Just look at the gorillas. They never eat meat, and their muscles are enormous. This proves that you can get all the protein you need without eating meat.

12. The vegetarian's reply to the carnivore depends upon

A. claiming all of the evidence cited by the carnivore is factually untrue.

B. citing evidence that calls the carnivore's conclusion into question.

C. pointing out that the carnivore's argument is a misapplication of a frequently acceptable way of arguing.

D. contradicting the carnivore's claim that protein is necessary for growth.

E. proposing a conclusion that is better supported by the carnivore's evidence than is the carnivore's conclusion.

13. Which of the following statements, if true, would most likely weaken the vegetarian's argument?

A. The top body builder in 2000 was a strict vegetarian.

B. To build muscles, gorillas require more essential amino acids than do humans.

C. Gorillas do not have the same appetite as humans.

D. Gorillas metabolize vegetation in a different way from humans.

E. Meat has a higher fat content than grains.

**14.** The benefits of psychotherapy result not only from the advice the therapist gives but also from the supportive relationship offered the patient. Even though this relationship may cost large amounts of money over many years, most patients interpret the therapist's concern for them as genuine and identify this caring relationship as the primary factor in improving their mental health. However, recent studies have found that only eight percent of therapist/patient relationships continue after the patient terminates formal paid visits.

If the statements above are true, then it must also be true that

**A.** therapists are equally concerned with moneymaking and their patients' well-being.

**B.** if therapy consists solely of reading a book, an important healing element will be missing.

**C.** therapists can treat mental illness without the use of prescription drugs.

**D.** therapists who terminate relationships are likely to benefit the mental health of their patients.

**E.** eight percent of patients will continue to improve after the termination of their therapy.

**15.** Unlike retail outlets where items are purchased in single units, club warehouse products are grouped in bulk packages usually consisting of a dozen units or more. This quantity buying offers savings to the customer. The option to take advantage of wholesale prices by buying in bulk makes club warehouse stores a practical choice for budget-conscious consumers.

Which of the following is an assumption necessary to the author's argument?

**A.** Club warehouse stores often have greater buying power and lower overhead costs, so they can offer a greater variety of products than regular retail outlets.

**B.** Club warehouse stores are often more conveniently located and have better parking facilities.

**C.** The emergence of club stores has caused many retail stores to close and thus eliminate competition for customers.

**D.** It is economically wise to buy single items since bulk packages seldom offer significant savings.

**E.** The financial savings from purchasing bulk packages may outweigh the inconvenience of being unable to purchase single items.

# Answers for Logical Reasoning Practice Questions

1. **A.** You need to find a statement that argues against the idea that low-rent housing options will end homelessness. The best choice here is A. If homelessness was a problem even when rents were low, then making rents low again logically won't solve the homeless problem. The next best choice is D, but without more information on what *some homeless people* means, A is a better choice because D implies that some homeless people *can* afford low-cost housing.

2. **D.** Your task here is to find an idea that one can safely infer from the passage. The best inference is D: a permeable container would not make an effective dry-ice bomb. The passage points out that the dry-ice bomb depends on a buildup of pressure inside a container. If a container were permeable, then the pressure inside would escape, and no explosion would take place.

3. **D.** The question asks you to find a statement that supports the claim of the current scholars—that behavior derives from an interaction of both experience and genotype. Choice D is the only option that does not weaken the current scholars' claim. It says that if identical organisms have identical experiences, then the organisms will always respond identically. This statement allows for both environmental and genetic factors to be tested at once. Note that this statement does not prove their claim; it merely provides more evidence that their thinking could be right.

4. **D.** Your task here is to find a statement that can be inferred from the evidence given in the passage. The most defensible conclusion is choice E. In the last sentence, the passage implies that advanced readers sometimes have to revert to the letter-by-letter approach to reading if they don't immediately recognize a word shape. Therefore, skillful readers cannot always use the word-shape strategy to read and must use the letter-by-letter system with unfamiliar words.

5. **A.** According to the conditions, the husband and wife can spend only the third week of March together, in France. Thus, choices C, D, and E are true. Because neither will visit Belize, B is also true, but A is not.

6. **D.** What you need to do here is find an answer choice that weakens the conclusion that the knuckler routine is the one thing causing errors in the programs. The best way is to find a case where the knuckler routine works without any problem. Choice E does just that. If the knuckler routine works well in a similar program, then it casts serious doubt on the conclusion that the knuckler routine is at fault. Of course, this is not perfect proof, but it does weaken the conclusion more than B does.

7. **D.** All of the flawed passages use a superlative, *best,* to describe a product based on a single quality, although other qualities should also be considered. In choice A, for example, the partial assumption is the higher the fiber content, the better the cereal. In E, the security is only *the most highly recommended,* not the *best* and is the recommendation of a specific brokerage.

8. **D.** Your task is to find a choice that is not supported by the statements of the three speakers. To do this, read through the answers and ask yourself, "Is this a plausible inference based on the three statements?" If your answer is "yes," eliminate that choice and keep looking. You'll see that all choices except D are derivable from the passage. Choice D is the least plausible because it says Yolanda and Xavier disagree *completely*. In fact, they may both agree that Eden existed in some past time, exists now, or will exist in the future.

9. **D.** Because the important differences between the Danes and Greenlanders are the cancer rate and the diet, citing qualities they have in common that might affect the cancer rate will strengthen the argument. Thus, choices A, B, and E support the argument, while C strengthens the connection between the Greenlanders' diet and cancer. But D, which at first seems to strengthen the case, adds that the Danes live chiefly in urban areas and so, possibly, are exposed to the carcinogens of the cities.

10. **C.** The statement is based on the assumption that the three years of accident-free flights are sufficient to guarantee continued safety in future flights. Choice A is possible, but it may be that the businessman sometimes travels by car. Choice E is also tempting, but it is possible another airline has as good a safety record in the same period but not in their entire period of operation. The primary assumption behind the statement is C.

11. **A.** This question asks you to draw a conclusion. You want to find the statement that must be true from the facts given in the passage. The best strategy is to read through each choice and evaluate whether it has to be true, eliminating those choices that are irrelevant or contradictory. Choice A basically combines information from the last two sentences. Candidates with work experience are hired either at entry level if they have an associate's degree or at management level if they have a bachelor's degree. Therefore, a new entry-level employee must have an associate's degree, not a bachelor's degree. If the candidate had a bachelor's degree, that person would be hired only as management.

12. **B.** Although the reply contradicts some of the statement *(We need to eat meat)*, it does not deny all of it. The vegetarian cites evidence that calls into question the carnivore's conclusion by pointing to an animal with large muscles that does not eat meat.

13. **D.** Choice A would support the vegetarian. Choices C and E do not essentially change the argument. If gorillas metabolize vegetation in a way different from humans D, it is possible that vegetables would not produce muscle growth in humans like that in great apes.

14. **B.** The relevant part of the passage is its first sentence, which claims the benefits of psychotherapy depend on both advice and the supportive relationship of therapist and patient. Books are unable to provide this kind of relationship and therefore lack an important healing element.

15. **D.** As stated in the passage, the advantage of shopping at club stores is the financial savings. However, what is sacrificed is the convenience of purchasing single items to suit one's needs. If the consumer feels that the money saved from buying in bulk outweighs the inconvenience of purchasing many items as opposed to single items at one time, then club stores are indeed the more practical option.

# A PATTERNED PLAN OF ATTACK
## *Logical Reasoning*

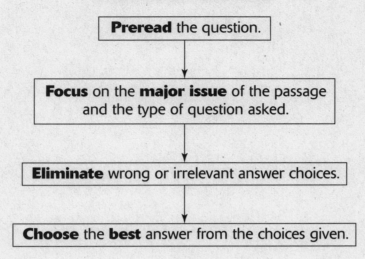

**Preread** the question.

↓

**Focus** on the **major issue** of the passage and the type of question asked.

↓

**Eliminate** wrong or irrelevant answer choices.

↓

**Choose** the **best** answer from the choices given.

# Introduction to Writing the Essay

## Ability Tested

This section tests your ability to express your opinion clearly and logically in writing, adhering to the rules and conventions of standard written English.

## Basic Skills Necessary

Basic organizational and writing skills are necessary for the Essay Writing section. Repeated practice in responding to LSAT essay topics should enrich and improve the skills you already possess.

## Directions

You are to plan and write a brief essay in no more than thirty minutes. Recent LSAT topics present two candidates or two items along with the criteria for considering both candidates or items and brief descriptions of each candidate's qualifications or each item's qualities. You must write an argument for hiring *one* of the candidates or choosing *one* of the items. YOU MUST WRITE ON THE GIVEN TOPIC ONLY.

The quality of your writing is more important than either the quantity of writing or the point of view you adopt. Your skill in organization, mechanics, and usage is important, although it is expected that your essay will not be flawless because of the time pressure under which you write.

You will be given an essay booklet that consists of a sheet of paper approximately 10 by 11 inches containing about 60 lines. Keep your writing within the lined area of your essay booklet. Write on every line, avoid wide margins, do not write any part of your essay on the back of the sheet, and write carefully and legibly. The sheets provided in this book approximate the size of the sheets provided during the test.

NOTE: On the actual LSAT, the essay topic is at the top of the essay writing page. Scratch paper for organizing and prewriting is provided.

## Analysis

1. You must respond only to the given topic. Your response will require no special knowledge in any area but will draw from your general knowledge and background.

2. You may choose to argue for either candidate or item; there is no "right" or "wrong" choice. Careful, clear writing, no matter what position you take, is most important.

3. Allow some time at the beginning of the thirty-minute period to plan your argument and some time to proofread your work before time is called. The time you will have for actually writing the argument will be brief; therefore, you should expect your finished essay to be brief—probably not completely filling the space provided.

4. Neat, legible handwriting (or printing) is important. Your readers will be distracted from the quality of your response if it is hard to read.

# Suggested Approach with Samples

This section uses the following sample topic to demonstrate approaches that work.

Read the following description of Fez and Durango, candidates for promotion from associate professor to full professor at I.Q. University. Write an argument for promoting either Fez or Durango. Use the information in this description and assume that two general policies guide the I.Q.U. decisions on promotion:

- Promotions are based on teaching effectiveness, professional growth, and service to the university.

- The publication of scholarly books and articles is recognized as professional growth.

Fez won the university award for distinguished teaching during both of his first two years at I.Q.U. Student evaluations of his classroom effectiveness have been consistently high; many students rate him the best teacher they have ever had. At the request of his department chairperson, Fez served for one year on the busy and challenging Faculty Development Committee, helping to prepare a lengthy report evaluating the year's work. Since arriving at I.Q., he has served on a less busy but important university committee, the President's Advisory Group. He has published a long and well-reviewed article in the most prestigious scholarly journal in his field and just recently contracted with a major publisher to complete a book summarizing the important research conducted over the last ten years by his most distinguished colleagues.

Durango has published three major books based on his own research and controversial ideas. One of the books was a best-seller for twenty weeks. Durango has a remarkable talent for writing, manifest not only in his major books, but also in the scores of articles he places in numerous scholarly journals. Because he is a controversial thinker and because of his generally abrasive personality, Durango is not popular with most students; however, a few very bright students have appreciated the refreshing quality of Durango's thought. Deeply concerned with the welfare of the university and curious about all the inner workings of the institution, Durango has volunteered over the years to serve on a number of university committees. However, his offer to serve has sometimes been refused by other committee members who have difficulty working with him.

# Read and Mark Relevant Criteria

In this case, the criteria are teaching effectiveness, professional growth, and service. Professional growth consists of scholarly publication.

# Make a Chart

Read the description of each candidate and chart his qualifications with reference to the criteria:

|  | *Fez* | *Durango* |
|---|---|---|
| Teaching | award/high evals | abrasive/bright like him |
| Growth | 1 prestige article/book in progress | 3 books/controversial/bestseller/many articles |
| Service | 2 committees | volunteer/hard to work with |

# Choose a Position or Candidate

In this example, you need to decide which candidate you support. Usually the two candidates' area of greatest strength will differ. For instance, Fez is superior in the teaching area; Durango is superior in the professional growth area. Choose either candidate, but be prepared to argue that his *greatest strength* should be a *primary criterion*. For instance, if you choose Fez, you must propose that teaching excellence is the most important factor to consider and tell *why*. If you choose Durango, you must propose that scholarly publication is the most important factor and tell *why*.

# Write the First Paragraph

Your first paragraph should

1. Emphasize the significance of the candidate's strength(s) and
2. Minimize the significance of the candidate's weaknesses.

The following because-although-therefore structure may be useful, but be aware that you may wish to adjust this method to fit your own writing style and the specific requirements of the topic.

(greatest strength) should be our primary consideration *because* (explain). *Although* (other criteria) must be considered, achievement in (greatest strength) shows (explain). *Therefore,* we should hire (promote, select, and so on) (name of candidate) based on his/her (achievement/strength).

**91**

Given the facts and criteria in this case, a *because-although-therefore* first paragraph might look as follows:

Excellence in teaching should be our primary consideration because if our professors are not effective in the classroom, they do not fulfill their responsibility—education. Although service and scholarship must also be considered, teaching effectiveness is the measure of success or failure "on the job." Therefore, we should promote Fez based on his teaching awards and evaluations.

An opening argument for Durango might proceed as follows:

Professional growth should be our primary consideration because without continuing research and publication, our faculty cannot contribute to the university's goal—increasing knowledge. Although teaching effectiveness and service must be considered, a candidate's scholarly writing best demonstrates strength and originality of intellect. Therefore, we should promote Durango based on his distinguished writing.

# Write a Middle Paragraph

In this paragraph, you need to:

1. Reiterate and reemphasize the candidate's or item's strength(s) and

2. Dismiss weaknesses as unimportant or turn weaknesses into strengths.

Note that the middle section may appropriately contain two or three paragraphs, each of which would contain a logical division of your argument. Following is a single paragraph argument for Fez.

Consistent student praise is an unmistakable indication of fine teaching; the praise Fez has received, along with his awards, shows that he has improved the quality of our students' intellectual lives. His professional growth is also distinctive. Fez chose to patiently compose a long essay of high quality rather than to publish numerous brief articles in unimportant journals. He knows his subject well as is evident from his grasp of a wide range of important research, research which will appear in his forthcoming book. He has been willing to serve the university on committees when called but has not let excessive attention to service weaken the quality of his teaching.

# Write a Conclusion (Optional)

Your conclusion summarizes the result of choosing your candidate or item. This statement may be only one or two sentences long.

By promoting Fez, we affirm our dedication to good teaching and show that the welfare of our students is our first concern.

# Reread and Edit

Neatly correct spelling, grammar, and usage errors in your essay. Do not make **major** changes at this time; such changes may weaken the legibility of your essay and require more time than you have remaining.

# Practice Writing Topics

Writing is a skill acquired almost exclusively through practice. So, the best way to prepare for the Essay section of the LSAT is to practice before you take the test. Using the blank essay pages provided, write on the topics in this section under the same time constraints you'll face during the test (30 minutes), then get feedback on your finished essays from a good, honest critic.

> NOTE: On the actual LSAT, the essay topic is at the top of the essay writing page. Scratch paper for organizing and prewriting is provided.

1. Read the following description of Wu and Bonilla, two candidates for conductor of the Pops Symphony Orchestra. Write an argument for hiring either Wu or Bonilla. The following facts are relevant to your decision:

   - The Pops Symphony conductor creates many of the orchestra's arrangements.
   - The hiring committee prefers a conductor with a national reputation and an entertaining stage personality.

Wu has been the first violinist of the Pops Symphony for three years, assisting the conductor. Late during the last Pops season, when the conductor fell ill and was forced to retire, Wu took over the baton for the final week of concerts. His entertaining, almost acrobatic, style won over every audience, and his final concert was aired on nationwide television and received an enthusiastic response from critics and viewers. During the off season, Wu has dedicated himself to arranging traditional American favorites for performance at the Pops debut next Independence Day. His talent as an arranger remains to be heard.

Trained in Europe, Bonilla has been guest conductor of several distinguished symphony orchestras, and his spirited performances of serious classical music have made him an international celebrity. His recent arrangements of Broadway show tunes, which he presented as an encore to the classical program, were well received throughout Europe. Critics admire the dignity with which Bonilla conducts the orchestra during serious classical works and marvel at the energy and enthusiasm he exhibits at the podium during lighter, brighter pieces.

**2.** Read the following description of Matson and O'Hara, who are seeking the position of city manager of a small California coastal community. Write an argument for appointing either Matson or O'Hara. Use the information in the following descriptions and assume that two general concerns will guide the City Council in making the appointment:

- The candidate's record as a supporter of a clean environment.

- The candidate's ability to strengthen community support and volunteer service for a program of urban beautification projects.

Matson has been a resident of California for six years. While in California, she has served as an officer in Friends of Wildlife, an organization that helps protect rare animal species, and has contributed heavily to the Committee to Prevent Offshore Oil Drilling. Matson's father owns a small oil company in Texas. Matson left a senior position with that company, as public relations director, to move to the West Coast. She just completed a year-long college course in landscape architecture, a subject that has always interested her. The course required that the students design three proposals for beautifying older sections of the city.

O'Hara is a native Californian who has lived in coastal communities all his life. Last year, while residing in Long Beach, he organized a large community protest against offshore drilling, managing to recruit a small staff, print and distribute hundreds of protest leaflets, and attract over 7,000 residents to a "Stop Oil" rally. He is a dues paying member of Save the Earth International, an environmental action group. For the last ten years, O'Hara has spent his vacation each year in the ghetto areas of Los Angeles, helping a community-sponsored group paint murals on the bare sides of tenement buildings. One of the murals has been highly praised by the senior art critic of the Los Angeles Tribune.

**3.** Ed and Diana Smith must decide on the purchase of one of two houses in the city suburbs at about the same price. Read the following information about the two houses. Then write an argument in support of buying either House A or House B, keeping the following two concerns in mind:

- The Smiths work in different sections of the city and have only one car.
- After making the down payment on the house, the Smiths will have to restrict their day-to-day expenses rigorously.

House A is a two-story, three-bedroom modern home with a two-car garage. There is a vacant, small, one-and-one-half room apartment above the garage that could be made rentable for a small amount of money. The house is a forty-minute drive from Diana's workplace, which is not accessible by public transportation. Ed's office is on the subway line, but the commute would require an hour and ten minutes.

House B is older than House A, but it is in a better neighborhood and is in excellent condition. It has a much larger yard that is attractively landscaped. The drive from House B to Diana's job would take about an hour and from there to Ed's office an additional forty minutes. The suburb in which House B is located has no access to public transportation that connects to the areas of the city where Ed and Diana are employed.

**4.** The City Council must decide how to use a large, vacant area near the downtown section of the city. Write an argument in favor of one of the two options, taking the following guidelines into account:

- The residents of the area are largely senior citizens with limited incomes.
- There are no funds in the city budget for continued support of the project after it has been completed.

The youth clubs of the city face a severe shortage of playing fields for their soccer and baseball leagues. The vacant area has space for two soccer and three baseball fields. The clubs would not be able to pay for the upkeep of the grounds, although they could supply funds for the equipment and necessary adult supervision by selling refreshments at the games.

The Senior Citizens Social Alliance in the city is looking for land for a community flower and vegetable garden. The small lots within the garden would be free to any senior residents of the city willing to plant and care for a garden. The Social Alliance would supply gardening tools and supplies, while the gardeners would supply whatever seeds or plants they chose to cultivate.

**5.** The owner of a midsize, largely upscale shopping center has a single vacancy and two applicants to rent the space. Bearing in mind the following two points, write an argument in favor of either Scepter Books or Elizabethan Hardware as renter.

- The owner hopes to increase the number of patrons who visit the center.
- The owner is eager to maintain the good will of his current tenants.

Scepter Books is a large chain of high-volume, discount bookstores that specialize in the sale of remaindered books and current bestsellers at reduced prices. The new store would compete for trade book sales with a small, privately owned bookshop in the center, but unlike the smaller store, Scepter would not sell expensive art books and most nonfiction titles. The smaller store now operates with a small but steady profit.

Elizabethan Hardware is a newcomer to the home supplies market, selling home decorating equipment and supplies, often at very high prices. There is no store like it in the center, although there is a huge Oscar's Home Repair about half an hour's drive away. Elizabethan is opening a number of new stores throughout the region, and so far almost all of them have prospered.

**6.** Kennedy, a studio art major in college, has just completed her teaching credential and is choosing between two job offers. Read the following descriptions of the offers. Then, write an argument in support of the offer from either Jackson City or Capital City, keeping the following two facts in mind:

- Kennedy regards teaching as secondary to her creative works as a sculptor.
- Kennedy has shown and sold some of her smaller bronzes at an exhibition at her college.

Jackson City, a small town three hundred miles north of the state capital, has offered Kennedy a very well paid job as director of the art programs in the high schools. The position requires eleven months of work, divided equally between teaching and administration. The cost of living in Jackson City is low.

Capital City, the largest city in the state, has an active art scene, with a number of museums, galleries, and foundries. It has offered Kennedy a part-time job teaching art in the middle schools. The beginning salary would not be equal to the expenses of living in the city, although there is a chance the job will become full time in six months.

**7.** The Naples Condominium Investment Club is choosing between two investment options. Read the description of the two options. Then, write an argument for choosing one of the options, considering these guidelines:

- The club wishes to make as much money as possible with a minimum amount of risk.
- The club plans to sell all of its assets and disband in two years.

Acme Securities has recommended the purchase of a conservative, no-load mutual fund with diversified holdings in stocks listed on the New York Stock Exchange. Since the fund is near its low for the year and market analysts are predicting a rise in stock prices, the security company believes the fund will produce a good profit with little risk.

Beta Securities has recommended the purchase of tax-free municipal bonds that will mature in two years. Since the bonds are such short-term investments, their cost is now three percent above their par value, but they are paying interest of six and a half percent and have top ratings from all of the major bond rating agencies.

# A PATTERNED PLAN OF ATTACK
## *Writing an Essay*

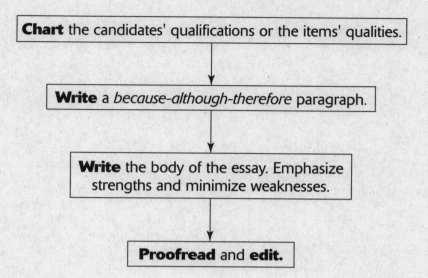

Chart the candidates' qualifications or the items' qualities.

Write a *because-although-therefore* paragraph.

Write the body of the essay. Emphasize strengths and minimize weaknesses.

Proofread and edit.

# THREE FULL-LENGTH PRACTICE TESTS

This part contains three full-length practice simulation LSATs. The practice tests are followed by complete answers, explanations, and analysis techniques. The format, levels of difficulty, question structure, and number of questions are similar to those on the actual LSAT. The actual LSAT is copyrighted and may not be duplicated, so these questions are not taken directly from the actual tests.

When taking these practice exams, try to simulate the test conditions by following the time allotments carefully.

# Practice Test 1

Section I:     Reading Comprehension—35 minutes; 27 questions

Section II:    Analytical Reasoning—35 minutes; 24 questions

Section III:   Logical Reasoning—35 minutes; 26 questions

Section IV:    Analytical Reasoning—35 minutes; 24 questions

Section V:     Logical Reasoning—35 minutes; 26 questions

Writing Essay—30 minutes

# Answer Sheet For Practice Test 1

(Remove This Sheet and Use It to Mark Your Answers)

## Section I

1 Ⓐ Ⓑ Ⓒ Ⓓ Ⓔ
2 Ⓐ Ⓑ Ⓒ Ⓓ Ⓔ
3 Ⓐ Ⓑ Ⓒ Ⓓ Ⓔ
4 Ⓐ Ⓑ Ⓒ Ⓓ Ⓔ
5 Ⓐ Ⓑ Ⓒ Ⓓ Ⓔ
6 Ⓐ Ⓑ Ⓒ Ⓓ Ⓔ
7 Ⓐ Ⓑ Ⓒ Ⓓ Ⓔ
8 Ⓐ Ⓑ Ⓒ Ⓓ Ⓔ
9 Ⓐ Ⓑ Ⓒ Ⓓ Ⓔ
10 Ⓐ Ⓑ Ⓒ Ⓓ Ⓔ
11 Ⓐ Ⓑ Ⓒ Ⓓ Ⓔ
12 Ⓐ Ⓑ Ⓒ Ⓓ Ⓔ
13 Ⓐ Ⓑ Ⓒ Ⓓ Ⓔ
14 Ⓐ Ⓑ Ⓒ Ⓓ Ⓔ
15 Ⓐ Ⓑ Ⓒ Ⓓ Ⓔ
16 Ⓐ Ⓑ Ⓒ Ⓓ Ⓔ
17 Ⓐ Ⓑ Ⓒ Ⓓ Ⓔ
18 Ⓐ Ⓑ Ⓒ Ⓓ Ⓔ
19 Ⓐ Ⓑ Ⓒ Ⓓ Ⓔ
20 Ⓐ Ⓑ Ⓒ Ⓓ Ⓔ
21 Ⓐ Ⓑ Ⓒ Ⓓ Ⓔ
22 Ⓐ Ⓑ Ⓒ Ⓓ Ⓔ
23 Ⓐ Ⓑ Ⓒ Ⓓ Ⓔ
24 Ⓐ Ⓑ Ⓒ Ⓓ Ⓔ
25 Ⓐ Ⓑ Ⓒ Ⓓ Ⓔ
26 Ⓐ Ⓑ Ⓒ Ⓓ Ⓔ
27 Ⓐ Ⓑ Ⓒ Ⓓ Ⓔ

## Section II

1 Ⓐ Ⓑ Ⓒ Ⓓ Ⓔ
2 Ⓐ Ⓑ Ⓒ Ⓓ Ⓔ
3 Ⓐ Ⓑ Ⓒ Ⓓ Ⓔ
4 Ⓐ Ⓑ Ⓒ Ⓓ Ⓔ
5 Ⓐ Ⓑ Ⓒ Ⓓ Ⓔ
6 Ⓐ Ⓑ Ⓒ Ⓓ Ⓔ
7 Ⓐ Ⓑ Ⓒ Ⓓ Ⓔ
8 Ⓐ Ⓑ Ⓒ Ⓓ Ⓔ
9 Ⓐ Ⓑ Ⓒ Ⓓ Ⓔ
10 Ⓐ Ⓑ Ⓒ Ⓓ Ⓔ
11 Ⓐ Ⓑ Ⓒ Ⓓ Ⓔ
12 Ⓐ Ⓑ Ⓒ Ⓓ Ⓔ
13 Ⓐ Ⓑ Ⓒ Ⓓ Ⓔ
14 Ⓐ Ⓑ Ⓒ Ⓓ Ⓔ
15 Ⓐ Ⓑ Ⓒ Ⓓ Ⓔ
16 Ⓐ Ⓑ Ⓒ Ⓓ Ⓔ
17 Ⓐ Ⓑ Ⓒ Ⓓ Ⓔ
18 Ⓐ Ⓑ Ⓒ Ⓓ Ⓔ
19 Ⓐ Ⓑ Ⓒ Ⓓ Ⓔ
20 Ⓐ Ⓑ Ⓒ Ⓓ Ⓔ
21 Ⓐ Ⓑ Ⓒ Ⓓ Ⓔ
22 Ⓐ Ⓑ Ⓒ Ⓓ Ⓔ
23 Ⓐ Ⓑ Ⓒ Ⓓ Ⓔ
24 Ⓐ Ⓑ Ⓒ Ⓓ Ⓔ

## Section III

1 Ⓐ Ⓑ Ⓒ Ⓓ Ⓔ
2 Ⓐ Ⓑ Ⓒ Ⓓ Ⓔ
3 Ⓐ Ⓑ Ⓒ Ⓓ Ⓔ
4 Ⓐ Ⓑ Ⓒ Ⓓ Ⓔ
5 Ⓐ Ⓑ Ⓒ Ⓓ Ⓔ
6 Ⓐ Ⓑ Ⓒ Ⓓ Ⓔ
7 Ⓐ Ⓑ Ⓒ Ⓓ Ⓔ
8 Ⓐ Ⓑ Ⓒ Ⓓ Ⓔ
9 Ⓐ Ⓑ Ⓒ Ⓓ Ⓔ
10 Ⓐ Ⓑ Ⓒ Ⓓ Ⓔ
11 Ⓐ Ⓑ Ⓒ Ⓓ Ⓔ
12 Ⓐ Ⓑ Ⓒ Ⓓ Ⓔ
13 Ⓐ Ⓑ Ⓒ Ⓓ Ⓔ
14 Ⓐ Ⓑ Ⓒ Ⓓ Ⓔ
15 Ⓐ Ⓑ Ⓒ Ⓓ Ⓔ
16 Ⓐ Ⓑ Ⓒ Ⓓ Ⓔ
17 Ⓐ Ⓑ Ⓒ Ⓓ Ⓔ
18 Ⓐ Ⓑ Ⓒ Ⓓ Ⓔ
19 Ⓐ Ⓑ Ⓒ Ⓓ Ⓔ
20 Ⓐ Ⓑ Ⓒ Ⓓ Ⓔ
21 Ⓐ Ⓑ Ⓒ Ⓓ Ⓔ
22 Ⓐ Ⓑ Ⓒ Ⓓ Ⓔ
23 Ⓐ Ⓑ Ⓒ Ⓓ Ⓔ
24 Ⓐ Ⓑ Ⓒ Ⓓ Ⓔ
25 Ⓐ Ⓑ Ⓒ Ⓓ Ⓔ
26 Ⓐ Ⓑ Ⓒ Ⓓ Ⓔ

CUT HERE

## Section IV

1 Ⓐ Ⓑ Ⓒ Ⓓ Ⓔ
2 Ⓐ Ⓑ Ⓒ Ⓓ Ⓔ
3 Ⓐ Ⓑ Ⓒ Ⓓ Ⓔ
4 Ⓐ Ⓑ Ⓒ Ⓓ Ⓔ
5 Ⓐ Ⓑ Ⓒ Ⓓ Ⓔ
6 Ⓐ Ⓑ Ⓒ Ⓓ Ⓔ
7 Ⓐ Ⓑ Ⓒ Ⓓ Ⓔ
8 Ⓐ Ⓑ Ⓒ Ⓓ Ⓔ
9 Ⓐ Ⓑ Ⓒ Ⓓ Ⓔ
10 Ⓐ Ⓑ Ⓒ Ⓓ Ⓔ
11 Ⓐ Ⓑ Ⓒ Ⓓ Ⓔ
12 Ⓐ Ⓑ Ⓒ Ⓓ Ⓔ
13 Ⓐ Ⓑ Ⓒ Ⓓ Ⓔ
14 Ⓐ Ⓑ Ⓒ Ⓓ Ⓔ
15 Ⓐ Ⓑ Ⓒ Ⓓ Ⓔ
16 Ⓐ Ⓑ Ⓒ Ⓓ Ⓔ
17 Ⓐ Ⓑ Ⓒ Ⓓ Ⓔ
18 Ⓐ Ⓑ Ⓒ Ⓓ Ⓔ
19 Ⓐ Ⓑ Ⓒ Ⓓ Ⓔ
20 Ⓐ Ⓑ Ⓒ Ⓓ Ⓔ
21 Ⓐ Ⓑ Ⓒ Ⓓ Ⓔ
22 Ⓐ Ⓑ Ⓒ Ⓓ Ⓔ
23 Ⓐ Ⓑ Ⓒ Ⓓ Ⓔ
24 Ⓐ Ⓑ Ⓒ Ⓓ Ⓔ

## Section V

1 Ⓐ Ⓑ Ⓒ Ⓓ Ⓔ
2 Ⓐ Ⓑ Ⓒ Ⓓ Ⓔ
3 Ⓐ Ⓑ Ⓒ Ⓓ Ⓔ
4 Ⓐ Ⓑ Ⓒ Ⓓ Ⓔ
5 Ⓐ Ⓑ Ⓒ Ⓓ Ⓔ
6 Ⓐ Ⓑ Ⓒ Ⓓ Ⓔ
7 Ⓐ Ⓑ Ⓒ Ⓓ Ⓔ
8 Ⓐ Ⓑ Ⓒ Ⓓ Ⓔ
9 Ⓐ Ⓑ Ⓒ Ⓓ Ⓔ
10 Ⓐ Ⓑ Ⓒ Ⓓ Ⓔ
11 Ⓐ Ⓑ Ⓒ Ⓓ Ⓔ
12 Ⓐ Ⓑ Ⓒ Ⓓ Ⓔ
13 Ⓐ Ⓑ Ⓒ Ⓓ Ⓔ
14 Ⓐ Ⓑ Ⓒ Ⓓ Ⓔ
15 Ⓐ Ⓑ Ⓒ Ⓓ Ⓔ
16 Ⓐ Ⓑ Ⓒ Ⓓ Ⓔ
17 Ⓐ Ⓑ Ⓒ Ⓓ Ⓔ
18 Ⓐ Ⓑ Ⓒ Ⓓ Ⓔ
19 Ⓐ Ⓑ Ⓒ Ⓓ Ⓔ
20 Ⓐ Ⓑ Ⓒ Ⓓ Ⓔ
21 Ⓐ Ⓑ Ⓒ Ⓓ Ⓔ
22 Ⓐ Ⓑ Ⓒ Ⓓ Ⓔ
23 Ⓐ Ⓑ Ⓒ Ⓓ Ⓔ
24 Ⓐ Ⓑ Ⓒ Ⓓ Ⓔ
25 Ⓐ Ⓑ Ⓒ Ⓓ Ⓔ
26 Ⓐ Ⓑ Ⓒ Ⓓ Ⓔ

CUT HERE

# Section I: Reading Comprehension

Time: 35 Minutes

27 Questions

**Directions:** Each passage in this group is followed by questions based on its content. After reading a passage, choose the best answer to each question and blacken the corresponding space on the answer sheet. Answer all questions following a passage on the basis of what is stated or implied in that passage. You may refer back to the passage.

*Questions 1 through 7 are based on the following passage.*

The history of religious liberty in the United States is unique and unparalleled in the rest of the world. The people populating the colonies in America were
(5) from societies where, for most of their recent past, the battle for social control was waged primarily by established churches and the secular governments. The role of the churches in those soci
(10) eties often was indistinguishable from that of the governments; indeed, there were many times in which a religion pitted the individual against the government. Notwithstanding the European
(15) experience, religious intolerance was also a major characteristic in the founding of certain American colonies, particularly Massachusetts and Pennsylvania.

While it is true that the concept of
(20) separation between church and state did not achieve immediate acceptance upon the establishment of the new colonies, several factors eventually led to the comprehensive religious freedom we
(25) enjoy today. Many of those involved in the early years of the colonies were there in search of greater political freedoms. Gradually, the connection between political freedom and religious
(30) freedom was comprehended. Moreover, the sheer numbers of religions practiced

prevented those in power from endorsing one without alienating a significant portion or the population. The New
(35) World required new institutions, and these institutions could grow in directions unfettered by past practices of institutions located thousands of miles away. All of these circumstances and
(40) more contributed to the idea that religion should be free from interference from the government.

Today, the new religions are called "cults," a term that carries negative con
(45) notations and implications. Most new religions share certain characteristics in common, which are not found in the older, more established religions. Among these traits are a lifestyle gener
(50) ally quite different from that of mainstream American life, a founder who is still living, and the operation of the new religion as a cult of personality.

As always, these new religions are
(55) seen as differing drastically in belief and practice from the major "established" religions. But this perceived difference is often a product of vantage point. For example, chanting and meditating seem
(60) foreign to various Western religions but are an integral part of various ancient, well-established Eastern religions. Aggressive proselytizing, while foreign to certain religions, is seen as a vital and
(65) necessary part of the Quaker religion.

GO ON TO THE NEXT PAGE

**115**

During the 17th and 18th centuries, Baptists (then viewed as a subversive "cult" but now second only to the Roman Catholic Church in terms of (70) membership) were jailed both in Massachusetts and Virginia.

The perceived differences between the new and old religions fade, however, in light of the United States (75) Constitution. In 1944, the Supreme Court held that inquiry into the veracity or validity of one's religious beliefs is precluded by the First Amendment. The Supreme Court stated:

(80) "The Fathers of the Constitution were not unaware of the varied and extreme views of religious sects, of the violence of disagreement among them, and the lack of any one religious creed on which (85) all men would agree. They fashioned a charter of government that envisaged the widest possible toleration of conflicting views. Man's relation to his God was made no concern of the state.... The First (90) Amendment does not select any one group or any one type of religion for preferred treatment. It puts them all in that position."

The significance of this is that in the (95) eyes of the law no religion whether "new" or "old" is more or less deserving of protection than any other religion. The "no establishment clause" of the First Amendment has been given an ex-(100) pansive interpretation by the court:

"The 'establishment of religion' clause of the First Amendment means at least this: Neither a state nor the Federal Government can set up a church. (105) Neither can pass laws that aid one religion, aid all religions, or prefer one religion over another. Neither can force nor influence a person to go to or to remain away from church against his will, or (110) force him to profess a belief or disbelief in any religion. No person can be punished for entertaining or professing religious beliefs or disbeliefs, for church attendance or non-attendance. No tax in (115) any amount, large or small, can be levied to support any religious activities or institutions, whatever they may be called, or whatever form they may adopt to teach or practice religion."

(120) Thus for the purposes of religious freedom, no distinction can be made between any religions. Those characteristics attributed to cults to distinguish new religions from old religions have no le-(125) gal significance.

1. According to the passage, religious freedom in the New World developed primarily because

   A. people perceived the connection between political and religious freedom.

   B. neither the state nor the federal government could establish a church.

   C. of the violent interaction between religious sects.

   D. of the development of "cults" with disparate lifestyles from the mainstream.

   E. the fathers of the Constitution had extreme views regarding religious sects.

2. According to the passage, religious intolerance was

   A. the reason for the first colonists' coming to America from England.

   B. more widespread in Europe than in America in the eighteenth century.

   C. often closely related to social or racial intolerance.

D. to be found in some of the early American colonies.

E. not present in the United States before the Civil War.

3. In order to avoid being branded as a cult, a new religion in the United States is at an advantage when its

A. recommended lifestyle is conventional.

B. founder and leader is still alive.

C. beliefs are common in Eastern churches.

D. fundamental tenets challenge Western dogma.

E. history and heritage contradict national norms.

4. According to the passage, which of the following religions was once regarded as a cult?

A. Roman Catholic

B. Baptist

C. Lutheran

D. Moslem

E. Anglican

5. Of the following, members of which church would be protected against arrest for proselytizing on public property?

A. Church of Scientology

B. Four Square Gospel Assembly

C. Quakers

D. Lutheran

E. Any religion

6. In the judgment of the Supreme Court, a new religion should be

A. more deserving of protection than an old religion.

B. less deserving of protection than an old religion.

C. subject to the same rules as an old religion.

D. subject to control by federal and state governments.

E. aided by either the federal or state government.

7. The Supreme Court regards the truth or falsehood of religious beliefs as

A. of no legal consequence.

B. the primary factor that determines whether they are protected under the First Amendment.

C. an issue to be determined by historical authorities.

D. the basis of individual moral responsibility.

E. the foundation of all legal systems.

*Questions 8 through 14 are based on the following passage.*

Pollution law, traditionally, has developed around litigation concerned with air pollution, and to a lesser extent with water pollution. This is a result of the
(5) more readily visible aspects of these types of pollution. Controversies surrounding these pollution forms gave rise to several theories upon which a plaintiff could recover. The nuisance theory is
(10) presented here.

The nuisance theory has been recorded since 1611. At common law

GO ON TO THE NEXT PAGE

the basis of the cause of action in nuisance was the interference with a right (15) to use property. Such interference must be both substantial and unreasonable and could arise through an intrusion of the land, or a disturbance of the occupant's health, his mental quiet, or his (20) comfort and habitation. The largest single problem that developed from the nuisance cause of action has been the courts' tendency to tolerate pollution in an effort to "balance equities." (25) Balancing the equities has led "... to the conclusion that the courts, while paying lip service to the landowner's right to pollution free air, have nevertheless recognized a right to do some polluting (30) of the air." This precluded recovery for air pollution as long as it is not unreasonable or unnecessary.

Unfortunately, the balancing concept "ignores" the permanent harm done to the (35) public. A better view would weight the public's economic injury caused by the abatement of the pollution against the physical harm caused to the public by the pollution." At present, it is only the (40) harm caused to the plaintiff that is weighed against the public economic interest. This view balances in favor of the polluter since virtually all pollution is caused by some socially useful activity.

(45) In addition to the major obstacles of balancing, certain technical aspects of the law of nuisance may prevent the obtaining of damages or injunctive relief. Nuisance is divided into public and pri- (50) vate types. If labeled "public," a showing of special injury is required before the private lawsuit will succeed. This special injury must be different in kind, not merely degree, and effectively limits (55) the action. If the nuisance is classified as "private," the plaintiff still faces another obstacle. Where the pollution continues for an extended period of time, the wrongdoer may become legally pro- (60) tected by way of a prescriptive right.

Another impasse within the private nuisance area is the doctrine of "coming to the nuisance":

"The plaintiffs are subject to an an- (65) noyance. This we accept, but it is an annoyance they have freely assumed. Because they desired and needed a residential proximity to their places of employment, they chose to found their (70) abode here."

Even if this doctrine is not applied as barring the plaintiff's litigation, it is a matter to be considered in "balancing the equities."

8. The main purpose of the passage is to

A. attack the judicial system.

B. explain the unfairness of "balancing the equities."

C. explain the nature and disadvantages of the nuisance theory.

D. reveal the partnership between polluters and the courts.

E. warn the public about a coming ecological disaster

9. According to the author, the courts' tendency to tolerate pollution and, thus, to favor polluters in court decisions, is a consequence of

A. balancing the equities.

B. protecting the public economic interest.

C. perceiving the plaintiff as a nuisance.

D. concern for permanent harm done to the public.

E. indifference to socially useful activity.

**10.** All of the following are mentioned as disadvantages of the nuisance theory EXCEPT:

A. the courts' tendency to tolerate pollution in an effort to balance equities.

B. ignoring the permanent harm done to the public.

C. the plaintiff's requirement to show "special injury" when a lawsuit is a public type.

D. invoking the "coming to the nuisance" doctrine.

E. the statute of limitations.

**11.** The passage argues that the cost of cleaning up or reducing pollution should be

A. borne by the private industries who were responsible for the pollution.

B. borne by the federal government, which failed to prevent the pollution.

C. borne by the state and federal governments.

D. weighed against the physical harm the pollution does.

E. divided between private industry and public agencies.

**12.** From lines 34–39, we can infer that courts would object to pollution more readily if it were

A. caused by activity that was socially useful.

B. caused by activity that was not socially useful.

C. harmful to the public but not to the polluter.

D. harmful to the polluter but not to the public.

E. equally harmful to the polluter and the public.

**13.** Which of the following points does the passage make regarding a "prescriptive right?"

A. A prescriptive right confers legal protection to a wrongdoer.

B. Pollution is not a crime as long as it serves "some socially useful activity."

C. Some illegal acts may become legally protected if they continue for a continuous period of time.

D. A prescriptive right provides courts with the means for "balancing the equities."

E. A prescriptive right must be in writing to be valid.

GO ON TO THE NEXT PAGE

**14.** With which of the following would the author of the passage most likely agree?

**A.** The courts have effectively recognized the landowner's basic right to pollution-free air.

**B.** A buyer of property in an area already polluted may not be able to obtain injunctive relief.

**C.** The effect of balancing the equities is a just distribution of responsibility and liability for pollution.

**D.** Pollution law has made no promising advances since 1611.

**E.** Controversies regarding pollution have all been resolved in recent years.

*Questions 15 through 20 are based on the following passage.*

Each method of counting bacteria has advantages and disadvantages; none is 100 percent accurate. Cell counts may be made with a counting chamber, a
(5) slide marked with a grid to facilitate counting of cells and to determine the volume of liquid in the area counted. Counts are made under a microscope and calculations made to determine the
(10) number of cells per ml of the original culture. Electronic cell counters can be used to count cells suspended in a liquid medium that passes through a hole small enough to allow the passage of only one
(15) bacterial cell at a time. The counter actually measures the rise in electric resistance of the liquid each time a cell passes through the hole. Smear counts are similar to cell counts: a known vol-
(20) ume of culture is spread over a known area (1 cm$^2$) of a slide and then stained. Counts are made from several microscope fields, and calculations are made.

In membrane filter counts a known
(25) volume of a culture is passed through a filter, which is then examined microscopically for cells. The advantage of cell counts, smear counts, and membrane filter counts is that they are
(30) quickly accomplished with little complicated equipment; however, both living and dead cells are counted.

The serial-dilution method involves the making of a series of dilutions,
(35) usually by a factor of 10, into a nutrient medium. The highest dilution producing growth gives a rough indication of the population of the original culture.

Plate counts are made by making ser-
(40) ial dilutions (usually in sterile tap water or an isotonic solution) of the original culture. Samples of known volume of the dilutions are transferred to petri dishes and mixed with nutrient agar.
(45) After a suitable incubation period, the colonies on the plates with between 30 and 300 colonies are counted. Because each colony is assumed to hive arisen from a single cell, calculations can be
(50) made to determine the original population size. Plate counts have the advantage of not including dead cells, and they can be used when the population is so low as to make other methods im-
(55) practical, but they require more time than direct counts, and they detect only those organisms that can grow under the conditions of incubation; the development of one colony from more than one
(60) cell is also a source of error.

A colorimeter or spectrophotometer is used in turbidimetric methods; the instrument measures the amount of light transmitted by test tubes with and with-
(65) out cultures; the difference represents the light absorbed or scattered by the bacterial cells and gives an indication of their concentration.

The total cell volume in a sample can
(70) be determined by centrifuging the sample

in a calibrated centrifuge tube. From the known volume of a single cell and the volume of the sample cells, the original population size can be calculated.

(75)    The dry weight of the washed, dehydrated cells gives a reliable indication of population size. Chemical assays for the concentration of nitrogen or other cell constituents present in cells in fairly
(80) constant amounts are used to calculate population size. Because living cells produce chemical changes in their environments, these changes may reflect the number of cells present; changes in pH
(85) or in the concentration of a substrate or product may be measured.

**15.** One method of counting bacteria that does NOT suffer from a major disadvantage of a "cell count" is a

    **A.** plate count.

    **B.** smear count.

    **C.** membrane filter count.

    **D.** serial-dilution count.

    **E.** turbidimetric count.

**16.** Which of the following is the most likely source of this passage?

    **A.** An illustrated introduction to science for middle school students

    **B.** A high school biology textbook

    **C.** A college biology textbook

    **D.** An advanced study of cellular biology

    **E.** A manual to accompany scientific equipment

**17.** According to the passage, the typical result of incubation is

    **A.** impractical.

    **B.** the precise population of the original culture.

    **C.** mutation of the nutrient agar.

    **D.** growth.

    **E.** 30 to 300 colonies.

**18.** Which of the following methods would a researcher whose primary concern is accuracy be most likely to employ?

    **A.** A smear or a membrane filter count

    **B.** A cell or a plate count

    **C.** A cell or a turbidimetric count

    **D.** A plate or a turbidimetric count

    **E.** A membrane filter or a plate count

**19.** The passage allows us to conclude that a biologist in a hurry to do a bacterial count may choose to

    **A.** seek out a spectrophotometer.

    **B.** estimate the total cell volume.

    **C.** perform a smear count.

    **D.** incubate.

    **E.** use a petri dish.

**20.** The purpose of this passage is to

    **A.** describe several methods of counting bacteria.

    **B.** demonstrate the disadvantages of the serial dilution count.

    **C.** recommend the use of the plate count method.

    **D.** justify the expense of bacterial cell counts.

    **E.** describe the advantages of cell counts, smear counts, and membrane filter counts.

GO ON TO THE NEXT PAGE

*Questions 21 through 27 are based on the following passage.*

Man has probably always been curious about himself. We can surmise that primitive man's dependence upon his environment would not have permitted (5) him to be indifferent to the effects of his surrounding world upon him. Very early in the history of mankind the living things that shared his world, especially other humans, must have aroused in him (10) a special interest. He must have speculated on their behavior and how he was alike of different from them. It is easy to imagine his asking the familiar questions, "What am I?" "How did I come to (15) be what I am?"

We suspect that somehow he stumbled upon the notion of attributing spirits to things that moved as an explanation for their motion. This *animistic* belief system was applied to fire, (20) water, clouds, plants, or to anything that moved. The conclusion that the leaf falls from the tree because the spirit of the leaf or the tree caused it to move may (25) lead us to smile, but animism was important as a first step man took toward understanding nature.

Similar explanations are provided by young children. When the child sees that (30) the trees move when the wind blows, he may come to believe that trees make the wind blow; thus, he is attributing volition to the trees. Although his premise, and consequently his conclusions, are (35) inaccurate, he is seeking causality, which too is an important first step.

It is not implausible to infer that early man eventually accepted the anthropomorphic viewpoint that his behavior as (40) well as that of all animals was accounted for in terms of purposive inner agents or spirits. From the immobility after death, for example, it was assumed that the spirit had left. This spirit that lacks

(45) physical dimensions came to be known as the soul, or "psyche" in Greek, the word from which psychology derives its name. In time, every aspect of behavior was attributed to a corresponding feature (50) in the mind or inner person. To some, the inner man was seen as driving the body, much as a person drives a car, and speculation on the nature of this inner person or personality was given considerable atten- (55) tion. Furthermore, how the "mind" or inner man related to the physical body and its actions became an important point of departure for those seeking answers to man's nature. The first conjectures about (60) this relationship were recorded by philosophers, eventually becoming known as the "mind-body problem."

Gradually in the course of inquiring into the nature of the universe by ancient (65) philosophers, there arose the question, "How can we know?" In other words, how can we be sure any knowledge is valid? Later, this concern for validity led to inquiries into the question, "How *do* (70) we know?"—the processes of knowledge. Very early philosophers had distinguished between knowledge gained by the senses and knowledge achieved by reason. They had noted, too, that knowl- (75) edge is *human* knowledge and therefore influenced by human ways of knowing. The question that arises next is whether any human mode of conceiving the world can have objective validity; (80) whether inquiring into the ultimate nature of reality is not, after all, quite futile.

Socrates considered the effort futile. But he believed that one kind of knowledge is obtainable—knowledge of the (85) self. This kind of knowledge is needed because it will reveal man's duty and enable him to lead a virtuous life. Socrates believed that virtue is the outcome of knowledge and that evil is fundamentally (90) ignorance. This is an early instance of the belief that the intellectual or rational is dominant in man and morally superior.

**21.** The primary purpose of this passage is to

 A.  speculate about the validity of ancient theories of being.

 B.  refute the premise that people are not curious about themselves.

 C.  show that the earliest beliefs about human nature and knowledge were naive and childlike

 D.  survey ancient viewpoints on human nature and human knowledge.

 E.  argue that ancient speculations about human nature culminated in the philosophy of Socrates.

**22.** Which of the following assumptions underlies the author's statement that animistic beliefs were "inaccurate" (line 35)?

 A.  There is no superhuman spirit in the universe.

 B.  The movement of inanimate objects is always caused by some external force.

 C.  Modern speculations about causality are accurate.

 D.  Ancient thinkers did not think carefully about causality.

 E.  The animistic belief system is practiced only by creatures of a lower order than human.

**23.** Which of the following questions is answered by the information in the passage?

 A.  Can any human mode of conceiving the world have objective validity?

 B.  Was Socrates virtuous?

 C.  Is *epistemology,* the study of knowledge, an exclusively modern interest?

 D.  Why is causality an insufficient explanation for natural events?

 E.  What is the nature of the universe and humans' mode of perceiving the world?

**24.** Socrates' point of view, as described in the passage, implies which of the following conclusions about evil people?

 A.  They are ignorant.

 B.  They are unable to achieve complete self-knowledge.

 C.  They are inherently virtuous, but incapable of showing it.

 D.  They are often either ignorant or irrational.

 E.  They often dominate those who are morally superior.

**25.** The "mind-body problem" (line 63), as described in the passage, is based upon which of the following assumptions?

 A.  Only when separated do the mind and body present no problem.

 B.  All outward appearance reflects the inner person.

 C.  While the body may change, the mind remains essentially unchanged.

 D.  No aspect of physical behavior is a purely physical reflex action.

 E.  "Mindlessness" is impossible.

GO ON TO THE NEXT PAGE

**26.** From the passage, we may conclude about the author's knowledge of the origins of the animistic belief system that he or she

   **A.** concludes that animism is a direct answer to the question, "What am I?"

   **B.** views animism as an outgrowth of earlier belief systems.

   **C.** is certain that animistic beliefs were acquired by accident.

   **D.** is not sure what the origins were.

   **E.** suspects that animism is not a step toward understanding nature.

**27.** Which of the following definitions of psychology best reflects the ancient Greek notion of psyche, as explained in the passage?

   **A.** The study of the mind-body problem

   **B.** The study of the mind

   **C.** The study of the soul

   **D.** The study of life after death

   **E.** The study of human behavior

IF YOU FINISH BEFORE TIME IS CALLED, CHECK YOUR WORK ON THIS SECTION ONLY. DO NOT WORK ON ANY OTHER SECTION IN THE TEST.

# Section II: Analytical Reasoning

Time: 35 Minutes

24 Questions

**Directions:** You will be presented with several sets of conditions. A group of questions follows each set of conditions. Choose the best answer to each question, drawing a rough diagram of the conditions when necessary.

*Questions 1 through 6 are based on the following information.*

A series of equal-sized pennants hangs from left to right on a horizontal wire that accommodates exactly ten pennants. The pennants each contain a different figure, six of which are numbers (1, 2, 3, 4, 5, and 6) and four of which are letters (A, B, C, D). The order of the pennants conforms to the following conditions:

The numbered pennants are not necessarily in numerical order, but the lettered pennants are arranged alphabetically from left to right.

No two lettered pennants are next to each other.

The first two pennants are the 4 and then the 6, respectively.

The pennant with the 2 is between the pennants with the B and the C.

The pennant with the D is between the pennant with the 1 and the pennant with the 3 and next to each of them.

**1.** Which of the following statements must be FALSE?

A. The pennant with the C is between the pennant with the 1 and the pennant with the 2, respectively.

B. The pennant with the B is next to the pennant with the 1 and the pennant with the A, respectively.

C. The pennant with the D is between the pennant with the 3 and the pennant with the 1, and next to each of them.

D. The pennant with the 5 is between the pennant with the A and the pennant with the B, and next to each of them.

E. The pennant with the 4 and the pennant with the 1 are each at the ends of the wire.

**2.** Which of the following must be true?

A. The pennant with the A is next to the pennant with the 3 but not next to the pennant with the 6.

B. The pennant with the 5 is next to the pennant with the A but not next to the pennant with the C.

C. The pennant with the 1 is next to the pennants with the C and the D.

D. The pennant with the 1 and the pennant with the 4 are at the two ends of the wire.

E. The pennant with the 1 and the pennant with the 3 are separated by three pennants between them.

GO ON TO THE NEXT PAGE

**125**

3. If the pennant with the 3 is at the extreme right end of the line,

   A. the pennant with the B is next to the pennant with the 1.

   B. the pennant with the C is between the pennants with the 2 and the 3 and next to each of them.

   C. the pennant with the A is between the pennants with the 4 and the 6 and next to each of them.

   D. the pennant with the C is next to the pennant with the 1.

   E. the pennant with the C is next to the pennant with the 4.

4. If the numbers of the pennants immediately adjacent to the pennant with the B are added together, their total would be

   A. 10.

   B. 7.

   C. 6.

   D. 4.

   E. 2.

5. Harold wishes to add two more pennants to the line, each containing a new letter. To do so, given the original conditions, which of the following is true?

   A. He can place one pennant with a letter between the pennants with the 4 and the 6.

   B. He can place one pennant with a letter at the extreme left of the line.

   C. He can rearrange only the first four pennants.

   D. He can place both new pennants at the extreme end of the line.

   E. He cannot add the two pennants without violating at least one of the original conditions.

6. Of the following, which pennant is most nearly in the middle of the line?

   A. The pennant containing the A

   B. The pennant containing the B

   C. The pennant containing the C

   D. The pennant containing the 5

   E. The pennant containing the 3

*Questions 7 through 12 are based on the following information.*

Adam attends a baseball-card show and is interested in purchasing five different baseball cards: an Aaron, a Berra, a Canseco, a Drysdale, and an Erskine. The cards have two different prices, retail and trading price.

The Aaron retails for the trading price of the Erskine, and the Erskine retails for the trading price of the Aaron.

   The Aaron's trading price is $65.

   The Aaron's trading price is $25 less than the Erskine's trading price.

   The Canseco's trading price is $10 less than the Berra's trading price.

   The Drysdale retails for $25 more than its trading price and $25 more than the Canseco retails.

   The Drysdale retails for $50 more than the trading price of the Berra.

7. If the Drysdale's trading price is $65, what is the Berra's trading price?

   A.  $75

   B.  $65

   C.  $55

   D.  $40

   E.  $30

8. If the Berra's trading price is $100, which of the following must be true?

   A.  The Drysdale's trading price is $125.

   B.  The Drysdale's trading price is $100.

   C.  The Canseco retails for $100.

   D.  The Canseco retails for $150.

   E.  The Drysdale retails for $200.

9. Which of the following must be true?

   A.  The Erskine retails for the trading price of the Canseco.

   B.  The Erskine retails for less than the trading price of the Aaron.

   C.  The Erskine retails for more than the trading price of the Aaron.

   D.  The Canseco retails for the trading price of the Drysdale.

   E.  The Drysdale retails for $50 less than the trading price of the Berra.

10. How much does the Erskine retail for?

   A.  $40

   B.  $50

   C.  $55

   D.  $60

   E.  $65

11. The Drysdale's trading price must be

   A.  $50 more than the Berra's trading price.

   B.  $50 less than the Berra's trading price.

   C.  $25 more than the Berra's trading price.

   D.  $25 less than the Berra's trading price.

   E.  the same as the Berra's trading price.

12. If the Canseco retails for $50, how much does the Drysdale retail for?

   A.  $75

   B.  $50

   C.  $25

   D.  $20

   E.  $15

Section II Analytical Reasoning

GO ON TO THE NEXT PAGE

*Questions 13 through 17 are based on the following information.*

The government is arranging an expedition to an underdeveloped area of the world and has to select a four-member team. Exactly two of the members must be engineers. The following professionals applied for the expedition:

A is an architect.

B is a biologist.

C is a chemist.

D is a doctor.

E is an engineer.

F is a field engineer.

G is a general engineer.

The architect and the engineer will not go together.

The doctor and the general engineer will not go together.

The biologist and the architect will not go together.

13. If A is selected, the rest of the expedition must be composed of

   A.  C, D, and F.

   B.  B, F, and G.

   C.  C, F, and G.

   D.  C, E, and F.

   E.  E, F, and G.

14. If the field engineer is rejected, then the others rejected would be

   A.  the chemist only.

   B.  the chemist or the biologist.

   C.  the architect, chemist, and engineer.

   D.  the architect and doctor.

   E.  the biologist, chemist, and doctor.

15. If the general engineer is selected, then which of the following must be true?

   A.  The biologist is selected.

   B.  The architect is not selected.

   C.  The chemist is selected.

   D.  The doctor is selected.

   E.  The engineer is not selected.

16. Which of the following CANNOT be true?

   A.  G and A do not both go on the same expedition.

   B.  C and E do not both go on the same expedition.

   C.  F and C both go on the same expedition.

   D.  A and B do not go on the same expedition.

   E.  B, C, and D can all go together.

17. If the doctor is selected and the chemist is not selected, the expedition will be composed of

   A.  A, E, and F.

   B.  B, E, and F.

   C.  A, F, and G.

   D.  B, E, and G.

   E.  A, B, and F.

*Questions 18 through 24 are based on the following information.*

Four runners—Arlene, Betty, Claire, and Doris—complete a ten-kilometer race. After the race, they record their times and notice the following:

> Arlene is faster than Betty.
>
> Claire is faster than Doris.
>
> Doris is slower than Betty.

**18.** Which of the following statements must be FALSE?

- **A.** Betty is slower than Claire.
- **B.** Doris is faster than Arlene.
- **C.** Betty is faster than Claire.
- **D.** Arlene is faster than Claire.
- **E.** Arlene is faster than Doris.

**19.** Which of the following statements must be true?

- **A.** Betty is faster than Claire.
- **B.** Doris is faster than Arlene.
- **C.** Betty is slower than Claire.
- **D.** Arlene is faster than Claire.
- **E.** Arlene is faster than Doris.

**20.** If a fifth runner, Edna, has a time faster than Claire's, which of the following CANNOT be true?

- **A.** Edna has the fastest time of the five runners.
- **B.** Arlene is faster than Claire.
- **C.** Doris is faster than Edna.
- **D.** Betty is faster than Edna.
- **E.** Claire is faster than Betty.

**21.** If Francine, whose time is slower than Claire's, joins the group, and if Betty is faster than Claire, which of the following must be true?

- **A.** Arlene is the fastest, and Francine is the slowest of the five.
- **B.** Arlene is the fastest, and Doris is the slowest of the five.
- **C.** Betty is the fastest, and Francine is the slowest of the five.
- **D.** Arlene is the fastest, and Betty is the second fastest of the five.
- **E.** Betty is the second fastest, and Doris is the slowest of the five.

**22.** Glenda and Helen join the original group of four runners, and Glenda's time is faster than Helen's. If Claire's time is faster than Glenda's, but Claire's is not the fastest time of the six runners, which of the following must be true?

- **A.** Arlene is the fastest of the six.
- **B.** Betty is the fastest of the six.
- **C.** Either Arlene or Betty is the fastest of the six.
- **D.** Helen is the slowest of the six.
- **E.** Doris is the slowest of the six.

**23.** If June and Kay join the original group, and June is faster than Claire, and Kay is faster than Betty but slower than Claire, Claire must be faster than

- **A.** one other runner.
- **B.** two other runners.
- **C.** three other runners.
- **D.** four other runners.
- **E.** five other runners.

GO ON TO THE NEXT PAGE

Section ■ Analytical Reasoning

**24.** If Sylvia enters the original group and is faster than Claire, which of the following is NOT a possible finishing order of times of the group, from fastest to slowest?

A.   Sylvia, Claire, Arlene, Betty, Doris

B.   Arlene, Sylvia, Betty, Claire, Doris

C.   Sylvia, Arlene, Claire, Betty, Doris

D.   Arlene, Betty, Sylvia, Claire, Doris

E.   Sylvia, Betty, Arlene, Claire, Doris

IF YOU FINISH BEFORE TIME IS CALLED, CHECK YOUR WORK ON THIS SECTION ONLY. DO NOT WORK ON ANY OTHER SECTION IN THE TEST.

# Section III: Logical Reasoning

**Time: 35 Minutes**

**26 Questions**

**Directions:** You will be presented with brief passages or statements and will be required to evaluate their reasoning. In each case, select the best answer choice, even though more than one choice may present a possible answer. Choices that are unreasonable or incompatible with common-sense standards should be eliminated.

1. Aristotle said that art represents "general truths" about human nature. Our city councilman is arguing in favor of the artistry—a giant mural in front of a Jeep dealership, portraying a variety of four-wheel-drive vehicles. He cites Aristotle's conception of art as his support.

   The preceding passage raises which of the following questions?

   A. Can a city councilman understand Aristotle?

   B. Which general truths about human nature does a four-wheel-drive mural not represent?

   C. Could Aristotle have predicted a modern society filled with sophisticated machines?

   D. To what extent are four-wheel-drive vehicles representative of a general advance in modern technology?

   E. What "general truth" about human nature does a mural of four-wheel-drive vehicles represent?

2. Speaker 1: The holy passion of friendship is of so sweet and steady and loyal and enduring a nature that it will last through a whole lifetime.

   Speaker 2: If not asked to lend money.

   The two speakers represent which of the following contrasting attitudes?

   A. Faith and despair

   B. Idealism and cynicism

   C. Idealism and optimism

   D. Socialism and capitalism

   E. Friendship and enmity

3. In 1933, a new industrial code was established to fix a minimum wage of 40 cents an hour in the United States.

   The above statement suggests which of the following maxims, or proverbs?

   A. You can fool some of the people some of the time.

   B. Don't count your chickens before they hatch.

   C. Times change.

   D. There's a sucker born every minute.

   E. Power to the people.

GO ON TO THE NEXT PAGE

4. Unfortunately, only 60 percent of the driving public uses regular seat belts. Automatic restraints are the answer, and the quicker they are required, the sooner highway deaths will be reduced.

The author's conclusion is based upon which of the following assumptions?

A. Only 60 percent of the driving public cares about passengers' lives.

B. The use of restraints reduces highway deaths.

C. Regular seat belts are inadequate safety devices.

D. It is unfortunate that 40 percent of the driving public does not use regular seat belts.

E. Highway deaths occur often enough so that reducing them is a necessity.

*Questions 5 and 6 are based on the following passage.*

Journalist: The heart and soul of our business is credibility. We get that credibility and respect, and the power that goes with it, only by being a socially and professionally responsible agent for the public. In some ways, we journalists have to have the same attitude to news as an employee of a bank has to money—it isn't ours. We're handling it on behalf of other people, so it cannot be converted to our own use. If we do, it's embezzlement.

5. Which of the following criticisms would most weaken the comparison between journalists and bank employees?

A. Different newspapers print different news, just as different banks hold assets from various sources.

B. Journalists are necessarily more creative individuals than bank employees.

C. The heart and soul of the banking business is money, not credibility.

D. A bank teller need not be credible, just responsible.

E. Embezzlement is properly a crime against the bank, not against the depositors.

6. The first sentence makes a point with which of the following techniques?

A. Metaphor

B. Sarcasm

C. Parody

D. Overstatement

E. Statistical support

7. The value of a close examination of the circumstances of an aircraft accident lies not only in fixing the blame but in learning lessons.

The above statement fits most logically into which of the following types of passages?

A. A survey of the "scapegoat phenomenon" in modern society

B. An argument in favor of including specific details in any academic essay

C. An argument against the usefulness of the National Transportation Safety Board

D. A brief history of aeronautics

E. A description of the causes of a particular aircraft accident

8. Consumers are not so easily manipulated as they are often painted. They may know what they want, and what they want may be greatly different from what other people believe they need.

Which of the following statements, if true, most weakens the above argument?

A. Most people continue to buy the same brand of a product year after year.

B. Companies that advertise the most sell the most products.

C. Store shelves packed with a variety of different brands have the potential to confuse the consumer.

D. Most consumers know which brand they are going to buy before entering a store.

E. People who shop with others rarely argue with their companions.

*Questions 9 and 10 are based on the following passage.*

The 1980 census showed a sharp rise during the 1970s in the number of Americans living together as unmarried couples, but an increase in the marriage rate in 1981 suggested that matrimony would make a comeback in the 1980s.

9. Which of the following best refutes the argument above?

A. One of the causes of more marriages was that the large population resulting from a baby boom was just reaching marriageable age.

B. Although information about the 1981 marriage rate was not complete, most analysts considered it to be reliable.

C. Many of those marrying in 1981 were couples who had lived together during the 1970s.

D. The number of Americans living together did not rise at a consistent rate during the 1970s.

E. The marriage rate increased dramatically in 1971 and fell even more dramatically in following years.

GO ON TO THE NEXT PAGE

**10.** With which of the following would the author be likely to agree?

   **A.** Americans should not live together as unmarried couples.

   **B.** Matrimony is preferable to living together.

   **C.** Economic circumstances have made matrimony attractive as a way of paying less income tax.

   **D.** The attitudes of young people in the 1980s were altogether different from the attitudes of young people in the 1970s.

   **E.** Prevailing attitudes toward marriage tend to persist for more than one year.

**11.** The shortsightedness of our government and our scientists has virtually nullified all of their great discoveries because of their failure to consider the environmental impact. The situation is far from hopeless, but our government agencies must become better watchdogs.

It can be inferred from the passage that blame is being placed upon

   **A.** consumers who prefer new technology to clean air.

   **B.** legal loopholes which allow industry abuse of government regulations.

   **C.** the intrinsic problematic nature of the technology itself.

   **D.** citizen and scientific groups responsible for overseeing safety concerns.

   **E.** the ability of government to actually police industry.

**12.** Voltaire once said, "Common sense is not so common."

Which of the following most nearly parallels Voltaire's statement?

   **A.** God must have loved the common man; he certainly made enough of them.

   **B.** The common good is not necessarily best for everyone.

   **C.** Jumbo shrimp may not actually be very big.

   **D.** Good people may not necessarily have good sense.

   **E.** Truth serum cannot contain the truth.

*Questions 13 and 14 are based on the following passage.*

The department store owned by my competitor sells green necklaces that glow in the dark. Only those customers of mine wearing those necklaces must be giving business to the competition.

**13.** The conclusion could best be strengthened by

   **A.** deleting "that glow in the dark."

   **B.** changing "sells" to "has sold."

   **C.** changing "the competition" to "my competitor."

   **D.** inserting "only" as the first word in sentence one.

   **E.** changing "wearing" to "owning."

**14.** The author foolishly assumes that

  A.  the customers might find the necklaces attractive.

  B.  customers are not buying other products from the competition.

  C.  customers will wear the necklaces in daylight.

  D.  a department store should not sell necklaces.

  E.  the competition is outselling the author.

**15.** Which of the following most logically completes the passage at the blank below?

Several of the survivors discussed their dilemma. They could remain on the island and attempt to survive as best they know how. Or they could attempt to escape, using the resources available to them. None of the group wished to venture away from their uncertain sanctuary, but all of them knew that help would be a long time coming. Their discussions were thus _____.

  A.  futile, arbitrary, and capricious

  B.  limited by their imagination and resolve

  C.  dampened by a sense of impending doom

  D.  possible, but by no means successful

  E.  courageous and honorable

*Questions 16 and 17 are based on the following letter.*

To the Chairman:

At the October 7th meeting, it was decided that no two officers would hold positions on the same committee. It has recently come to my attention that both Charles S. Smith and Arnold Krunkle will be serving in some capacity on the Building and Maintenance Committee, and both have been nominated for officer status. As you know, this is in direct disregard for the rules as voted by the membership last October 7th. I would hope that sufficient action be taken by the Disciplinary Committee (on which committee both of the above are members) so that this problem will be remedied.

Sincerely,

Irving H. Fortnash

**16.** Which of the following is the essential flaw that the writer of the letter fails to notice?

  A.  Smith and Krunkle are already serving together on the Disciplinary Committee.

  B.  The Chairman has no power in the matter.

  C.  The membership cannot pass rules limiting members.

  D.  Smith and Krunkle are not yet officers.

  E.  Building and Maintenance is actually two committees.

Section **Logical Reasoning**

GO ON TO THE NEXT PAGE

17. Which of the following most completely and reasonably describes actions that may occur in the near future?

    A.  Fortnash resigns his membership.

    B.  Either Smith or Krunkle resigns his membership.

    C.  Krunkle resigns his committee post on the Building and Maintenance Committee.

    D.  Smith resigns his position on the Building and Maintenance Committee.

    E.  One of the two (Smith or Krunkle) resigns his position on the Building and Maintenance committee, and the other resigns his position on the Disciplinary Committee.

18. Radio announcer: Flamo Lighters when you need them! Always reliable, always dependable. In all weather, with ten-year guarantee. Don't get caught without a light—keep a Flamo in your pocket wherever you go!

    All of the following are claims for Flamo Lighters made or implied by the announcer's copy EXCEPT:

    A.  Convenience

    B.  Dependability

    C.  Longevity

    D.  Winter-proof

    E.  All-purpose

19. Investigative reporter: All records of births, deaths, and marriages are doubtful because all records are open to question.

    The investigative reporter uses which of the following techniques to support his or her argument?

    A.  Deductive reasoning

    B.  Inductive reasoning

    C.  Symbolic reasoning

    D.  Circular reasoning

    E.  Providing examples

20. The top salesperson at a large sporting goods store always advises her customers to buy snow skis instead of a snowboard. She points out that because skis are longer, they provide greater stability, control, and stopping power. Besides, she points out, because skiers outnumber snowboarders by seven to one, there must be something inherently better about skiing.

    Which of the following, if true, is the strongest logical objection to the argument that the salesperson makes based on the comparative number of skiers and snowboarders?

    A.  The salesperson probably makes more profit selling skis than selling snowboards.

    B.  When given two choices, people usually select the choice that is inherently better.

    C.  More people buy economy cars than luxury cars, but this difference doesn't make the economy cars inherently better.

**D.** The dangers of skiing are much greater than the dangers of snowboarding.

**E.** Individuals are bound to have different ability levels in any given sport.

21. Exobiology is the search for extraterrestrial life. Traditionally, theorists have speculated that life could exist elsewhere if six factors prove suitable: temperature, water, pressure, salinity, acidity, and oxygen. However, a new line of thinking suggests that radically different life forms—such as those based on silicon rather than carbon—could exist without all six factors present. This new theory would increase the possible number of planets supporting life in our galaxy from fifty thousand to nearly two billion.

Which statement, if true, supports the idea that noncarbon life forms may exist?

**A.** Life forms have been found only on earth.

**B.** Like carbon, silicon promotes the formation of polypeptides, essential components of life.

**C.** The statistical possibility of life on two billion planets is much greater than that of life on fifty thousand planets.

**D.** The six factors required for carbon-based life have been debated for the last four hundred years.

**E.** Silicon atoms are much less reactive than carbon atoms.

22. All race-car lovers enjoy classical music.

No backgammon players enjoy classical music.

All those who enjoy classical music also enjoy fine wine.

If each of the above statements is true, which of the following must also be true?

**A.** Everyone who plays backgammon enjoys fine wine.

**B.** No one who enjoys fine wine plays backgammon.

**C.** No backgammon players are race-car lovers.

**D.** No backgammon players enjoy fine wine.

**E.** No race-car lover enjoys fine wine.

*Questions 23 and 24 are based on the following passage.*

It has been proven that the "lie detector" can be fooled. If one is truly unaware that one is lying, when in fact one is, then the "lie detector" is worthless.

23. This argument would be strengthened most by

**A.** demonstrating that one's awareness of truth or falsity is always undetectable.

**B.** showing that the "truth" of any statement always relies on a subjective assessment.

GO ON TO THE NEXT PAGE

C. citing evidence that there are other means of measuring truth that are consistently less reliable than the lie detector.

D. citing the number of cases in which the lie detector mistook falsehood for truth.

E. claiming that ordinary, unbiased people are the best "lie detectors."

24. Without contradicting his or her own statements, the author might present which of the following arguments as a strong point in favor of the lie detector?

A. The methodology used by investigative critics of lie detectors is itself highly flawed.

B. Law-enforcement agencies have purchased too many detectors to abandon them now.

C. Circumstantial evidence might be more useful in a criminal case than is personal testimony.

D. The very threat of a lie-detector test has led a significant number of criminals to confess.

E. People are never "truly aware" that they are lying.

25. Radial Keratotomy (RK) is a technology giving visually impaired people the opportunity to attain perfect vision. RK can free people from the burden of wearing glasses or having to maintain contact lenses. The risks of this delicate operation have decreased significantly since the procedure's creation, and success rates have risen such that eight out of every ten people undergoing RK surgery can achieve perfect vision. Although the cost of the procedure is high ($3,000 per eye), all visually impaired individuals should take advantage of RK to attain the perfect vision that everyone deserves and thus improve their quality of life.

Which of the following assumptions underlies the passage above?

A. The benefits of perfect vision are numerous, and visually impaired individuals should undergo RK surgery.

B. Visually impaired individuals cannot improve their sight unless RK surgery is used to correct their disability.

C. RK technology will decrease in cost in the future.

D. The possibility of achieving perfect vision outweighs the costs and risks of RK surgery.

E. RK provides perfect vision for all individuals, regardless of their genetic background and visual disabilities.

26. The best way to get rid of the common cold is to stop eating. That way the cold will starve to death and voila! You're cured!

Which of the following is an assumption that supports the conclusion in the passage above?

A. When one begins fasting, the cold will increase in severity because its bacteria will begin to rapidly multiply to try to stay alive.

B. The body's immune system will not become weakened by the lack of food.

C. The body's immune system will be reduced in strength in response to the reduced energy intake.

D. Bacteria causing a cold will begin to grow in number regardless of the amount of food intake.

E. Bacteria causing the common cold are present not only in our bodies but also throughout the environment.

IF YOU FINISH BEFORE TIME IS CALLED, CHECK YOUR WORK ON THIS SECTION ONLY. DO NOT WORK ON ANY OTHER SECTION IN THE TEST.

Section III Logical Reasoning

# Section IV: Analytical Reasoning

Time: 35 Minutes

24 Questions

**Directions:** You will be presented with several sets of conditions. A group of questions follows each set of conditions. Choose the best answer to each question, drawing a rough diagram of the conditions when necessary.

*Questions 1 through 6 are based on the following information.*

There are seven players on a basketball team—A, B, C, D, E, F, and G. The team photographer is trying to place them in order of height so that he can arrange the players for a team photograph. As he starts to arrange the players, he notices the following relationships:

A is taller than B.

B is taller than C.

A is taller than D.

D is taller than E.

F is not taller than C.

G is not taller than D.

1. How many players must be shorter than A?

    **A.** Six

    **B.** Five

    **C.** Four

    **D.** Three

    **E.** None

2. All of the following could be true EXCEPT:

    **A.** B is taller than E.

    **B.** D is taller than C.

    **C.** C is taller than D.

    **D.** C is taller than E.

    **E.** F is taller than B.

3. How many players must be taller than F?

    **A.** None

    **B.** One

    **C.** Two

    **D.** Three

    **E.** Four

4. Which of the following CANNOT be true?

    **A.** B is taller than F.

    **B.** G is not shorter than B.

    **C.** B is taller than C.

    **D.** G is taller than A.

    **E.** E is shorter than C.

**5.** If F is taller than G, which of the following must be true?

   **A.** G is the shortest of the seven players.

   **B.** F is the shortest of the seven players.

   **C.** D is taller than F.

   **D.** D is taller than G.

   **E.** C is taller than G.

**6.** To determine with certainty the relative height of all seven players, in addition to the original conditions, how many additional single-condition statements of height relationship must there be?

   **A.** One

   **B.** Two

   **C.** Three

   **D.** Four

   **E.** Five

*Questions 7 through 12 are based on the following information.*

Four football games will be played this weekend among eight teams. In each game, one team plays another team, and only one of the two teams can win. In this league there can be no ties. Three sportswriters—Stevens, Cardenas, and Blume—wrote predictions for their respective newspapers. The predictions and additional facts about the games are as follows:

   Stevens predicted that the Packers, Rams, Bears, and Redskins would win.

   Cardenas predicted that the Raiders, Bears, Jets, and Packers would win.

   Blume predicted that the Redskins, Packers, Cowboys, and Jets would win.

   The Colts played in one of the four games but were not picked to win by any of the sportswriters.

   The Cowboys and Raiders played on different days.

   The Rams played the Jets.

**7.** Using only the information given in the first paragraph and the predictions by Stevens and Cardenas, which one of the following teams could the Rams play?

   **A.** The Packers

   **B.** The Bears

   **C.** The Redskins

   **D.** The Chargers

   **E.** The Raiders

**8.** The only team picked to win by all the sportswriters was the

   **A.** Bears

   **B.** Cowboys

   **C.** Jets

   **D.** Packers

   **E.** Redskins

**9.** If the Colts win, which of the following must lose?

   **A.** The Jets

   **B.** The Bears

   **C.** The Cowboys

   **D.** The Raiders

   **E.** The Packers

GO ON TO THE NEXT PAGE

10. Which of the following must be true?

    A. The Cowboys play the Raiders.

    B. The Bears play the Redskins.

    C. The Jets play the Bears.

    D. The Rams play the Raiders.

    E. The Redskins play the Raiders.

11. If the Jets and Cowboys win, which of the following must be true?

    A. Stevens predicted the most winners.

    B. Cardenas predicted the most winners.

    C. Blume predicted the most winners.

    D. If the Redskins lose and the Raiders win, Cardenas will have predicted the most winners.

    E. If the Redskins win and the Raiders lose, Blume will have predicted the most winners.

12. Which of the following must be FALSE?

    A. The Bears play the Cowboys.

    B. The Redskins play the Rams.

    C. The Colts play the Packers.

    D. The Raiders play the Redskins.

    E. The Rams play the Jets.

*Questions 13 through 18 are based on the following information.*

Five planets—A, B, C, D, and E—are orbiting around a central sun, each in its own circular orbit but not necessarily in the order given. Each planet is in its own circular orbit, and none of the orbits cross paths.

The smallest orbit is not planet A's or planet B's.

Planet D has the largest orbit.

Planet C is not in an orbit next to planet E's or D's.

Planet E is closest to the sun.

13. Which of the following must be true?

    A. Planet C's orbit is not second from the sun.

    B. Planet D's orbit is next to planet E's orbit.

    C. Planet A's orbit is next to planet B's orbit.

    D. Planet A's orbit is closer to the sun than planet B's orbit.

    E. Planet B's orbit is next to planet D's orbit.

**14.** Which of the following must be FALSE?

A. The orbit of planet D is between planet C's orbit and planet E's orbit.

B. The orbit of planet B is between planet C's orbit and planet E's orbit.

C. The orbit of planet C is between planet B's orbit and planet D's orbit.

D. The orbit of planet E is smaller than planet D's orbit.

E. The orbit of planet A is farther from the sun than the orbit of planet B.

**15.** Which of the following statements can be derived from the other four statements?

A. The smallest orbit is not planet A's or B's.

B. Planet D has the largest orbit.

C. Planet C is not in an orbit next to planet E's or D's.

D. Planet E is closest to the sun.

E. None of the statements above can be derived.

**16.** If planet B's orbit is next to planet C's orbit, which of the following must be true?

A. Planet A's orbit is closer to the sun than planet C's orbit.

B. Planet B's orbit is closer to the sun than planet C's orbit.

C. Planet A's orbit is next to planet B's orbit.

D. Planet A's orbit is not next to planet B's orbit.

E. Planet C's orbit is closer to the sun than planet E's orbit.

**17.** If planet A's orbit is next to planet E's,

A. planet D's is next to planet E's.

B. planet B's is next to planet D's.

C. planet C's is next to planet E's.

D. planet A's is between planet C's and planet D's.

E. planet B's is between planet C's and planet A's.

**18.** If a new planet is discovered, planet F, and its circular orbit around the sun is next to planet C's orbit, then planet F's orbit must be

A. between the orbits of planet B and planet C.

B. between the orbits of planet A and planet B.

C. between the orbits of planet C and planet D.

D. between the orbits of planet C and planet E.

E. between the orbits of planet A and planet C.

GO ON TO THE NEXT PAGE

*Questions 19 through 24 are based on the following information.*

Jennifer arranges her daily schedule of seven high school classes, each of which is fifty minutes in length, and the first of which begins at 7 a.m. Each class begins on the hour, lunch is at 1:15 p.m., and the final class of the day begins at 2 p.m. She arranges her classes as follows:

> She takes Psychology sometime after English.
>
> She takes Spanish sometime after Science.
>
> She takes Science exactly three hours after Calculus.
>
> She takes English at either 7 a.m. or 9 a.m.
>
> Her final class of the day is Music, not PhysEd.

19. If Jennifer takes PhysEd and Psychology consecutively, but not necessarily in that order, then she must take Calculus from

    A.  7:00–7:50.
    B.  8:00–8:50.
    C.  9:00–9:50.
    D.  10:00–10:50.
    E.  11:00–11:50.

20. If at 7:15 a.m. Jennifer is in English, in which class must she be at 12:15 p.m.?

    A.  Spanish
    B.  PhysEd
    C.  Science
    D.  Psychology
    E.  Calculus

21. Which of the following subjects can be taken at either of two times: 9 a.m. or 11 a.m.?

    A.  Spanish
    B.  English
    C.  Science
    D.  Psychology
    E.  Calculus

22. Which of the following is a complete and accurate list of classes that Jennifer could schedule at 8 a.m.?

    A.  PhysEd
    B.  Calculus
    C.  PhysEd, Calculus
    D.  PhysEd, Psychology
    E.  PhysEd, Psychology, Calculus

**23.** Which of the following is a complete and accurate list of times at which PhysEd could begin?

A. 8 a.m., 9 a.m., 11 a.m.

B. 8 a.m., 11 a.m., 12 noon

C. 7 a.m., 8 a.m., 9 a.m.

D. 8 a.m., 9 a.m., 10 a.m., 12 noon

E. 7 a.m., 8 a.m., 9 a.m., 10 a.m.

**24.** If Jennifer takes English at 9 a.m., which of the following is possible?

A. She takes PhysEd after Spanish.

B. She takes PhysEd after Psychology.

C. She takes Psychology after Spanish.

D. She takes Calculus after Spanish.

E. She takes Calculus after Psychology.

IF YOU FINISH BEFORE TIME IS CALLED, CHECK YOUR WORK ON THIS SECTION ONLY. DO NOT WORK ON ANY OTHER SECTION IN THE TEST.

# Section V: Logical Reasoning

Time: 35 Minutes

26 Questions

**Directions:** You will be presented with brief passages or statements and will be required to evaluate their reasoning. In each case, select the best answer choice, even though more than one choice may present a possible answer. Choices that are unreasonable or incompatible with common-sense standards should be eliminated.

1. A woman planning to travel by jet to Europe was arrested at the airport for attempting to carry a deactivated bomb onto the airplane. She pleaded with authorities that her actions were caused by her fear of a terrorist sabotaging the plane. Upon being questioned, she explained that, since the probability of one bomb being on the plane was small, the probability of *two* bombs being on the same plane would be miniscule, and so she brought her own to decrease the odds of sabotage from a terrorist bomb.

   The woman's reasoning about her lessening the chances of a real bomb being aboard her plane contains faulty logic because

   A. there was little chance that any bomb could pass the metal detector.

   B. her deactivated bomb cannot be logically equated in the same circumstances with a live bomb.

   C. her attempting to bring any bomb aboard a plane actually jeopardized her own life.

   D. her actions are unrelated to and independent of any particular terrorist's activities.

   E. a terrorist, knowing one bomb is already aboard, would necessarily avoid putting a second bomb on the same plane.

2. English automobiles leak oil. All sportscars need some repair every month. Since the vehicle I recently purchased leaks oil and needs repair every month, I must have purchased an English sportscar.

   Which of the following, if true, would logically weaken the conclusion above?

   A. Only English sportscars need repair every month.

   B. Not all English sedans leak oil.

   C. Some sportscars need repair every two weeks.

   D. Danish automobiles also leak oil.

   E. American sportscars never need repair.

**3.** Business consultant: The Norton Corporation needs its trash removed throughout the year. Hilldale Trash Removal picks up every week, whereas Suburban Haulers pick up twice a month. Since Hilldale's monthly charges are equal to Suburban's, it differs little to the Norton Corporation which service it uses.

Which of the following, if true, would most strengthen the consultant's conclusion in the passage above?

A. Only half as many corporations use Suburban as use Hilldale.

B. Hilldale's dumpsters are slightly larger than those of Suburban.

C. The Norton Corporation generates no more than one-half dumpster of trash per month.

D. Frequency of pickup during the month is of significance to the Norton Corporation.

E. Hilldale provides more reliable service than Suburban.

**4.** The number of pristine wilderness preserves in this country, as well as in the world, is quickly diminishing. Species extinction is fifty times more rapid today than twenty years ago. Despite recent environmentalists' efforts to work within the legal system to halt the rapid exploitation of wilderness, little is being done to protect endangered species or their environments. Therefore, radical environmentalists are justified in taking any actions—even illegal ones—to stop the destruction of the environments.

Which of the following is an unstated assumption of the author?

A. The importance of the protection of endangered species and their environments transcends that of strictly legal issues.

B. The number of pristine wilderness preserves should be increased beyond those that presently exist.

C. The number of species disappearing reflects the survival of the fittest in order that only the heartiest ought to survive.

D. Radical environmental action will be much more effective than orthodox measures in reversing environmental damage.

E. The legal system is slow to effect change but will eventually respond to the needs of the people.

Section **V** Logical Reasoning

GO ON TO THE NEXT PAGE

**5.** All computer geniuses are also brilliant mathematicians. Therefore, some computer geniuses don't require calculators for simple multiplication facts.

Which of the following is the LEAST necessary assumption for the conclusion above to be logically correct?

**A.** Some brilliant mathematicians don't require calculators for simple multiplication facts.

**B.** All brilliant mathematicians don't require calculators for simple multiplication facts.

**C.** Some brilliant mathematicians require calculators for simple multiplication facts.

**D.** All computer geniuses who require calculators for simple multiplication facts are brilliant mathematicians.

**E.** Only computer geniuses are also brilliant mathematicians.

*Questions 6 and 7 are based on the following passage.*

Only a few decades ago, parents were encouraged to enroll their children as early as possible in sports activities. In fact, in the 1960s, it was deemed highly unlikely that any child could become a champion in his or her field without having started training before the age of five or six. However, sports physiologists have recently discovered that, since the muscular and skeletal development of pre-teenaged children is incomplete, some types of training prior to adolescence place unnatural stresses on the growing body and may cause serious, permanent injury. Sports physiologists now advise that strenuous training not begin until the teenage years.

**6.** Which of the following can reasonably be inferred from the passage above to be a viewpoint commonly held in the 1960s?

**A.** Strenuous sports training will be unlikely to cause permanent injuries in teenage athletes.

**B.** An athlete beginning sports training in the teenage years will be unlikely to become a champion.

**C.** Sports champions are likely to become permanently and seriously injured.

**D.** Preteenage athletes require less sports training than teenage athletes.

**E.** Teenage athletes can become champions only if they undertake strenuous and serious training.

**7.** A sports training program is being established today to develop young athletes. If the information in the passage above is true, which additional information would be directly useful in the establishment of the training program?

**A.** Which types of sports training place unnatural stresses on a young body

**B.** How many teenagers undergoing strenuous training went on to become sports champions

**C.** How many sports physiologists advise that strenuous training not begin until the teenage years.

**D.** Which present-day sports champions enjoyed their preteenage training

**E.** Whether preteenage and teenage athletes were offered the same sports training program

8. A telephone survey conducted weekends in late December of 2,000 residents of Knoxberg indicated strong opposition to a proposed local tax to rebuild the old civic stadium complex. Over 70% of those respondents indicated that they would oppose a tax for such a purpose. Yet a poll taken of 2,000 random spectators at the Knoxberg Sports Center in mid-July found almost the opposite sentiment. Nearly 75% of those questioned indicated approval of the proposal, despite the necessity to increase taxes for the new complex.

All of the following, if true, would reasonably explain the marked difference in the results of the two surveys EXCEPT:

A. Respondents polled just after Christmas, when bank accounts are typically low, would be inclined to oppose a proposed tax hike.

B. Spectators at a sports center would tend to be sports fans and thus more favorable to a tax for rebuilding the sports stadium.

C. Telephone respondents found at home on the weekend would be those stay-at-homes less interested in attending sporting events.

D. The six-month interval between the two surveys would account for wear on the old stadium to warrant its renovation.

E. A poll of 2,000 random spectators conducted in the summertime at a sporting event would include many children who don't pay taxes.

9. We have been warned that if we stop watering our lawn, then not only will our grass die and our trees turn brown, but also the gophers will find the dry, hard soil a stimulus for ravaging whatever vegetation happens to survive. Therefore, we have decided to continue to water our lawn.

All of the following can be reasonably inferred as goals of the author EXCEPT:

A. The grass not dying

B. The trees not turning brown

C. The gophers not ravaging remaining vegetation

D. The soil not becoming dry and hard

E. Water conservation

10. Purchasers of large amounts of prescription drugs have often received discounts from the pharmaceutical companies. Health maintenance organizations, private and public hospitals, and government agencies such as the Defense Department have saved millions of dollars by buying in quantity and insisting upon discounted prices. But Medicaid has not taken advantage of the free market, despite the billions it spends on prescription drugs each year. After a fierce battle between Congress and the drug companies, some changes will be made. Congress has asked for mandatory rebates on commonly used drugs paid for by Medicaid, and they have asked for generic equivalents to be substituted for more expensive name-brand drugs when generics are available.

Section V Logical Reasoning

GO ON TO THE NEXT PAGE

All of the following are objections that might be used by pharmaceutical companies arguing against the congressional proposals EXCEPT:

A. Lower prices will reduce the money available for research on new prescription drugs.

B. Substitution of generic drugs will create a system where richer patients will receive superior drugs.

C. Mandatory rebates are a form of price fixing—in this case, by the government.

D. The price of prescription drugs has increased at a rate three times that of the national inflation rate during the past three years.

E. A federally required program may jeopardize discount drug programs for the elderly already negotiated by many states.

*Questions 11 and 12 are based on the following passage.*

The Laffer curve shows that when income tax rates are reduced, there is an increase in taxable income, and an increase in taxable income results in increased total tax revenues for the government.

11. Which of the following most closely parallels the argument above in terms of its logical features?

A. If the city increases its sales taxes on luxury goods from 6.5% to 7.5%, it will raise tax revenues, which can be used to improve traffic congestion in the downtown area.

B. The senator argued that by limiting the import of Japanese automobiles, the number of American cars sold will increase.

C. Orrin's law holds that an advertisement using more than 25 words of text will not be read, and when an advertisement is not read, the product is not sold. Therefore, the fewer words an advertisement has, the more effective it will be in promoting its product.

D. Business magazines claim that the balance of payment will be improved if Americans reduce their use of gasoline and buy only American-made electrical appliances. In two years, they argue, the United States will no longer be a debtor nation.

E. If taxpayers earning more than $30,000 pay a tax rate increased from 28% to 33%, taxpayers earning less than $10,000 can be exempted from federal taxes without decreasing the federal revenues.

12. If the statements in the passage are true, which of the following must also be true?

A. Unless Congress reduces the income tax rate, the government revenues will decrease.

B. If Congress reduces the income tax rates, the revenues that the government receives from income taxes will increase.

C. The reduction of the income tax rates may produce an increase in the total tax income received by the government.

**D.** If Congress raises the income tax rates, the revenues that the government receives from income taxes will decrease.

**E.** Congress will lower the income tax rates only if the lower rates will produce increased revenues.

13. Political analyst: The large vote, invariably heavily Democratic, that unions are able to get out on election days is a target of Republicans in Congress. Unions use telemarketing methods to see to it that their members vote for union-endorsed candidates. And they pay for these with union dues. Republicans hope to "protect the rights of the working person" by passing laws that will prohibit the use of union dues to support these election tactics.

The analyst puts the phrase "protect the rights of the working person" in quotation marks in order to—

**A.** indicate that it is the words of the Republican platform.

**B.** indicate the analyst's sympathy with the working person.

**C.** call attention to the Republicans' concern for the working person's rights.

**D.** suggest that the Republicans' stated motive is specious.

**E.** encourage support from congressional representatives of both parties.

14. No high jumper entered the track meet unless he or she was a track club member. No track club member both entered the meet and was a high jumper.

Which of the following conclusions can be correctly drawn from the two sentences above?

**A.** No one but high jumpers entered the meet.

**B.** Only track club members entered the meet.

**C.** No track club members entered the meet.

**D.** No high jumper entered the meet.

**E.** Some track club members entered the meet.

15. David Smith, a loan officer at Lyon Savings Bank, has been found guilty of embezzlement. This must mean that the bank cannot be trusted by its clients.

Which of the following, if true, would best call into question the conclusion above?

**A.** The nature of a whole may greatly differ from that of its parts.

**B.** People tend to seek out a society that shares their own values.

**C.** Organizations reflect characteristics of their members.

**D.** The whole is equal to the sum of all of its parts.

**E.** No bank has only completely honest employees.

Section **V** Logical Reasoning

GO ON TO THE NEXT PAGE

**16.** It is greatly to our political and economic advantage to continue our alliance with South Korea. But it is time to establish diplomatic relations with North Korea. The first barrier to improved relations with the North is nuclear policy. They insist on our removing the nuclear weapons they claim we have stationed in South Korea. We insist that they negotiate safeguards with the International Atomic Energy Agency on their nuclear facilities.

Diplomatic agreements are almost always based upon what is good for both sides and what is important to them both. We should, therefore, recognize the possibility of a future Korean reunification, renew our pledges of support, and agree to cooperative efforts to combat international terrorism.

The passage suggests that agreement between North Korea and the United States may be possible because

**A.** both countries are opposed to international terrorism.

**B.** we recognize that reunification is now possible.

**C.** an agreement with North Korea will be more beneficial to South Korea than to North Korea.

**D.** a reunification of North and South Korea would greatly benefit both countries and the United States.

**E.** our mutual self-interests may coincide.

**17.** If I do not get at least a B on the final exam, I will definitely fail my geology course.

From the statement above, it most logically follows that if I do get a B on the final exam in geology, I then

**A.** may or may not pass the course.

**B.** will definitely pass the course.

**C.** will probably not pass the course.

**D.** will probably pass the course.

**E.** will definitely not pass the course.

**18.** The United States is not the only country with a huge trade imbalance with Japan. Thailand's trade deficit with Japan this year has increased by 60%. Despite large increases in exports to Japan, Taiwan's deficit balance continues to increase. So does that of South Korea, home of Samsung Electronics, the world's largest manufacturer of microwave ovens. Among Asian nations, only Indonesia has a trade surplus with Japan.

If all of the above is true, which of the following would be inconsistent with the passage?

**A.** Japan is the largest manufacturer of parts of microwave ovens in Asia.

**B.** Total imports by Taiwan have grown increasingly insignificant.

**C.** Indonesia's chief exports are natural resources, especially oil.

**D.** No other nations in Asia have a trade surplus with Japan.

**E.** Japan may have a trade imbalance with other nations not mentioned in the passage.

19. Yours free! Simply send $2 in cash or money order for our illustrated catalog and take $2 off the price of your first order.

Which of the following is most similar in its logical structure to the advertisement above?

A. Clip and mail this coupon with two proofs of purchase from Diamond Soap, and we will send you two coupons worth 50 cents off your next two bars of Diamond Soap.

B. Free for a limited time only! Simply buy two of the compact discs listed below, and we will send a third compact disc of your choice absolutely free.

C. Free! Send the enclosed postage-free card with your name and address, and we'll send you two free samples of sugarfree breath mints.

D. Buy two pounds of Japan Rice, remove the proof-of-purchase labels, and take them to your grocer with this coupon to receive $1 off a can of Cranby cranberries.

E. Complete money-back guarantee! Your full purchase price back without question if the surface of your new Dynamel frying pan ever wears off.

20. Five percent of Americans earning less than $15,000 a year say they have achieved the American dream. Six percent of Americans earning more than $500,000 a year say they have achieved the American dream.

If the information above is true, which of the following can be inferred from the passage?

A. At least eleven percent of all Americans believe that they have achieved the American dream.

B. Five percent of Americans believe that the American dream can be realized without amassing great wealth.

C. Achieving a huge salary may be only incidental to realizing the American dream.

D. The American dream is achieved primarily by those who earn between $15,000 a year and $500,000 a year.

E. The American dream is an unattainable goal that ought not to be sought.

*Questions 21 and 22 are based on the following passage.*

1991 magazine article: Wall Street optimists believe that the generation coming to maturity in the 1990s will save more than the generations of the previous decades, and the increase in the savings rate will mean higher investments in stocks and bonds. The savings rate reached a 9% high in the early 1970s but fell to as low as 3% in 1987. It rose slightly in 1988 and 1989 to 4.5%. One Wall Street forecaster predicts that savings will rise to 10% by 1996 and the Dow Jones average will rise with it to 5000.

GO ON TO THE NEXT PAGE

In fact, the savings rate fell in 1990 to 4%, and most economists believe that it will not begin to rise again for at least four years. The expectation that the generation of the 1990s would spend less for homes and on their children and more for retirement has not yet been justified. The threat of a recession makes a decreased savings rate even more likely.

21. All of the following would logically explain Wall Street's desire for a rise in the savings rate EXCEPT:

    A. With greater savings, more money would be invested in stocks and bonds.

    B. With more demand for stocks and bonds, the price of stocks and bonds will rise.

    C. With more investment in stocks and bonds, the commissions of Wall Street brokers will increase.

    D. Changes in savings rates will be indicative of the particular inflationary condition of the economy.

    E. With a growth in savings, more discretionary funds are available for market speculation.

22. All of the following would support the argument of the second paragraph of the passage EXCEPT:

    A. The rise in wages annually is much greater than the annual rise in prices.

    B. Excise and income tax rates will rise this year and next.

    C. The unemployment rate shows a very slight but steady rise each month.

D. The savings rate in the third quarter of this year was 0.2% less than the savings rate in the third quarter of last year.

E. The threat of a severe oil shortage could greatly increase the inflation rate.

23. Since this country enjoys far superior air power, we should have no trouble driving any enemy from a country it has invaded. Even if we did not bomb the invaded nation out of concern for killing its citizens, there is nothing to prevent our leveling the country of the invaders. With our superior air force, we are invincible, and there is no need to risk forces on the ground.

Which of the following, if true, would strengthen the argument of the passage above?

    A. The offensive against Germany, 1943–1945, demonstrates that air power alone is not enough to win a war.

    B. Superior air power can do no more than assure control of the air over a land invasion route.

    C. Heavy bombing of an enemy will increase the determination of its people to continue a war.

    D. Better military tactics can provide the advantage that inexperienced military forces often require.

    E. With superior air power, land invasion has often proved to be unnecessary.

**24.** Only truck drivers are courteous driving on interstates. Some motorists are truck drivers. Therefore, some motorists are courteous driving on interstates.

Which of the following most closely parallels the reasoning in the argument above?

A. Only ducks can fly. Some feathered animals can't fly. Therefore, some ducks are feathered animals.

B. Only homes are built out of brick. Some office buildings are built out of brick. Therefore, some office buildings are homes.

C. Only roads made out of concrete are safe. Only highways are safe. Therefore, some concrete highways are safe.

D. Only mothers can give birth to future presidents. Some kangaroos are mothers. Therefore, some kangaroos can give birth to future presidents.

E. Only secretaries can type letters. Some who type letters are men. Therefore, some secretaries are men.

**25.** All the shoppers at the mall return home at the end of the day with newly purchased items. Some of these items will be necessities for home or office, others will be gifts purchased for loved ones, and still others will be trinkets of no practical use but which were simply purchased by compulsive shoppers with money to burn.

If the above passage is true, which of the following statements must also be true?

A. All of the gifts brought home at the end of the day will have been purchased at the mall.

B. Some of the items purchased at the mall will not be necessities for the home or office, gifts for loved ones, or trinkets of no practical use.

C. Some of the gifts purchased for loved ones will also be trinkets of no practical use.

D. Items brought home at the end of the day will be both gifts purchased for loved ones and trinkets of no practical use.

E. Not all of the gift items in the mall will be purchased by the end of the day.

GO ON TO THE NEXT PAGE

**26**. Mr. Frederick:  I don't know whether to take my umbrella or leave it home. What's the weather forecast for today?

Ms. Johnson:  The weatherperson said that it's a typical desert day—not a chance for rain.

Mr. Frederick:  That's a mistake. There's not a cloud in the sky.

Mr. Frederick's final comment indicates that he has <u>inferred</u> that Ms. Johnson means that

**A.** the weather is beautiful and will remain that way for the rest of the day.

**B.** the weatherperson is undecided about the forecast for the rest of the day.

**C.** the weatherperson indicated some kind of cloudy or rainy weather to be imminent.

**D.** the weatherperson indicated that the sunny, cloudless sky will remain that way.

**E.** the weather is changeable and could become sunny at any time.

IF YOU FINISH BEFORE TIME IS CALLED, CHECK YOUR WORK ON THIS SECTION ONLY. DO NOT WORK ON ANY OTHER SECTION IN THE TEST.

# Writing Essay

Time: 30 Minutes

**Directions:** You are to complete a brief essay on the given topic. You may take no more than 30 minutes to plan and write your essay. After reading the topics carefully, you should probably spend a few minutes planning and organizing your response. YOU MAY NOT WRITE ON A TOPIC OTHER THAN THE GIVEN TOPIC.

The quality of your writing is more important than either the quantity of writing or the point of view you adopt. Your skill in organization, mechanics, and usage is important, although it is expected that your essay will not be flawless because of the time pressure under which you write.

Keep your writing within the lined area of your essay booklet. Write on every line, avoid wide margins, and write carefully and legibly.

NOTE: On the actual LSAT, the essay topic is at the top of the essay writing page. Scratch paper for organizing and prewriting is provided.

# Essay Topic

*Read the following descriptions of Mariano and Matisse, two applicants for the position of banquet manager at the St. Germaine hotel. Then, write an argument for hiring either Mariano or Matisse. The following criteria are relevant to your decision:*

The banquet manager must plan parties for a variety of ethnic, religious, community, and business groups.

The banquet manager coordinates all the elements of each party (food, music, liquor, special presentations, etc.) and serves as master of ceremonies at the guests' request.

GO ON TO THE NEXT PAGE

Mariano has been a popular independent bandleader and entertainer in the local area for twenty years. He and his musicians have performed at hundreds of wedding receptions, bar mitzvahs, anniversary celebrations, and holiday parties. Mariano prides himself on the scope of his musical knowledge: No guest has ever requested a song that he could not play. Mariano has worked closely with the caterer and the bartender at each party to make sure that, for example, the band plays soft, unobtrusive music when dinner is served. Mariano has never worked at the St. Germaine hotel.

Matisse has been the chef in the St. Germaine hotel restaurant for twelve years and is widely known for the wide range of tasty dishes he offers, from lasagna to Veal Cordon Bleu. The restaurant features a piano bar, and Matisse has been known to step out of the kitchen and sing to customers for whom he has prepared a special dish. When he last served Beef Stroganoff to a visiting Russian couple, he sent the customers a complimentary bottle of vodka and accompanied the waiter's entrance by bellowing the "Song of the Volga Boatmen." The restaurant accepts a few large parties (up to twelve people). Such parties often phone ahead days in advance to request that Matisse cook them a special dinner.

# Answers and Complete Explanations For Practice Test 1

## Answer Key for Practice Test 1

| Section I | Section II | Section III | Section IV | Section V |
|---|---|---|---|---|
| Reading Comprehension | Analytical Reasoning | Logical Reasoning | Analytical Reasoning | Logical Reasoning |
| 1. A | 1. B | 1. E | 1. A | 1. D |
| 2. D | 2. B | 2. B | 2. E | 2. D |
| 3. A | 3. D | 3. C | 3. C | 3. C |
| 4. B | 4. B | 4. B | 4. D | 4. A |
| 5. E | 5. E | 5. E | 5. E | 5. A |
| 6. C | 6. B | 6. A | 6. C | 6. B |
| 7. A | 7. D | 7. E | 7. E | 7. A |
| 8. C | 8. A | 8. B | 8. D | 8. D |
| 9. A | 9. D | 9. E | 9. E | 9. E |
| 10. E | 10. E | 10. E | 10. E | 10. D |
| 11. D | 11. C | 11. E | 11. E | 11. C |
| 12. B | 12. A | 12. C | 12. B | 12. B |
| 13. C | 13. C | 13. D | 13. A | 13. D |
| 14. B | 14. D | 14. B | 14. A | 14. D |
| 15. A | 15. C | 15. C | 15. A | 15. A |
| 16. C | 16. E | 16. D | 16. D | 16. E |
| 17. D | 17. B | 17. E | 17. B | 17. A |
| 18. D | 18. B | 18. E | 18. B | 18. B |
| 19. C | 19. E | 19. D | 19. B | 19. B |
| 20. A | 20. C | 20. C | 20. A | 20. C |
| 21. D | 21. D | 21. B | 21. D | 21. D |
| 22. C | 22. A | 22. C | 22. C | 22. A |
| 23. C | 23. C | 23. D | 23. E | 23. E |
| 24. A | 24. E | 24. D | 24. A | 24. D |
| 25. D | | 25. D | | 25. D |
| 26. D | | 26. B | | 26. C |
| 27. C | | | | |

# How to Score Your Exam

Your score on the actual LSAT is simply the number of questions you answered correctly (minus a small adjustment factor) scaled to a 120–180 scoring range. There is no penalty for incorrect answers other than no credit. The experimental section (in this case, one of the Analytical Reasoning sections) would not count toward your score.

# Analyzing Your Test Results

Use the charts on the following pages to carefully analyze your results and spot your strengths and weaknesses. You should complete the entire process of analyzing each subject area and each individual problem for each Practice Test. Then examine these results for trends in types of errors (repeated errors) or poor results in specific subject areas. THIS REEXAMINATION AND ANALYSIS IS IMPORTANT TO YOU: IT SHOULD ENABLE YOU TO RECOGNIZE YOUR AREAS OF WEAKNESS AND IMPROVE THEM.

## Tally Sheet

Use the Answer Key to mark the number of questions you finished, got right, and got wrong in the following grid.

| | Possible | Completed | Right | Wrong | |
|---|---|---|---|---|---|
| Section I: Reading Comprehension | 27 | All | 17 | 10 | |
| Section II: Analytical Reasoning | 24 | All | 14 | 10 | |
| Section III: Logical Reasoning | 26 | All | 14 | 8 | 4² |
| Section IV: Analytical Reasoning | 24 | | | | |
| Section V: Logical Reasoning | 26 | All | 15 | 8 | 3² |
| OVERALL TOTALS | 127 | | | | |

## Analysis Sheet for Problems Missed

One of the most important parts of test preparation is analyzing why you missed a problem so that you can reduce the number of future mistakes. Now that you have taken Practice Test 1 and corrected your answers, carefully tally your mistakes by marking them in the proper column.

## Reason for Mistake

| | Total Missed | Simple Mistake | Misread Problem | Lack of Knowledge |
|---|---|---|---|---|
| Section I: Reading Comprehension | | | | |
| Section II: Analytical Reasoning | | | | |
| Section III: Logical Reasoning | | | | |
| Section IV: Analytical Reasoning | | | | |
| Section V: Logical Reasoning | | | | |
| OVERALL TOTALS | | | | |

Reviewing this data should help you determine WHY you are missing certain problems. Now that you have pinpointed the type of error, take the next practice test and focus on avoiding your most common type of error.

# Section I: Reading Comprehension

1. **A.** Choices B and C may have been ideas stated in the passage, but they do not address a *primary* reason for the development of religious freedom in the New World. The best answer is A.

2. **D.** The first paragraph points out the intolerance in Massachusetts and Pennsylvania.

3. **A.** The new religion is less likely to be suspected as aberrant if its founder is safely dead and its beliefs are Western rather than Eastern.

4. **B.** The fourth paragraph reminds the reader that two hundred years ago, the Baptists were regarded with suspicion.

5. **E.** All religions would receive equal protection.

6. **C.** The court makes no legal distinctions between an old and a new religion.

7. **A.** The court makes no inquiries into the truth or falsehood of a religious belief.

8. **C.** After an introductory paragraph, the passage focuses upon the nature of the disadvantages to a plaintiff of the nuisance theory.

9. **A.** The second and third paragraphs discuss the effect of balancing to the advantage of the polluters.

10. **E.** The passage cites each of the first four options but makes no mention of the statute of limitations.

11. **D.** The passage does not deal explicitly with who should pay for pollution cleanup. In the third paragraph, it does argue for weighing the *economic injury caused by the abatement of the pollution* against the harm caused to the public.

**163**

**12. B.** The passage points out the balance in favor of polluters who are engaged in a *socially useful activity*.

**13. C.** The next-to-last paragraph's final sentence makes this point.

**14. B.** The author would disagree strongly with choices A and C. Choices D and E contain absolutes (*no* and *all*) which make them problematic. Choice B, the correct response, is an instance of *coming to the nuisance* described in the last paragraph of the passage.

**15. A.** According to the first paragraph, a disadvantage of cell counts, smear counts, and membrane filter counts is that *both living and dead cells are counted*. This is not true of plate counts, which *have the advantage of not including dead cells* (paragraph 3).

**16. C.** The passage assumes a vocabulary and knowledge beyond those of most high school biology students but not beyond those of a college student. A more advanced student would probably have already mastered this material.

**17. D.** The third paragraph shows that incubation produces colonies, which means that there is a population *growth*. Choice E describes only the range of colonies that are counted; it is too limited to be the best choice.

**18. D.** According to the first paragraph, cell counts, smear counts, and membrane filter counts are quick and less costly, but they cannot discriminate between live and dead cells.

**19. C.** The smear count is one of the methods that is *quickly accomplished*. The other choices are related to more time-consuming procedures.

**20. A.** Although the passage cites the advantages and disadvantages of several methods of cell counting, it does not recommend or condemn any single method. It attempts to describe what each entails.

**21. D.** Each of the other choices is a secondary rather than a primary purpose of the passage. Only choice D reflects the general nature of the passage.

**22. C.** A criticism of ancient theories assumes that modern theories are more adequate; otherwise no basis for the criticism exists.

**23. C.** The passage raises the questions stated in choices A and B but does not answer either of them. By explaining throughout the passage that ancient people were interested in the nature of knowledge, the author indicates that such an interest is not exclusively modern and thus answers the question addressed by choice C.

**24. A.** This question draws from a simple, explicit statement in the final paragraph: *Socrates believed . . . that evil is fundamentally ignorance*. Each of the other choices is an unwarranted complication or extension of this statement.

**25. D.** This choice essentially reiterates the first sentence of paragraph 5, which states the ancient assumption underlying the *mind-body problem*.

**26. D.** The first sentence of the second paragraph expresses the author's uncertainty about the origins of animism, uncertainty especially apparent in the phrase *we suspect that somehow. . . .*

**27. C.** *Soul* is the definition given for the Greek use of *psyche*, and this leads us to define psychology as the study of the soul.

# Section II: Analytical Reasoning

To construct a chart for questions 1 through 6, it is easiest to list the letters consecutively (A, B, C, and D), leaving room between them to place in numbers. Your chart should then look like this:

$$4 \ 6 \ A \ 5 \ B \ 2 \ C \ \tfrac{1}{3} \ D \ \tfrac{3}{1}$$

**1. B.** Only choice B must be false. All the other choices are true or could be true.

**2. B.** From the chart, only choice B must be true. Notice that the pennant with the 1 may, but not necessarily must, be at the right end of the wire.

**3. D.** If the pennant with the 3 is at the extreme right end of the line, the pennant with the 1 is third from the right.

**4. B.** The pennants next to the B contain the numbers 5 and 2, for a total of 7.

**5. E.** To add two more pennants with different letters, both pennants must go to the right of the D to remain true to the original condition regarding alphabetical order. However, in such a case, the two pennants with letters would be next to each other, thus violating an original condition.

**6. B.** The pennants most nearly in the middle are B and 2. Only B is among the choices given.

From the information given for questions 7 through 12, you can write the following relationships or equations:

$$Ar = Et$$

and

$$Er = At \text{ (first condition)}$$

$$At = 65 \text{ (second condition)}$$

Using the first and second conditions, you now also know that

$$Er = 65$$

$$At = Et - 25 \text{ (third condition)}$$

Using the second and third conditions, you now also know that

$$Et = 90$$

$$Ct = Bt - 10 \text{ (fourth condition)}$$

$$Dr = Dt + 25$$

and

$$Dr = Cr + 25$$

Using the two parts of the fifth condition, you also know that

$$Dt + 25 = Cr + 25 \text{ or } Dt = Cr$$

$$Dr = Bt + 50 \text{ (sixth condition)}$$

**7. D.** If the Drysdale's trading price is $65, according to the first part of the fifth condition given *(the Drysdale retails for $25 more than its trading price)*, the Drysdale retails for $90. Now using the sixth condition *(the Drysdale retails for $50 more than the trading price of the Berra)*, $90 is $50 more than $40, so the Berra's trading price would be $40.

**8. A.** Using the sixth condition,

$$Dr = Bt + 50$$

If the Berra's trading price is $100,

$$Dr = 100 + 50$$

The Drysdale retails for $150. Now using the fifth condition,

$$Dr = Dt + 25$$

Since you now know that the Drysdale retails for $150,

$$150 = Dt + 25$$

The Drysdale trading price must be $125. So A is true.

**9. D.** D is true. From the statements contained in the fifth condition,

$$Dr = Dt + 25$$

and

$$Dr = Cr + 25$$

All these amounts are equal to each other, so

$$Dt + 25 = Cr + 25$$

Therefore,

$$Dt = Cr$$

**10. E.** Using the first and second conditions,

$$At = 65$$
$$Er = At$$

Therefore,

$$Er = 65$$

**11. C.** Scanning all the answers shows that we must deduce a relationship between Dt and Bt. Using the fifth condition, we know that

$$Dr = Dt + 25$$

Using the sixth condition, we know that

$$Dr = Bt + 50$$

Therefore,

$$Dt + 25 = Bt + 50$$

Using some simple algebra, we subtract equal amounts from each side of the equation, in this case 25, and get

$$Dt = Bt + 25$$

Therefore, the Drysdale's trading price is $25 more than the Berra's trading price. This is a difficult question.

12. **A.** Using the second part of the fifth condition, we know that

$$Dr = Cr + 25$$

Therefore, if the Canseco retails for $50,

$$Dr = 50 + 25$$

$$Dr = 75$$

So the Drysdale retails for $75.

For questions 13 through 17, a simple connection diagram will be helpful. The lines connect those professionals who would not go together. From the given information, the chart is as follows:

13. **C.** If A is selected, then F and G are selected, and E and B are not selected. If G is selected, then D is not selected; therefore, the team is A, C, F, and G.

14. **D.** If the field engineer is rejected, the engineer and the general engineer are selected; therefore, the architect and doctor would be rejected.

15. **C.** If the general engineer (G) is selected, the doctor D cannot be selected. Therefore, from A, B, and C, either pair A and C or pair B and C can be chosen, depending upon which other engineer (E or F) is chosen along with G. In either event, the chemist C will be selected.

16. **E.** From the diagram, A and B each could be true. An expedition can be selected without both G and A, and one can be selected without both C and E together. Choice C also can be true, as an expedition may contain both F and C. Choice D is simply a restatement of the third statement. Choice E cannot be true, because this would preclude two engineers (a stated requirement) from going on the trip.

17. **B.** If the doctor is selected, the general engineer is not selected, and the engineer and the field engineer are selected. If the engineer is selected, the architect is not selected, and since the chemist is not selected, the biologist is selected. Therefore, the team would consist of the biologist, doctor, engineer, and field engineer, or B, D, E, and F. The other three are therefore B, E, and F.

From the information given for questions 18 through 24, the following diagram can be drawn:

*fastest*
A
B
C?
D
*slowest*

**18. B.** From the chart, we can see that Doris is the slowest of the four runners. (Note: For this and several other problems, Claire *may* be fastest of all or faster than only Doris.)

**19. E.** Again, Doris is the slowest of all.

**20. C.** Entering Edna on our chart for this problem gives us

A
B
E?
C?
D

Doris will still be slowest of all.

**21. D.** Including Francine and the new information gives us

A
B
C
F?
D

Arlene, Betty, and Claire will be the fastest, second fastest, and third fastest, respectively. Of Francine and Doris, however, it cannot be determined who is fourth fastest and who is slowest of all.

**22. A.** If C is not the fastest, A *must* be.

A
B
C?
G?
H?
D

**23. C.** Claire will be faster than three runners: Kay, Betty, and Doris. The diagram would now look like this:

A
J?
C?
K?
B
D

**24. E.** From the original statements, Arlene is faster than Betty.

# Section III: Logical Reasoning

**1. E.** This choice raises the question relevant to establishing the mural as art in Aristotelian terms.

**2. B.** The first speaker puts forth a "perfect" view of friendship (idealistic), and the second questions the endurance of friendship (cynicism).

**3. C.** Answering A or D requires the unsupported assumption that the 1933 minimum wage was too low and unfair to the workers. The statement describes a circumstance in the past that is obviously much different from present circumstances, thus suggesting choice C.

**4. B.** The conclusion that highway deaths will be reduced with the advent of automatic restraints is necessarily based upon the assumption that such restraints reduce highway deaths. None of the other choices focuses on the conclusion; E is an assumption that could motivate the passage as a whole, rather than just the conclusion.

**5. E.** Choices C and D do not address the comparison between journalists and bank employees; and A and B use the comparison in statements irrelevant to the points in the passage. E criticizes the term that links bad journalists with bad bank employees—embezzlement—by pointing out that bank embezzlement does not so directly affect the customers of a bank in the same way as biased or false journalism affects the customers (readers) of a newspaper.

**6. A.** *Heart and soul* is a metaphor, employing terms normally associated with another subject, humans, to refer to a nonhuman entity, business.

**7. E.** This choice is related most fully to the subject matter of the original statement.

**8. B.** This suggests that exterior forces, such as advertising, influence consumer choices and undercuts the contention that consumers know what they want. Each of the other choices is either irrelevant or strengthens rather than weakens the argument.

**9. E.** Choices A, C, and D are irrelevant to the argument, and B actually strengthens the argument. E suggests that the evidence from one year cannot reliably predict a long-term trend.

**10. E.** This is implied in the final sentence. Each of the other choices requires assumptions or beliefs extraneous to the passage.

**11. E.** Neither consumers, citizen groups, nor legal loopholes are mentioned in the statement.

**12. C.** Voltaire's statement shows the irony that the descriptive word used *(common)* may not, in reality, be so. Likewise, the adjective describing the shrimp *(jumbo)* indicates that the shrimp are large; this may not be the case.

**13. D.** Making *only* the first word of sentence 1 does not solve all of the logical problems in the passage but does strengthen the passage by indicating that customers with green necklaces must have bought them from the competition.

**14. B.** The author does not realize that customers not wearing green necklaces may have bought other items from the competition.

**15. C.** The passage establishes that the survivors were caught in a life and death "survival" situation. While B may be a possible choice, answer C logically follows the sense of their dilemma, clouded by uncertainty and the possibility of death.

**16. D.** The letter fails to note that the decision concerns *officers,* and Smith and Krunkle have been merely nominated to be officers and are not yet such. The other choices are either not stated in the letter or are not essential to the argument.

**17. E.** Answers B, C, and D are only partial descriptions and, although may be correct, are not as complete a description of possible future action as answer E. Nothing in the letter would imply the action stated in A.

**18. E.** The announcer claims that Flamo Lighters are convenient (*in your pocket wherever you go*), have longevity (*ten-year guarantee*), are winterproof (*all-weather*), and are dependable (*always reliable, always dependable*). The announcer does not suggest, however, that they are all-purpose.

**19. D.** Because *doubtful* and *open to question* mean nearly the same thing, the reporter is using circular reasoning to support the argument.

**20. C.** You are looking for the choice that most *weakens* the passage. The correct response, C, directly attacks the salesperson's logic that the number of consumers of a given product is a measure of the inherent quality of that product. The comparison between the economy and luxury cars follows the same logic, pointing out that numbers do not necessarily indicate quality. More people buy the economy cars because of their affordable price, even though the luxury cars may have better quality. Other factors besides quality (such as cost, availability, and so forth) are obviously involved in winter-sports choices, as well as in automobile purchases.

**21. B.** This question asks you to find a statement that supports the idea that noncarbon life forms may exist. Of the choices given, only B strengthens the argument. Choice B states that silicon atoms can build essential components of life—polypeptides. This supports the idea that life could exist without carbon.

**22. C.** All racecar lovers enjoy classical music. Since there are no backgammon players who enjoy classical music, then none of the backgammon players are racecar lovers. D is false because the third statement does not necessarily exclude those who don't enjoy classical music from enjoying fine wine.

**23. D.** The argument is *It has been* proven *that the 'lie detector' can be fooled.* The best choice is the one which provides such proof—D. A and B are too general, and C weakens the argument.

**24. D.** Only this choice both represents a *strong* point *and* is not contradictory. A, C, and E contradict the argument, and B is not a relatively strong point.

**25. D.** Although the costs of RK surgery are high and the risk of failure is still quite significant (20%), the possible benefits of a lifetime of perfect vision outweigh all of these cons and justify the risks. At least that's what you can be sure the author assumes because the author encourages those visually impaired to undergo the operation.

**26. B.** Without food, the body's immune system could likely become weakened, thus making it more susceptible to sickness. The assumption in choice B—that the immune system will *not* become weakened—is an important premise for the conclusion that only the cold will weaken and die when one stops eating, not the body's immune system.

# Section IV: Analytical Reasoning

From the information given, the following diagram can be drawn:

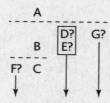

**1. A.** A is the tallest of the seven.

**2. E.** If from the statements B is taller than C, and F is not taller than C, then choice E, *F is taller than B,* cannot be true. All of the other statements are possible.

**3. C.** Only two players must be taller than F: player A and player B.

**4. D.** Since from the chart we can see that A is tallest of all, G cannot be taller than A. All the other statements can (though not necessarily must) be true.

**5. E.** From the new information, the diagram would look like this:

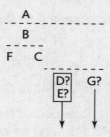

C is equal to or taller than F, and F is taller than G. Therefore, since G is not taller than D, C must be taller than G.

**6. C.** There must be at least three additional statements—for example, C is taller than D, E is taller than F, F is taller than G.

Using the given information, you can construct the following chart or Venn diagram to help answer questions 7 through 12:

|  | *Stevens* | *Cardenas* | *Blume* |
|---|---|---|---|
| Packers vs. Colts | Packers | Packers | Packers |
| Rams vs. Jets | Rams | Jets | Jets |
| Bears vs. Cowboys | Bears | Bears | Cowboys |
| Redskins vs. Raiders | Redskins | Raiders | Redskins |

*or*

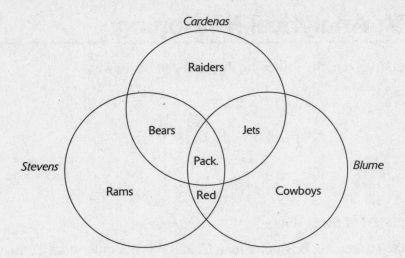

7. **E.** Using the first statement, Stevens predicted that, of the four games, the Packers, Rams, Bears, and Redskins will win. Therefore, the Rams cannot possibly be playing the Packers, Bears, or Redskins. From the second statement, we learn that Cardenas believes that the Raiders and Jets will win, instead of the Rams and Redskins as Stevens had predicted. Therefore, the Rams must be playing either the Raiders or the Jets. Note that the Chargers, choice D, are not among the options.

8. **D.** The first, second, and third statements tell us that each sportswriter picked the Packers to win.

9. **E.** From the chart, we can see that if the Colts win, the Packers must lose.

10. **E.** From the chart, we can see that the Redskins play the Raiders.

11. **E.** If the Jets and the Cowboys win, then Blume has picked at least two games correctly. Since all the sportswriters picked the Packers, we may discount that game, since it won't have any bearing on who picked the most winners. However, if the Raiders win and the Redskins lose (Blume picked the Redskins), Cardenas will have predicted as many winners as Blume. But if the Redskins win and the Raiders lose, Blume will have predicted the most winners.

12. **B.** From the chart, we can see that choice B is false. The Redskins do not play the Rams; the Redskins play the Raiders.

From the information given, you can construct the following chart to help you answer questions 13 to 18:

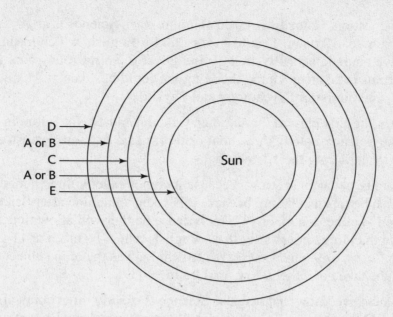

**13. A.** Since planet E is closest to the sun and planet C's orbit is not next to planet E's, planet C is not second from the sun.

**14. A.** Since planet D has the largest orbit, it is farthest from the sun. Thus, its orbit cannot be between the orbits on any of the other planets. From the information given, we cannot pinpoint planet B's orbit. Planet B's orbit *may* be between those of planets C and E. Planet C's orbit *may* be between those of planets B and D.

**15. A.** From the initial information and the fourth statement 4, we know that planet E is closest to the sun. Thus, we can deduce that the smallest orbit is not planet A's or planet B's.

**16. D.** We already know that planet B's orbit has to be next to planet C's, since planet C is the center orbit and the only available orbits for B are on either side of C's orbit.

**17. B.** If planet A's orbit is next to planet E's, then planet B's must be the next to last orbit away from the sun, or B, next to planet D's.

**18. B.** If planet F's orbit is discovered next to planet C's, its orbit will lie between planet A's and planet B's because planet A's orbit and planet B's orbit are on either side of C's.

From the facts given, you can draw the following notes, which enable you to more easily answer questions 19 to 24:

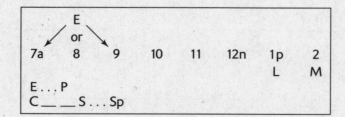

Notice that because Science is exactly three hours after Calculus, and Spanish is taken after Science, then Calculus must be taken at either 7 a.m. or 8 a.m.

**19. B.** If, for this question, Calculus is taken at 7 a.m., then Science is at 10 a.m. and Spanish is at either 11 a.m. or 12 noon. That leaves 9 a.m. for English, which means there are no two consecutive hours left for Psychology and PhysEd. So rule out 7 a.m. for Calculus. If, however, Calculus is taken at 8 a.m., then English could be taken at 7 a.m., leaving the 9 a.m. and 10 a.m. hours for Psychology and PhysEd.

**20. A.** If English is the first class at 7 a.m., then Calculus must be at 8 a.m. in order for Jennifer to take Science exactly three hours later (at 11 a.m.) and Spanish after Science. So Spanish is taken during the 12 noon hour.

**21. D.** Science cannot be taken at 9 a.m. because it comes exactly three hours after Calculus. Nor can Spanish be taken at 9 a.m. because it is taken sometime after Science. Calculus cannot be taken at either 9 a.m. or 11 a.m. because neither will allow time for Spanish to be taken (more than three hours after that). English cannot be taken at 11 a.m. because it is taken at either 7 a.m. or 9 a.m. That leaves Psychology as the only subject of the five listed that can be taken at either 9 a.m. or 11 a.m.

**22. C.** From the facts, we know that because Science is exactly three hours after Calculus, and Spanish is taken after Science, then Calculus must be taken either at 7 a.m. or 8 a.m. So Calculus is among the list of subjects that could be taken at 8 a.m. Psychology cannot be taken at 8 a.m. because this would put English at 7 a.m., leaving neither 7 a.m. nor 8 a.m. for Calculus, which must be taken at either of those two hours. PhysEd can also be taken at 8 a.m., as long as Calculus is taken at 7 a.m.

**23. E.** PhysEd cannot be at 11 a.m. or 12 noon, and here's why: If English is at 7 a.m., then Calculus must be at 8 a.m. This puts Science at 11 a.m. and Spanish after that at 12 noon. If, however, English is at 9 a.m., then Calculus could be at 7 a.m. This puts Science at 10 a.m., with both Psychology and Spanish taking the 11 a.m. and 12 noon spots, not necessarily in that order. So PhysEd cannot be at 11 a.m. or 12 noon, which eliminates choices A, B, and D. The only difference between the remaining two choices, C and E, is that E contains 10 a.m. Can PhysEd be taken at 10 a.m.? Yes, if English is at 7 a.m. and Calculus is at 8 a.m.

**24. C.** If English is taken at 9 a.m., then Calculus is taken at either 7 a.m. or 8 a.m. So the two possible schedules look like this.

| 7a | 8 | 9 | 10 | 11 | 12n | 1p | 2 |
|----|----|----|----|------|------|----|----|
| C | PE | E | Sc | P/Sp | Sp/P | L | M |

| 7a | 8 | 9 | 10 | 11 | 12n | 1p | 2 |
|----|----|----|----|----|-----|----|----|
| PE | C | E | P | Sc | Sp | L | M |

The only possible choice is C.

# Section V: Logical Reasoning

1. **D.** Choice E is incorrect because there is nothing in the passage to suggest that the woman's actions would be known by a terrorist. The presence of her bomb would not affect whether or not a terrorist would place another bomb on the plane. Therefore, her actions have no effect on whether or not another bomb might be aboard.

2. **D.** The passage does not state that *only* English automobiles leak oil. If Danish automobiles also leak oil, the conclusion would no longer necessarily be true.

3. **C.** Choice C strengthens the conclusion, since it indicates that the Norton dumpster is large enough to accommodate Norton's trash, regardless of the frequency of each company's pickup. The other choices weaken or have no impact on the strength of the conclusion.

4. **A.** By condoning any actions—even illegal ones—that radical environmentalists may take to stop environmental erosion, the author assumes that such protection of endangered species is so important that it takes priority over even legal issues. Choice D is incorrect; *reversing* environmental damage is never addressed.

5. **A.** Although choice B (*All brilliant mathematicians . . .*) is an assumption necessary for the conclusion to logically follow, it is not the *least necessary assumption*. Choice A, *Some* [but not all] *brilliant mathematicians don't require calculators . . .*, would also suffice to support the conclusion, if that population of *some mathematicians* happened to include some computer geniuses. Therefore, choice B, requiring only a part of the population (*some*) rather than the total population (*all*) is the least assumption necessary for the conclusion to logically follow. This is a difficult, tricky question.

6. **B.** Since the passage states that it is unlikely that any child can become a champion without having started training before age fix or six, then it necessarily follows that an athlete beginning training in the teenage years will be unlikely to become a champion.

7. **A.** Only A is directly useful. Since certain types of training place unnatural stresses and cause permanent injury, it would no doubt be useful to know which types. Since the training program in question mentions nothing about turning out champions, B is irrelevant. Choice E has only remote bearing, if any, on the question.

8. **D.** All the other choices would help explain the marked difference in opinions in the two surveys. A six-month lapse of time, however, would not cause an old stadium to deteriorate appreciably.

9. **E.** Since the author has decided to continue to water the lawn, it can be reasonably concluded that all the results stated in the passage are desired goals of the author. Water conservation is not one of those goals.

10. **D.** Drug companies would not use an inordinate rise in drug prices to support their case. All the other choices support their side.

11. **C.** Choice C and the original passage both describe a cause and effect that are apparent contradictions: the less tax, the more tax revenues received; the less advertising, the more effective the advertisement.

**12. B.** Laffer's law holds that a reduction in income tax rates will increase government income tax revenues. Choice C, because it refers to overall tax (not only income tax), is not necessarily true.

**13. D.** Since the vote in question is *invariably Democratic*, the stated Republican motive is doubtful, and the quotation marks make this clearer.

**14. D.** If no club member who entered was a high jumper and no high jumper except club members entered, no high jumper can have entered. None of the other choices are certain.

**15. A.** Choices B, C, D, and E support the conclusion of the passage, but choice A suggests that this bank cannot be judged by the behavior of one of its parts (employees).

**16. E.** The passage asserts that agreements are usual when both sides benefit.

**17. A.** The statement makes clear that failure is certain without a B, but it does not state that passing is certain with the B.

**18. B.** It would be inconsistent that Taiwan would have a trade deficit with Japan and yet have relatively insignificant imports. Each of the other statements is consistent with the passage.

**19. B.** The claim of *Free!* Is specious in the passage and in choice B. Both require a purchase, which is not free.

**20. C.** Since approximately the same percentage of high-income and low-income Americans claim to have achieved the American dream, the income factor may be unimportant when Americans say they've achieved the American dream. In choice B, the reference is to 5% of *all* Americans, not 5% of those earning less than $15,000.

**21. D.** Choices A, B, C, and E are each a sensible account of the advantages to Wall Street of a rise in the savings rate. Only choice D is not directly relevant to the issue.

**22. A.** The second paragraph argues that the saving rate will not rise, and choices B, C, D, and E support this prediction. But if the rise in wages is greater than the inflation rate, more money is available for savings.

**23. E.** Choices A, B, and C all weaken the argument of the passage, which contends that superior air power makes a land invasion unnecessary and supposes that *leveling the country* will bring capitulation. Choice D is irrelevant. Only E strengthens the argument.

**24. D.** The correct answer will simply parallel the logic of the original statement; its relative truth in real life is irrelevant. The original logic is structured as follows:

Only truck drivers A are courteous driving on interstates B.

Some motorists C are truck drivers A.

Therefore, some motorists C are courteous driving on interstates B.

The correct answer will parallel:

Only A are B.

Some C are A.

Therefore, some C are B.

The only choice that exactly parallels this logic is choice D.

**25. D.** Since items brought home at the end of the day will be necessities, gifts, and trinkets, then it must be true that items brought home will be both gifts and trinkets. Note that this statement does not exclude the necessities.

**26. C.** Frederick's final statement (*That's a mistake. There's not a cloud in the sky.*) indicates that he must have thought Johnson's remark about the weatherperson implied some sort of cloudy or inclement weather. The key words in the question are *he inferred—he inferred what Ms. Johnson means,* even though his inference is incorrect.

# Practice Test 2

Section I:    Analytical Reasoning—35 minutes; 24 questions

Section II:   Logical Reasoning—35 minutes; 25 questions

Section III:  Reading Comprehension—35 minutes; 28 questions

Section IV:   Logical Reasoning—35 minutes; 26 questions

Section V:    Analytical Reasoning—35 minutes; 24 questions

Writing Essay—30 minutes

# Answer Sheet For Practice Test 2

(Remove This Sheet and Use It to Mark Your Answers)

## Section I

1 Ⓐ Ⓑ Ⓒ Ⓓ Ⓔ
2 Ⓐ Ⓑ Ⓒ Ⓓ Ⓔ
3 Ⓐ Ⓑ Ⓒ Ⓓ Ⓔ
4 Ⓐ Ⓑ Ⓒ Ⓓ Ⓔ
5 Ⓐ Ⓑ Ⓒ Ⓓ Ⓔ
6 Ⓐ Ⓑ Ⓒ Ⓓ Ⓔ
7 Ⓐ Ⓑ Ⓒ Ⓓ Ⓔ
8 Ⓐ Ⓑ Ⓒ Ⓓ Ⓔ
9 Ⓐ Ⓑ Ⓒ Ⓓ Ⓔ
10 Ⓐ Ⓑ Ⓒ Ⓓ Ⓔ
11 Ⓐ Ⓑ Ⓒ Ⓓ Ⓔ
12 Ⓐ Ⓑ Ⓒ Ⓓ Ⓔ
13 Ⓐ Ⓑ Ⓒ Ⓓ Ⓔ
14 Ⓐ Ⓑ Ⓒ Ⓓ Ⓔ
15 Ⓐ Ⓑ Ⓒ Ⓓ Ⓔ
16 Ⓐ Ⓑ Ⓒ Ⓓ Ⓔ
17 Ⓐ Ⓑ Ⓒ Ⓓ Ⓔ
18 Ⓐ Ⓑ Ⓒ Ⓓ Ⓔ
19 Ⓐ Ⓑ Ⓒ Ⓓ Ⓔ
20 Ⓐ Ⓑ Ⓒ Ⓓ Ⓔ
21 Ⓐ Ⓑ Ⓒ Ⓓ Ⓔ
22 Ⓐ Ⓑ Ⓒ Ⓓ Ⓔ
23 Ⓐ Ⓑ Ⓒ Ⓓ Ⓔ
24 Ⓐ Ⓑ Ⓒ Ⓓ Ⓔ

## Section II

1 Ⓐ Ⓑ Ⓒ Ⓓ Ⓔ
2 Ⓐ Ⓑ Ⓒ Ⓓ Ⓔ
3 Ⓐ Ⓑ Ⓒ Ⓓ Ⓔ
4 Ⓐ Ⓑ Ⓒ Ⓓ Ⓔ
5 Ⓐ Ⓑ Ⓒ Ⓓ Ⓔ
6 Ⓐ Ⓑ Ⓒ Ⓓ Ⓔ
7 Ⓐ Ⓑ Ⓒ Ⓓ Ⓔ
8 Ⓐ Ⓑ Ⓒ Ⓓ Ⓔ
9 Ⓐ Ⓑ Ⓒ Ⓓ Ⓔ
10 Ⓐ Ⓑ Ⓒ Ⓓ Ⓔ
11 Ⓐ Ⓑ Ⓒ Ⓓ Ⓔ
12 Ⓐ Ⓑ Ⓒ Ⓓ Ⓔ
13 Ⓐ Ⓑ Ⓒ Ⓓ Ⓔ
14 Ⓐ Ⓑ Ⓒ Ⓓ Ⓔ
15 Ⓐ Ⓑ Ⓒ Ⓓ Ⓔ
16 Ⓐ Ⓑ Ⓒ Ⓓ Ⓔ
17 Ⓐ Ⓑ Ⓒ Ⓓ Ⓔ
18 Ⓐ Ⓑ Ⓒ Ⓓ Ⓔ
19 Ⓐ Ⓑ Ⓒ Ⓓ Ⓔ
20 Ⓐ Ⓑ Ⓒ Ⓓ Ⓔ
21 Ⓐ Ⓑ Ⓒ Ⓓ Ⓔ
22 Ⓐ Ⓑ Ⓒ Ⓓ Ⓔ
23 Ⓐ Ⓑ Ⓒ Ⓓ Ⓔ
24 Ⓐ Ⓑ Ⓒ Ⓓ Ⓔ
25 Ⓐ Ⓑ Ⓒ Ⓓ Ⓔ

## Section III

1 Ⓐ Ⓑ Ⓒ Ⓓ Ⓔ
2 Ⓐ Ⓑ Ⓒ Ⓓ Ⓔ
3 Ⓐ Ⓑ Ⓒ Ⓓ Ⓔ
4 Ⓐ Ⓑ Ⓒ Ⓓ Ⓔ
5 Ⓐ Ⓑ Ⓒ Ⓓ Ⓔ
6 Ⓐ Ⓑ Ⓒ Ⓓ Ⓔ
7 Ⓐ Ⓑ Ⓒ Ⓓ Ⓔ
8 Ⓐ Ⓑ Ⓒ Ⓓ Ⓔ
9 Ⓐ Ⓑ Ⓒ Ⓓ Ⓔ
10 Ⓐ Ⓑ Ⓒ Ⓓ Ⓔ
11 Ⓐ Ⓑ Ⓒ Ⓓ Ⓔ
12 Ⓐ Ⓑ Ⓒ Ⓓ Ⓔ
13 Ⓐ Ⓑ Ⓒ Ⓓ Ⓔ
14 Ⓐ Ⓑ Ⓒ Ⓓ Ⓔ
15 Ⓐ Ⓑ Ⓒ Ⓓ Ⓔ
16 Ⓐ Ⓑ Ⓒ Ⓓ Ⓔ
17 Ⓐ Ⓑ Ⓒ Ⓓ Ⓔ
18 Ⓐ Ⓑ Ⓒ Ⓓ Ⓔ
19 Ⓐ Ⓑ Ⓒ Ⓓ Ⓔ
20 Ⓐ Ⓑ Ⓒ Ⓓ Ⓔ
21 Ⓐ Ⓑ Ⓒ Ⓓ Ⓔ
22 Ⓐ Ⓑ Ⓒ Ⓓ Ⓔ
23 Ⓐ Ⓑ Ⓒ Ⓓ Ⓔ
24 Ⓐ Ⓑ Ⓒ Ⓓ Ⓔ
25 Ⓐ Ⓑ Ⓒ Ⓓ Ⓔ
26 Ⓐ Ⓑ Ⓒ Ⓓ Ⓔ
27 Ⓐ Ⓑ Ⓒ Ⓓ Ⓔ
28 Ⓐ Ⓑ Ⓒ Ⓓ Ⓔ

CUT HERE

## Section IV

1 Ⓐ Ⓑ Ⓒ Ⓓ Ⓔ
2 Ⓐ Ⓑ Ⓒ Ⓓ Ⓔ
3 Ⓐ Ⓑ Ⓒ Ⓓ Ⓔ
4 Ⓐ Ⓑ Ⓒ Ⓓ Ⓔ
5 Ⓐ Ⓑ Ⓒ Ⓓ Ⓔ
6 Ⓐ Ⓑ Ⓒ Ⓓ Ⓔ
7 Ⓐ Ⓑ Ⓒ Ⓓ Ⓔ
8 Ⓐ Ⓑ Ⓒ Ⓓ Ⓔ
9 Ⓐ Ⓑ Ⓒ Ⓓ Ⓔ
10 Ⓐ Ⓑ Ⓒ Ⓓ Ⓔ
11 Ⓐ Ⓑ Ⓒ Ⓓ Ⓔ
12 Ⓐ Ⓑ Ⓒ Ⓓ Ⓔ
13 Ⓐ Ⓑ Ⓒ Ⓓ Ⓔ
14 Ⓐ Ⓑ Ⓒ Ⓓ Ⓔ
15 Ⓐ Ⓑ Ⓒ Ⓓ Ⓔ
16 Ⓐ Ⓑ Ⓒ Ⓓ Ⓔ
17 Ⓐ Ⓑ Ⓒ Ⓓ Ⓔ
18 Ⓐ Ⓑ Ⓒ Ⓓ Ⓔ
19 Ⓐ Ⓑ Ⓒ Ⓓ Ⓔ
20 Ⓐ Ⓑ Ⓒ Ⓓ Ⓔ
21 Ⓐ Ⓑ Ⓒ Ⓓ Ⓔ
22 Ⓐ Ⓑ Ⓒ Ⓓ Ⓔ
23 Ⓐ Ⓑ Ⓒ Ⓓ Ⓔ
24 Ⓐ Ⓑ Ⓒ Ⓓ Ⓔ
25 Ⓐ Ⓑ Ⓒ Ⓓ Ⓔ
26 Ⓐ Ⓑ Ⓒ Ⓓ Ⓔ

## Section V

1 Ⓐ Ⓑ Ⓒ Ⓓ Ⓔ
2 Ⓐ Ⓑ Ⓒ Ⓓ Ⓔ
3 Ⓐ Ⓑ Ⓒ Ⓓ Ⓔ
4 Ⓐ Ⓑ Ⓒ Ⓓ Ⓔ
5 Ⓐ Ⓑ Ⓒ Ⓓ Ⓔ
6 Ⓐ Ⓑ Ⓒ Ⓓ Ⓔ
7 Ⓐ Ⓑ Ⓒ Ⓓ Ⓔ
8 Ⓐ Ⓑ Ⓒ Ⓓ Ⓔ
9 Ⓐ Ⓑ Ⓒ Ⓓ Ⓔ
10 Ⓐ Ⓑ Ⓒ Ⓓ Ⓔ
11 Ⓐ Ⓑ Ⓒ Ⓓ Ⓔ
12 Ⓐ Ⓑ Ⓒ Ⓓ Ⓔ
13 Ⓐ Ⓑ Ⓒ Ⓓ Ⓔ
14 Ⓐ Ⓑ Ⓒ Ⓓ Ⓔ
15 Ⓐ Ⓑ Ⓒ Ⓓ Ⓔ
16 Ⓐ Ⓑ Ⓒ Ⓓ Ⓔ
17 Ⓐ Ⓑ Ⓒ Ⓓ Ⓔ
18 Ⓐ Ⓑ Ⓒ Ⓓ Ⓔ
19 Ⓐ Ⓑ Ⓒ Ⓓ Ⓔ
20 Ⓐ Ⓑ Ⓒ Ⓓ Ⓔ
21 Ⓐ Ⓑ Ⓒ Ⓓ Ⓔ
22 Ⓐ Ⓑ Ⓒ Ⓓ Ⓔ
23 Ⓐ Ⓑ Ⓒ Ⓓ Ⓔ
24 Ⓐ Ⓑ Ⓒ Ⓓ Ⓔ

CUT HERE

# Section I: Analytical Reasoning

**Time: 35 Minutes**

**24 Questions**

**Directions:** You will be presented with several sets of conditions. A group of questions follows each set of conditions. Choose the best answer to each question, drawing a rough diagram of the conditions when necessary.

*Questions 1 through 7 are based on the following information.*

Within a national park, there are five ranger stations—Q, R, S, T, and U. A communications system links the stations, but messages can be sent or relayed only according to the following plan:

> From T to Q
>
> From Q to R and from Q to U
>
> From S to R and from S to U
>
> From R to S and from R to T

1. Which is the only station that CANNOT relay a message?

   A. Q

   B. R

   C. S

   D. T

   E. U

2. The quickest way of getting a message from station R to station Q is by way of

   A. S.

   B. T.

   C. U.

   D. S to U.

   E. U to T.

3. With one relay, all of the following connections could be made EXCEPT:

   A. From R to Q.

   B. From T to U.

   C. From S to Q.

   D. From Q to T.

   E. From Q to S.

4. If station T is destroyed by a forest fire, all of the following connections could be made, with relays or not, EXCEPT:

   A. From Q to R.

   B. From S to U.

   C. From S to R.

   D. From R to Q.

   E. From R to U.

5. Which of the following is possible using exactly two other relay stations?

   A. From Q to U

   B. From Q to S

   C. From U to R

   D. From T to U

   E. From T to R

GO ON TO THE NEXT PAGE

6. The largest number of times that a message could be relayed without going through a station for a second time is

   A. 0.

   B. 1.

   C. 2.

   D. 3.

   E. 4.

7. Stations W and V are added to the communications system. If W can send messages only to S and receive messages only from U, and if V can send messages only to T, all the following will be true EXCEPT:

   A. V can get a message to W.

   B. U can get a message to Q.

   C. R can get a message to W.

   D. W can get a message to S.

   E. W can get a message to V.

*Questions 8 through 13 are based on the following information.*

Five yachts representing Australia, Belgium, Canada, Denmark, and England compete in a six-race regatta. The following are the results in all of the six races:

Belgium always finishes ahead of Canada.

Australia finishes either first or last.

England finishes either first or last.

Every yacht finishes each race.

There are no ties in any race.

In each race, ten points are awarded for a first-place finish, eight points for second, six points for third, four points for fourth, and two points for fifth.

8. If Denmark finishes third in the third race, which of the following must be true of that race?

   A. Australia finishes first.

   B. England finishes first.

   C. Belgium finishes second.

   D. Canada finishes second.

   E. Australia finishes fifth.

9. If England finishes two places ahead of Canada in the first race, all of the following will be true of that race EXCEPT:

   A. Belgium finishes ahead of Denmark.

   B. Canada finishes two places ahead of Australia.

   C. Denmark finishes fourth.

   D. Belgium finishes immediately behind England.

   E. Canada finishes ahead of Belgium.

10. If Australia finishes first only once, and Denmark finishes second exactly twice, the lowest total number of points that the Belgium yacht can earn in the regatta is

   A. 36.

   B. 38.

   C. 44.

   D. 46.

   E. 48.

**11.** If England's total for the six races is 36 points, which of the following must be true?

    **A.** Belgium's total is more than 36 points.

    **B.** Canada's total is less than 36 points.

    **C.** Australia's total is 36 points.

    **D.** Denmark's total is less than 36 points.

    **E.** Denmark's total is 36 points.

**12.** If Australia finishes first in four races, which of the following could earn a total of fewer than 26 points in the six races?

    **A.** Belgium only

    **B.** Canada only

    **C.** Denmark only

    **D.** England or Canada

    **E.** Denmark or Canada

**13.** If a sixth boat, Finland, enters the third race and finishes behind Canada and France, which of the following must be true of that race?

    **A.** England finishes first.

    **B.** Australia finishes sixth.

    **C.** Denmark finishes second.

    **D.** Canada finishes third.

    **E.** Finland finishes fifth.

*Questions 14 through 19 are based on the following information.*

A university committee is to be made up of four members, with an equal number of men and women, an equal number of natural scientists and social scientists, and an equal number of instructors and professors. The four members are to be selected from seven people—A, B, C, D, E, F, and G. Facts about the seven people are as follows:

    B, C, and D are men; the others are women.

    A, B, and C are natural scientists; the others are social scientists.

    A, D, E, and G are instructors; the others are professors.

**14.** If B and D are chosen for the committee, the women members of the committee must be

    **A.** A and F.

    **B.** A and G.

    **C.** A and E.

    **D.** G and E.

    **E.** G and F.

**15.** If the instructors chosen for the committee are A and D, which of the following must be a member of the committee?

    **A.** B

    **B.** C

    **C.** E

    **D.** F

    **E.** G

GO ON TO THE NEXT PAGE

**16.** If F is chosen for the committee, which of the following must be a member of the committee?

  **A.** G

  **B.** B

  **C.** C

  **D.** D

  **E.** E

**17.** Each of the following pairs could serve together on the committee EXCEPT:

  **A.** A and B.

  **B.** A and C.

  **C.** C and D.

  **D.** D and E.

  **E.** E and G.

**18.** If G is chosen for the committee, which of the following pairs must also be chosen for the committee?

  **A.** A and C

  **B.** B and C

  **C.** D and E

  **D.** B and D

  **E.** B and F

**19.** If A is chosen for the committee, which of the following CANNOT be chosen a member of the committee?

  **A.** F

  **B.** B

  **C.** C

  **D.** D

  **E.** E

*Questions 20 through 24 are based on the following statements.*

Sam is getting dressed to go to a party, but he is having trouble deciding on what clothes to wear.

> He will not wear any color combination that does not go well together.
>
> He has two pairs of slacks, brown and blue; three dress shirts, white, aqua, and gray; four pairs of socks, red, black, brown, and blue; and two pairs of shoes, black and brown.
>
> Blue slacks cannot be worn with red or brown socks.
>
> Gray does not go well with brown.
>
> Black does not go well with brown.

Assuming that Sam can wear only one pair of shoes, slacks, socks, and one shirt at a time, answer the following questions.

**20.** If Sam wears black shoes he will NOT wear

  **A.** blue socks.

  **B.** a white shirt.

  **C.** an aqua shirt.

  **D.** blue slacks.

  **E.** red socks.

**21.** If Sam wears brown slacks and a white shirt, he could

  **A.** not wear blue socks.

  **B.** wear black socks.

  **C.** wear aqua socks.

  **D.** not wear brown shoes.

  **E.** not wear black socks.

**22.** Which one of the following is a combination of colors that Sam will NEVER wear together?

   **A.** Blue and red

   **B.** Blue and brown

   **C.** White and black

   **D.** Gray and blue

   **E.** White and red

**23.** Suppose that Sam buys a brown tie. If he wears this new tie, then he CANNOT wear which one of the following?

   **A.** A white shirt

   **B.** Brown slacks

   **C.** Blue socks

   **D.** Black shoes

   **E.** Red socks

**24.** Suppose that Sam buys a pair of gray shoes and black slacks and decides that the red socks do not go well with the black slacks. If he decides to wear the gray shoes and the black slacks, which one of the following is a complete and accurate list of the possible colors he could wear?

   **A.** Aqua, gray, black

   **B.** Aqua, white, gray, black

   **C.** White, gray, black, brown

   **D.** Aqua, white, blue, red, black

   **E.** Aqua, white, blue, gray, black

IF YOU FINISH BEFORE TIME IS CALLED, CHECK YOUR WORK ON THIS SECTION ONLY. DO NOT WORK ON ANY OTHER SECTION IN THE TEST.

# Section II: Logical Reasoning

**Time: 35 Minutes**

**25 Questions**

**Directions:** You will be presented with brief passages or statements and will be required to evaluate their reasoning. In each case, select the best answer choice, even though more than one choice may present a possible answer. Choices that are unreasonable or incompatible with common-sense standards should be eliminated.

1. Which of the following most logically completes the passage at the blank below?

   The English language, lacking the rigidity of most European tongues, has been bent and shaped in at least as many ways as there are countries or regions where it is spoken. Though purists often argue that "standard" English is spoken only in certain high-minded enclaves of the American northeast, the fact is that it is the most widely used language in the world and is not likely to yield that distinction for a very long time, if ever. Nevertheless, _____.

   A. it remains one of the most widely spoken languages throughout the world

   B. it can be understood in just about every corner of the globe

   C. even making allowances for regional peculiarities, English as it is spoken has been much abused in recent times

   D. though we may be proud of these facts, English remains one of the most difficult languages to master

   E. English, as it is spoken, lacks the rigidity of the classical and more historic European languages

2. Life imitates art.

   Which of the following, if true, most strongly supports the above statement?

   A. When Warren Beatty filmed *Reds,* he tried to suggest not only the chaos of the Russian Revolution, but also its relationship to the present.

   B. The number of professional ballet companies has increased over the last five years, but the number of dance majors has decreased.

   C. On Tuesday, the business section of the newspaper had predicted the drop in interest rates that occurred on Friday.

   D. Truman Capote wrote *In Cold Blood* as a result of a series of brutal slayings by two crazed killers.

   E. Soon after the advent of color television, white shirts became less popular as dressy attire for men, and pastel-colored shirts began to sell well.

3. When President Lyndon Johnson signed the Voting Rights Act in 1965, he used fifty pens, handing them out as souvenirs to a joyous gathering in the President's Room of the Capitol, where Abraham Lincoln had signed the Emancipation Proclamation on January 1, 1863. When President Reagan signed an extension of the Voting Rights Act in 1982, he spoke affectionately of the "right to vote," signed with a single pen, then concluded the four-minute ceremony by rising from his desk, announcing, "It's done."

If the passage above is true, which of the following is most probably true?

A. The Voting Rights Act did not require an extension.

B. The Voting Rights Act is not significantly related to the Emancipation Proclamation.

C. President Reagan saw himself as more like Lincoln than did Johnson.

D. President Reagan did not regard the extension of the act as an occasion for fanfare.

E. President Reagan objected strenuously to an extension of the Voting Rights Act.

4. Congressperson: Serving a few months as a Capitol page can be an exciting and enriching experience for high school students from around the country.

Student: If the circumstances are right.

The student's response suggests which of the following?

A. Belligerence

B. Acquiescence

C. Skepticism

D. Disbelief

E. Ignorance

*Questions 5 and 6 are based on the following passage.*

On average, federal workers receive salaries 35.5% higher than private-sector salaries. For instance, federal workers in California average $25,206 a year, 25% higher than the average pay in the private sector, which is $20,365.

5. This information would best support which of the following opinions?

A. Private-sector salaries in California are above average.

B. The private sector is being paid fairly.

C. Federal jobs are more secure than private-sector jobs.

D. Public-sector work is more difficult than private-sector work.

E. Federal pay is out of line.

6. Which of the following statements is consistent with the information in the passage?

A. Salaries of California federal workers more nearly approximate the salaries in the private sector than do the salaries of federal workers nationwide.

B. There are more generous vacation leave privileges for private workers than for federal workers.

C. Social programs have been curtailed in the face of large state deficits.

GO ON TO THE NEXT PAGE

**D.** State workers in California receive salaries comparable to those of private workers.

**E.** Recently, federal workers have begun demanding higher compensation benefits.

**7.** Political columnist: Money talks as never before in state and local elections, and the main cause is TV advertising. Thirty seconds can go for as much as $20,000. Political fundraising is one of the few growth industries left in America. The way to stop the waste might be for television to be paid by state and local government, at a standard rate, to provide airtime to all candidates to debate the issues. This might be boring at first, but eventually candidates might actually brush up their debating skills and electrify the TV audience with content, not style.

Which of the following presuppositions is necessary to the political columnist's argument above?

**A.** Candidates do not yet spend too much money on television advertising.

**B.** Television is the most effective medium to reach the public.

**C.** Freedom of speech does not abridge the freedom to spend.

**D.** Television can be used to educate and inform the public.

**E.** The television audience desires exciting political candidates.

*Questions 8 and 9 are based on the following passage.*

According to a recent study by the National Academy of Public Administration, postal patrons are regularly affronted by out-of-order stamp vending machines, branch post office lobbies locked at night, and 34-cent letters that take as long to get there as 13-cent letters did nearly two decades ago.

**8.** Which of the following, if true, would weaken the implication of one of the writer's observations?

**A.** Most out-of-order vending machines are located in run-down neighborhoods.

**B.** Late-night vandalism has plagued post offices nationwide.

**C.** Postage rates rose over a hundred percent from 1983 to 2001, but the cost of first class mail is still cheaper in the U.S. than anywhere else.

**D.** As a public corporation, the Postal Service has increased its capital assets by $3 billion.

**E.** Two decades ago, most letters reached their destination within twenty-four hours.

**9.** Which of the following transitions probably begins a sentence critical of the argument above?

**A.** However

**B.** In addition

**C.** Despite

**D.** In reality

**E.** Therefore

**10.** Of all the petty little pieces of bureaucratic arrogance, it's hard to imagine one smaller than that of the city schools in not admitting a British subject whose father is working—as a legal alien—for a nearby petrochemical company. Someone apparently decided that if the boy had been an illegal alien, a recent U.S. Supreme Court decision in a Texas case would have required the district to admit him, but since he is legal, there is no such requirement. That is nonsense.

Which of the following best expresses the point of the author's argument?

A. The city schools outside Texas should not base decisions on a precedent set in Texas.

B. The stability of a parent's job should have no bearing on the educational opportunity offered his or her child.

C. Bureaucratic arrogance has resulted in unsound legal interpretation.

D. Legal sense and nonsense are sometimes indistinguishable.

E. Both legal and illegal aliens should receive equal treatment.

**11.** By appropriating bailout money for the depressed housing industry, Congress is opening the door to a flood of special relief programs for other recession-affected businesses.

The author's attitude toward Congress's action is probably

A. neutral.

B. disapproving.

C. confused.

D. happy.

E. irate.

**12.** A researcher has concluded that women are just as capable in math as men are, but that their skills are not developed because society expects them to develop other and more diverse abilities.

Which of the following is a basic assumption of the researcher?

A. Ability in math is more important than ability in more diverse subjects.

B. Ability in math is less important than ability in more diverse subjects.

C. Women and men should be equally capable in math.

D. Women might be more capable than men in math.

E. Women tend to conform to social expectations.

*Questions 13 and 14 are based on the following passage.*

Beginning this fall, Latino and Asian students will not be allowed to transfer out of bilingual classes (that is, courses given in a student's native language) until they pass strict competency tests in math, reading, and writing—as well as spoken English. The board and its supporters say this will protect children from being pushed out of bilingual programs before they are ready. They have hailed this as a victory for bilingual education.

GO ON TO THE NEXT PAGE

13. Which of the following, if true, is the strongest criticism of the position of the board?

    A. A foreign student may be quite competent in math without being competent in English.

    B. Some native students already in English-speaking classes are unable to pass the competency tests.

    C. Most foreign students require many months of practice and instruction before mastering English skills.

    D. Many students prefer to transfer out of bilingual classes before they have achieved competency in English.

    E. Holding back students will double the number of students in bilingual classes—twice as many Latino and Asian children isolated from the English-speaking mainstream.

14. The argument above would be most strengthened if the author were to explain

    A. how efficient the bilingual program is.

    B. how well staffed the bilingual program is.

    C. whether the community supports the bilingual program.

    D. whether any board members do not support the bilingual program.

    E. how the students feel about the bilingual program.

15. The $464 million "reserve" in the 2001–2002 budget adopted by the legislature in June turns out to have been based mainly on wishful thinking. Because of tax cuts approved by voters on the June ballot, along with the continuing recession and other events affecting income and expenses, the actual reserve in prospect may be as low as $7 million.

    The author is probably leading to which of the following conclusions?

    A. These facts warrant an investigation into who squandered $457 million.

    B. A reserve in the budget is not so necessary as we might wish it to be.

    C. The legislature would be wise not to add any new spending to the budget adopted in June.

    D. The recession will probably not last much longer, but while it does the legislature must adjust the budget accordingly.

    E. Legislative budgets are typically careless and unheeding of variable factors that may affect their accuracy.

*Questions 16 and 17 are based on the following passage.*

"The sum of behavior is to retain a man's dignity without intruding upon the liberty of others," stated Sir Francis Bacon. If this is the case, then not intruding upon another's liberty is impossible.

**16.** The conclusion strongly implied by the author's arguments is that

    **A.**  retaining one's dignity is impossible without intruding upon another's liberty.

    **B.**  retaining dignity never involves robbing others of liberty.

    **C.**  dignity and liberty are mutually exclusive.

    **D.**  there is always the possibility of a "dignified intrusion."

    **E.**  B. F. Skinner's *Beyond Freedom and Dignity* takes its cue from Bacon.

**17.** The author's argument would be weakened if it were pointed out that

    **A.**  Bacon's argument has been correctly interpreted.

    **B.**  retaining dignity always involves a reduction of liberty.

    **C.**  liberty is also an impossibility.

    **D.**  Bacon himself intruded on others' liberties.

    **E.**  neither liberty nor dignity can be discussed in absolute terms.

**18.** Jonathan Swift said, "Laws are like cobwebs which may catch small flies but let wasps and hornets break through."

Jonathan Swift would most probably believe that

    **A.**  prosecutors should be tough on criminals.

    **B.**  pesticides should be used to deter large insects.

    **C.**  small crimes should not be prosecuted.

    **D.**  the powerful can often avoid serious criminal sentences.

    **E.**  laws do not stop people from committing crimes.

**19.** Which of the following most logically completes the passage at the blank below?

In a civilized society, members of the community will often defer to others, even against their own better judgment. This situation may occur in public, in gatherings with strangers, or in the household with one's family or friends. It is a sign of a more sophisticated culture that one's immediate interests are thought to be secondary to those of another. On first examination, this may seem to be selflessness, but _____.

    **A.**  actually it is not; it is just ignorance

    **B.**  rather it may take many names

    **C.**  actually it is

    **D.**  to some extent it does serve the ends of the individual concerned

    **E.**  sometimes it can harbor animosities and hostility

**20.** The following letter was sent to a candidate applying for entrance to Nathford University.

Thank you for your interest in Nathford University. We regret to say that your application for entrance has been rejected. Unfortunately, because of the unusually high number of candidates

GO ON TO THE NEXT PAGE

Section **II** Logical Reasoning

this year, we were not even able to accept all those with SAT scores of 1000 or above, as has been our practice in the past. We have only a limited number of openings and must accept entering students accordingly.

Which of the following can be validly concluded from the letter?

A.  The student receiving the letter had SAT scores of 1000 or above.

B.  The student receiving the letter did not have SAT scores of 1000 or above.

C.  Nathford University accepted only those students with SAT scores of 1000 or above.

D.  Nathford University rejected many students with SAT scores of 1000 or above.

E.  Nathford University had constraints other than SAT scores that affected selection of candidates.

21.  The Verdex Code for Plumbers states that before beginning repair work on a sewage line in a house, the incoming water valve must be turned off. However, if the house uses a septic tank instead of city sewage, the Verdex Code is superseded by an older code (called the Stipex Code) that allows incoming water to be either off or on. In either case, the rule for turning incoming water off does not apply when working on commercial property.

If the statements above are true, which of the following statements must also be true?

A.  The Verdex Code is widely observed by professional plumbers.

B.  Plumbers working on commercial property must turn the incoming water supply off.

C.  Plumbers must turn the incoming water supply off when working on houses with septic tanks.

D.  Incoming water is considered potable, whereas sewage water is nonpotable.

E.  The Stipex Code does not apply to houses connected to city sewage systems.

*Questions 22 and 23 are based on the following passage.*

The older we get, the less sleep we should desire. This is because our advanced knowledge and capabilities are most enjoyable when used; therefore, "mindless" sleep becomes a waste of time.

22.  This author's statement might be strengthened if he or she pointed out that

A.  advanced knowledge is often manifested in creative dreams.

B.  the mind is quite active during sleep.

C.  few empirical studies have concluded that sleep is an intellectual stimulant.

D.  advanced capabilities are not necessarily mind-associated.

E.  dreams teach us how to use waking experiences more intelligently.

**23.** The author's statement might be weakened by pointing out that

    **A.**  eight hours of sleep is a cultural, not a physical, requirement.

    **B.**  the most capable people rarely sleep.

    **C.**  rest is a positive contribution to knowledge and capability.

    **D.**  young children enjoy themselves less than knowledgeable adults.

    **E.**  people rarely waste time during their waking hours.

**24.** Don't spend the night tossing and turning! Take Eezy-Z's for a sound, restful sleep . . . you'll wake up refreshed, energized, with no drugged-up hangover. Remember . . . Eezy-Z's when you need that sleep!

Which of the following is NOT a claim of Eezy-Z's?

    **A.**  A good night's sleep

    **B.**  Added energy

    **C.**  No aftereffects

    **D.**  Quickly falling asleep

    **E.**  A restful slumber

**25.** College student: Whenever I need to study but feel sleepy, all I do is take a few of those caffeine pills, and I'm completely awake. According to the label, these pills are perfectly safe to use, since I could get the same amount of energizing caffeine by drinking a few cups of coffee.

Which of the following statements weakens the argument expressed by the student?

    **A.**  Pills that can help prevent drowsiness often contain caffeine, a natural substance that can increase "awakenesss" and provide the user with a sudden boost of energy.

    **B.**  Since caffeine is a natural substance found in many common foods such as chocolate, pills that are caffeine-based may be just as safe.

    **C.**  One subconsciously limits intake of caffeine through its method of intake; for example, most people can drink only a few cups of coffee before they feel full.

    **D.**  Many students tend to pull "all nighters" in school, and caffeine pills are an ideal way to reduce drowsiness and study through the night.

    **E.**  In the last decade, many pharmaceutical companies have released caffeine-based pills that have been widely sold over the counter in drugstores.

IF YOU FINISH BEFORE TIME IS CALLED, CHECK YOUR WORK ON THIS SECTION ONLY. DO NOT WORK ON ANY OTHER SECTION IN THE TEST.

# Section III: Reading Comprehension

Time: 35 Minutes

28 Questions

**Directions:** Each passage in this group is followed by questions based on its content. After reading a passage, choose the best answer to each question and blacken the corresponding space on the answer sheet. Answer all questions following a passage on the basis of what is *stated* or *implied* in that passage. You may refer back to the passage.

*Questions 1 through 7 are based on the following passage.*

Arbitration is nothing more than an orderly and practical settlement of a controversy by skilled and impartial persons whose decision, called an award, is final
(5) and binding. The provision for resolving disputes by arbitration is quite often part of the original contract for services. If the parties do not have such a contract clause, they may make a "submission
(10) agreement" to initiate arbitration.

Although there may be superficial resemblance, arbitration and compromise are not the same. The arbitrator, most frequently one thoroughly familiar with
(15) the field or industry, judges the rights of the parties. For example, a buyer demands a dollar-per-unit price reduction due to alleged inferior quality of a product. The seller denies the inferiority and
(20) disavows any reduction. A compromise would split the difference. An arbitration award, reflecting expert and independent evaluation of the product might grant no allowance or a specific amount.
(25) That an arbitration decision legally binds the parties stands as one of its most important characteristics. In its 1854 milestone decision, the United States Supreme Court declared that
(30) "if an [arbitration] award is within the submission and contains the honest decision of the arbitrators, after a full and fair

hearing of the parties, a court of equality will not set it aside for error, either in law
(35) or in fact. A contrary course . . . would make an award the commencement, not the end, of litigation."

Besides delivering a legally binding decision, the arbitration process has
(40) other equally notable features. It's quick, economical, practical, self-regulated, and objective. Even more important, arbitration decisions are rendered by those with expertise and competence
(45) in the given industry. In construction cases, for instance, the arbitrators are architects, engineers, general contractors, subcontractors, landscape architects, and attorneys skilled in construction
(50) matters. Locally, the American Arbitration Association (AAA) lists about 1,400 individuals from these professions who have volunteered to arbitrate construction cases. Nationally, that
(55) number is about 10,000.

Arbitrations are administered nationwide by the AAA through its 22 regional offices. Once the parties agree to arbitrate, the arbitration site is chosen. The
(60) parties may agree on the site, or it may be determined by the AAA or the arbitrators.

Arbitrators are generally selected by mutual agreement of the parties who review lists of volunteers carefully
(65) screened by the AAA. Depending upon the complexity of the case and the amount of the claim, one arbitrator may

suffice or three may be enlisted. As a general rule, in claims of less than \$35,000, (70) one person arbitrates. These arbitrators, usually nominated by the leaders in their industries and professions, serve under AAA rules, and their conduct is guided by a written manual of the AAA which is (75) sent to them on their appointment to a case. Arbitrators' objectivity is paramount. A person appointed as neutral arbitrator must disclose any circumstance or condition linking him in any way to (80) one of the parties. Such a connection may disqualify the arbitrator.

The hearing, where both parties tell their sides of the issue, takes as much time as necessary for all relevant infor- (85) mation to be presented. In a survey of the last 200 construction arbitrations filed as of the end of 1995, the AAA found that 87 were settled or withdrawn before the hearing stage, and of the 113 remaining, (90) 91, or 81%, required only one hearing. In the same survey, 82% of the cases necessitated only one arbitrator.

During the hearing, the parties may be represented by attorneys, but this is (95) not required. In presenting the material, parties are not bound by the rules of evidence which characterize regular court proceedings. The arbitrator determines what testimony is relevant. The so- (100) called "burden of proof" obligation rests equally on both parties. Ordinary rules of courtesy and a cooperative attitude govern these hearings. Neither party may confer with any arbitrator outside (105) the presence of the other party.

The arbitration panel must render its award within 30 days after the final hearing. The award must be written, clear, definite, complete—that is, all (110) questions answered—and within the scope of the arbitration.

1. According to the passage, the number of arbitrators in a hearing reflects the degree of

    A. objectivity of the given industry.

    B. state interference.

    C. simplicity of the claim.

    D. professional requirements of the industry.

    E. burden-of-proof obligation.

2. If, according to the author, a party in an arbitration believes that its award, though honest, was incorrectly determined, it

    A. may appeal the settlement to another arbitrator.

    B. may appeal the settlement to a court of law.

    C. may seek redress through a compromise settlement.

    D. may reverse the decision through due process.

    E. has no recourse, since the decision is final.

3. Which of the following would the author most probably consider the best candidate for arbitration?

    A. An AIDS patient seeking damages from an impure blood transfusion

    B. A middle-age construction foreman accused of negligence at a housing site

    C. A college freshman seeking damages because of a university's discrimination practices

GO ON TO THE NEXT PAGE

Section ■■■ Reading Comprehension

**D.** A young mother whose infant son was abducted and returned by her estranged husband

**E.** A 40-year old police chief fined $180,000 for violating a citizen's due-process rights

4. It can be inferred that the author would probably consider arbitration similar to litigation in that in both instances

**A.** many disputes are ultimately settled by the parties themselves.

**B.** judgment is rendered by a specialist from the parties' own field.

**C.** an impartial decision is reached that is binding and final.

**D.** traditional rules of evidence bind both parties.

**E.** procedures often become time consuming and expensive.

5. It can be inferred from the passage that, when disputes reach the hearing stage, less than half the time

**A.** only one arbitrator may be used.

**B.** more than one hearing may be required.

**C.** lawyers may represent the parties.

**D.** regional offices administer the arbitration.

**E.** an award is rendered within thirty days.

6. The author would probably disagree with which of the following statements about a party in a dispute?

**A.** A party in a dispute settled by arbitration may be granted absolutely nothing.

**B.** A party in a dispute settled by arbitration may be granted half of what he or she claimed was due him or her.

**C.** A party in a dispute settled by arbitration may be granted more than what he or she claimed was due him or her.

**D.** A party in a dispute settled by arbitration may be granted less than what he or she claimed was due him or her.

**E.** A party in a dispute settled by compromise may be granted more than what he or she claimed was due him or her.

7. Which of the following qualities would the author value in a prospective arbitrator hearing a claim made by a recording star for proper compensation against a recording company?

**A.** A working knowledge of the legal system

**B.** Strong connections within the given industry

**C.** An understanding of evidentiary proceedings

**D.** Expertise in the recording industry

**E.** Knowledge of the laws of compensation

*Questions 8 through 14 are based on the following passage.*

Juvenile delinquency is an imprecise and nebulous legal and social label for a wide variety of norm-violating behaviors. There are as many legal definitions for (5) the term as there are jurisdictions. In a criticism of the wide limits used in identifying juvenile delinquency, the Second United Nations Congress on the Prevention of Crime and the Treatment of (10) Offenders adopted the following in 1960:

"The Congress considers that the scope of the problem of juvenile delinquency should not be unnecessarily inflated. Without attempting to formulate (15) a standard definition of what should be considered to be juvenile delinquency in each country, it recommends (1) that the meaning of the term *juvenile delinquency* should be restricted as far as (20) possible to violations of the criminal law and (2) that even for protection, specific offenses which would penalize small irregularities or maladjusted behavior of minors, but for which adults would not (25) be prosecuted, should not be created."

In general, a juvenile delinquent in Africa is one who commits an act defined by law as illegal and/or who is adjudicated "delinquent" by an appropriate (30) court. The legal definition in most African countries is usually restricted to persons under the age of 21 years. The exact lower and upper age limits differ from country to country. For example, in (35) most of the East African countries, the age is 8 years. In Tanzania, all crimes committed by persons below the age of criminal responsibility can be legally defined as juvenile delinquency. The applicable (40) Penal Code of Tanzania states:

A person under the age of 7 years is not criminally responsible for any act or omission. A person under the age of 12 is not criminally responsible for an act (45) or omission unless it is proved he had capacity to know that he ought not to do the act or make the omission.

Similarly, in Kenya a juvenile delinquent is a child between the statutory ju-(50) venile court age of 7 and 16 years who commits an act which, when committed by persons beyond this statutory juvenile court age, would be punishable as a crime or as an act injurious to other indi-(55) viduals or the public, In this country, a person is considered an adult when he is 19 years old or above. At this age, if he commits a crime, he is tried in court as an adult and not as a juvenile.

(60) Despite official claims to the contrary, juvenile delinquency is not merely increasing in Africa but is already widespread. There is the constant fear in Africa today that delinquents may grad-(65) uate to become hardened criminals of the future. The fact that 45 percent of the population of Africa is below 15 years of age or that the proportion of young persons aged 25 years and below was esti-(70) mated to be 63 percent in 1975 makes crime in Africa largely a problem involving young people.

Various reasons have been suggested as likely causes of juvenile delinquency (75) in African countries. Among these are rapid urbanization in the new states, instability within family structure, lack of employment and educational opportunities, urban migration, the impersonality (80) of urban life, lack of parental control, and individual maladjustment. Turbulence in family relations, emotional instability, and the spread of urban culture appear to be far more important for crime and (85) delinquency in the country than any local cultural or tribal influence. We should look to urban pressures on the family rather than to subcultures in our efforts to explain crime.

GO ON TO THE NEXT PAGE

Section III Reading Comprehension

(90)    Participants in the First West African Conference in Comparative Criminology listed three broad causes of juvenile delinquency in Africa. First, they suggested that delinquency in the region is a
(95) "result of a tragic loss of family life and emotional security." They suggested that changes in family relations and parental roles which occur in the city are destroying the traditional tribal family. The re-
(100) sult, they explained, is a loss of harmony and communication both between the parents themselves and between parents and children. Second, delinquency in Africa was attributed to lack of an
(105) adequate state prevention policy. Third, the participants in the conference suggested that lack of individual medical-psychosocial resources in the African countries is responsible for juvenile
(110) delinquency. They explained that in most African countries, there is a lack of sufficient and competent personnel, specialized institutions, and cooperation between the various public/private ser-
(115) vices charged with providing care for the juveniles. The result is that "some of Africa's juveniles who suffer from epilepsy, are problem children, or are pathologically disturbed are not given
(120) specialized therapy which would facilitate their treatment and care."

**8.** Which of the following would be the most appropriate title for this passage?

**A.** The Causes and Control of Juvenile Delinquency

**B.** Juvenile Delinquency in Africa and the West

**C.** Possible Causes of Juvenile Delinquency

**D.** Juvenile Delinquency in Africa and Some Causes

**E.** Dealing with Juvenile Delinquency in Africa

**9.** The United Nations Congress on the Prevention of Crime recommended that

**A.** juvenile delinquency be used as the term to describe the behavior of young persons who have violated civil or criminal laws.

**B.** maladjusted behavior of minors not be called juvenile delinquency.

**C.** minors should be prosecuted for offenses that would not be prosecuted in adults.

**D.** the tragic loss of life resulting from delinquency should be addressed.

**E.** radical changes in parental roles must be mandated.

**10.** In Africa, the age of a juvenile delinquent is

**A.** the same in all the countries.

**B.** between the ages of 8 and 21 years.

**C.** between the ages of 7 and 21 years.

**D.** between the ages of 12 and 21 years.

**E.** different from one country to another.

**11.** From information in the passage, we can infer that Kenya and Tanzania

**A.** would hold a seven-year-old criminally responsible.

**B.** would not hold a nine-year-old criminally responsible.

**C.** are in East Africa.

**D.** have identical juvenile criminal codes.

**E.** restrict the legal definition of juvenile delinquency to persons under the age of 21.

**12.** One reason the passage suggests for the large number of young people who are involved in crime in Africa is the

A. high percentage of young people in the African population.

B. failure of European countries to support anticrime measures in the Third World.

C. failure of parents to control children at an impressionable age.

D. failure to distinguish between physical and mental illness.

E. lack of tribal laws to deal with problems of juvenile wrongdoing.

**13.** The passage suggests all of the following as possible causes of African juvenile delinquency EXCEPT:

A. lack of employment.

B. excessive parental control.

C. urban migration.

D. individual maladjustment.

E. lack of education.

**14.** According to the passage, which of the following is likely to have an effect in reducing juvenile delinquency in Africa?

A. An increase in the population of the cities

B. An increase in state expenditure for medicine

C. An increase in state expenditure for transportation

D. An increase in recreational activities for adults

E. An increase in severity of criminal sentences

*Questions 15 through 21 are based on the following passage.*

In economics, demand implies something slightly different from the common meaning of the term. The layman, for example, uses the term to mean the
(5) amount that is demanded of an item. Thus, if the price were to decrease and individuals wanted more of the item, it is commonly said that demand increases. To an economist, demand is a
(10) relationship between a series of prices and a series of corresponding quantities that are demanded at these prices. If one reads the previous sentences carefully, it should become apparent that there is a
(15) distinction between the quantity demanded and the demand. This distinction is often a point of confusion and we all should be aware of and understand the difference between these two terms.
(20) We repeat, therefore, that demand is a relationship between price and quantities demanded, and therefore suggests the effect of one (e.g., price) on the other (e.g., quantity demanded). Therefore,
(25) knowledge of the demand for a product enables one to predict how much more of a good will be purchased if price decreases. But the increase in quantity demanded does not mean demand has
(30) increased, since the relationship between price and quantity demanded (i.e., the demand for the product) has not changed. Demand shifts when there is a change in income, expectations, taste,
(35) etc., such that a different quantity of the good is demanded at the same price.

In almost all cases, a consumer wants more of an item if the price decreases. This relationship between price and
(40) quantity demanded is so strong that it is referred to as the "law of demand." This "law can be explained by the income and substitution effects. The income effect

GO ON TO THE NEXT PAGE

(45) occurs because price increases reduce the purchasing power of the individual and, thus, the quantity demanded of goods must decrease. The substitution effect reflects the consumer's desire to get the "best buy." Accordingly, if the (50) price of good A increases, the individual will tend to substitute another good and purchase less of good A. The negative correlation between price and quantity demanded is also explained by the law of (55) diminishing marginal utility. According to this law, the additional utility the consumer gains from consuming a good decreases as successively more units of the good are consumed. Because the (60) additional units yield less utility or satisfaction, the consumer is willing to purchase more only if the price of the good decreases.

Economists distinguish between indi-(65) vidual and market demand. As the term implies, individual demand concerns the individual consumer and illustrates the quantities that individuals demand at different prices. Market demand in-(70) cludes the demand of all individuals for a particular good and is found by summing the quantities demanded by all individuals at the various prices.

The other side of the price system is (75) supply. As in the case of demand, supply is a relationship between a series of prices and the associated quantities supplied. It is assumed that as price increases the individual or firm will (80) supply greater quantities of a good. There is a positive correlation between quantity supplied and product price.

Economists also distinguish between a change in supply and quantity sup-(85) plied. The distinction is similar to the one made with respect to demand. Also, as in the case of demand, economists distinguish between individual firm supply and market supply, which is the (90) summation of individual supply.

Taken together, supply and demand yield equilibrium prices and quantity. Equilibrium is a state of stability, with balanced forces in which prices and (95) quantity will remain constant. In reality, equilibrium is seldom attained, for the factors affecting the market are constantly changing.

15. Assume that firms develop an orange-flavored breakfast drink high in vitamin C that is a good substitute for orange juice but sells for less. Based upon assertions in the passage, which of the following would occur with respect to the demand for orange juice?

   A. Health food stores would resurrect the law of diminishing marginal utility.

   B. Assuming that the price of fresh orange juice remained constant, more orange juice would be consumed.

   C. The law of demand would prevail.

   D. Assuming that the price of fresh orange juice remained constant, the demand would not change.

   E. There is not enough information in the passage to answer this question.

16. According to the passage, a group of individuals will

   A. derive less satisfaction from a product.

   B. exert individual demand under appropriate conditions.

   C. shift the demand line to the right.

   D. constitute a market.

   E. emphasize supply over demand.

**17.** According to the passage, a change in demand would occur in which of the following situations?

    **A.** The gasoline price increases, resulting in the increased sale of Nissans (whose price remains stable).

    **B.** The gasoline price increases, resulting in the increased sale of Nissans (which go on sale in response to increased gas prices).

    **C.** The gasoline price decreases on the same day that a new 43-mpg car enters the market.

    **D.** A federal order imposes a price ceiling on gasoline.

    **E.** A federal order lifts price regulations for gasoline.

**18.** According to the passage, quantity supplied and product price are not

    **A.** correlative.

    **B.** disjunctive.

    **C.** related.

    **D.** symbiotic.

    **E.** consequential.

**19.** Assume that the demand for houses increases. Drawing from the passage, decide which of the following would most likely cause such a shift.

    **A.** Interest rates on mortgages increase.

    **B.** The government predicts a large increase in the extent of unemployment.

    **C.** In a poverty area, a new government program provides jobs for all who need them.

    **D.** A low-priced type of mobile home is announced that is a good substitute for houses.

    **E.** The cost of lumber increases.

**20.** Which of the following is the most appropriate title for the passage?

    **A.** Equilibrium: The Key to Economics

    **B.** Economics and the Laws of Supply and Demand

    **C.** Market Price: The Essential Elements of Economics

    **D.** The Role of Government in the Economy

    **E.** The Market System in an Ideal Economy

**21.** All of the following issues are mentioned in the passage EXCEPT:

    **A.** why economic equilibrium is seldom achieved.

    **B.** how illegal price fixing affects the marketplace.

    **C.** if there exists a distinction between firm supply and market supply.

    **D.** how the "law of demand" can be explained.

    **E.** the functions of a market price.

GO ON TO THE NEXT PAGE

*Questions 22 through 28 are based on the following passage.*

"There is no security"—to quote his own words—"against the ultimate development of mechanical consciousness, in the fact of machines possessing
(5) little consciousness now. A mollusc has not much consciousness. Reflect upon the extraordinary advance which the machines have made during the last few hundred years, and note how slowly the
(10) animal and vegetable kingdoms are advancing in comparison. The more highly organised machines are creatures not so much of yesterday as of the last five minutes, so to speak, in comparison with
(15) past time. Assume for the sake of argument that conscious beings have existed for some twenty million years: See what strides machines have made in the last thousand! May not the world last twenty
(20) million years longer? If so, what will they not in the end become? Is it not safer to nip the mischief in the bud and to forbid them further progress?"

"But who can say that the vapour en-
(25) gine has not a kind of consciousness? Where does consciousness begin, and where end? Who can draw the line? Who can draw any line? Is not everything interwoven with everything? Is not machin-
(30) ery linked with animal life in an infinite variety of ways? The shell of a hen's egg is a machine as much as an egg-cup is; the shell is a plan for holding the egg as much as the egg-cup for holding the
(35) shell: Both are phases of the same function; the hen makes the shell in her inside, but it is pure pottery. She makes her nest outside of herself for convenience's sake, but the nest is not more of a machine than
(40) the egg-shell is. A 'machine' is only a 'device'"

. . . "Even a potato in a dark cellar has a certain low cunning about him which serves him in excellent stead. He knows
(45) perfectly well what he wants and how to get it. He sees the light coming from the cellar window and sends his shoots crawling straight thereto: They will crawl along the floor and up the wall and out at
(50) the cellar window; if there be a little earth anywhere on the journey, he will find it and use it for his own ends. What deliberation he may exercise in the matter of his roots when he is planted in the earth is a
(55) thing unknown to us, but we can imagine him saying, 'I will have a tuber and a tuber there, and I will suck whatsoever advantage I can from all my surroundings. This neighbour I will overshadow, and
(60) that I will undermine; and what I can do shall be the limits of what I will do. He that is stronger and better placed than I shall overcome me, and him that is weaker I will overcome.' The potato says
(65) these things by doing them, which is the best of language. What is consciousness if this is not consciousness? We find it difficult to sympathise with the emotions of a potato; so we do with those of an
(70) oyster. Neither of these things makes a noise on being boiled or opened, and noise appeals to us more strongly than anything else, because we make so much about our own sufferings. Since then they
(75) do not annoy us by any expression of pain we call them emotionless; and so *qua* mankind they are; but mankind is not everybody."

. . . "*Either,*" he proceeds, "a great
(80) deal of action that has been called purely mechanical and unconscious must be admitted to contain more elements of consciousness than has been allowed hitherto (and in this case, germs of con-
(85) sciousness will be found in many actions of the higher machines)—*Or* (assuming the theory of evolution but at the same time denying the consciousness of vegetable and crystalline action)
(90) the race of man has descended from things which had no consciousness at

all. In this case, there is no *a priori* im- probability in the descent of conscious (and more than conscious) machines (95) from those which now exist, except that which is suggested by the apparent ab- sence of anything like a reproductive system in the mechanical kingdom."

**22.** When the speaker uses *qua* at the conclusion of the third paragraph, he probably means

    **A.** against.

    **B.** compared to.

    **C.** as well as.

    **D.** with the help of.

    **E.** unaffected by.

**23.** We can conclude that the author of this passage

    **A.** believes that certain plants may display the characteristics of consciousness.

    **B.** believes that the consciousness of machines is comparable to the consciousness of humans.

    **C.** is not the same as the speaker, and therefore may not share any of the speaker's views.

    **D.** is writing this passage amidst the twentieth-century boom in high technology.

    **E.** holds that machines cannot reproduce themselves.

**24.** The primary purpose of this speaker is to

    **A.** argue that machines and other presumably unconscious things do possess a sort of consciousness.

    **B.** describe the widespread proliferation of machines and the effects of it.

    **C.** ridicule those who have not thought deeply about the relationship between consciousness and lack of consciousness.

    **D.** show that creatures may be both cunning and silent.

    **E.** express fear that the machine age may displace human, animal, and plant life.

**25.** The main argument of the passage is summarized in which of the following places?

    **A.** The first sentence of the first paragraph, line 1

    **B.** The first sentence of the second paragraph, line 24

    **C.** The first sentence of the third paragraph, line 42

    **D.** The first sentence of the fourth paragraph, line 79

    **E.** The last sentence of the third paragraph, line 74

GO ON TO THE NEXT PAGE

Section ▌▌▌ Reading Comprehension

**26.** From the second paragraph, lines 24–41, we may infer the speaker's belief that

   **A.** the vapour engine thinks for itself.

   **B.** mechanical life and animal life are mirror images of each other.

   **C.** nothing is certain.

   **D.** the creation of egg-cups was as natural as the creation of eggs.

   **E.** the world is a system of interrelationships.

**27.** From the speaker, we may infer which of the following conclusions about silent creatures such as potatoes and oysters?

   **A.** They do not suffer.

   **B.** They have feelings.

   **C.** Their behavior is well known to the author.

   **D.** They do not speak because speaking is not the best of languages.

   **E.** They are not related to mankind.

**28.** The speaker implies that one of the causes of the limited human understanding of consciousness and lack of consciousness is

   **A.** the fact that humans descended from things that never had any consciousness at all.

   **B.** the unlikelihood that any human has ever listened to a potato.

   **C.** the human tendency to characterize other creatures with reference only to human characteristics.

   **D.** the human avoidance of machines that are able to think.

   **E.** the breach of security that occurs when machines, which are presumably amoral, take over many of the moral duties of advanced society.

IF YOU FINISH BEFORE TIME IS CALLED, CHECK YOUR WORK ON THIS SECTION ONLY. DO NOT WORK ON ANY OTHER SECTION IN THE TEST.

# Section IV: Logical Reasoning

Time: 35 Minutes

26 Questions

**Directions:** You will be presented with brief passages or statements and will be required to evaluate their reasoning. In each case, select the best answer choice, even though more than one choice may present a possible answer. Choices that are unreasonable or incompatible with common-sense standards should be eliminated.

1. Dr. Maizels, having administered an extensive examination, was unable to find any specific physical ailment causing the patient's pain. Therefore, he concluded that there must not be a physical reason for the patient's pain.

A critique of the logic used by Dr. Maizels would probably emphasize that his reasoning

   A. uses an important term unclearly.

   B. tries to make its point by citing an inexperienced authority.

   C. assumes something to be true simply because it has not been proven otherwise.

   D. attempts to use a general answer to address a specific problem.

   E. mistakes a necessary condition for a sufficient one.

2. Because postage stamps are often gummed on their reverse side and perforated and because the items in this collection are gummed on their reverse side and perforated, this collection most likely consists of postage stamps.

Which of the following most closely parallels the reasoning used in the argument above?

   A. Because legal scholars are often in demand and earn high salaries, legal scholarship most likely causes high incomes.

   B. Because legal scholars are often in demand and earn high salaries and because Suzanne is a legal scholar, Suzanne most likely earns a high salary and is in demand.

   C. Because baseball players are often both strong and agile and because Adam is undoubtedly strong and agile, Adam is most likely a baseball player.

   D. Because postage stamps are often gummed on their reverse side and perforated, postage stamps are most likely in collections.

   E. Because rare and vintage automobiles typically cost more than a thousand dollars and this appears to be a rare and vintage automobile, this will most likely cost more than a thousand dollars.

GO ON TO THE NEXT PAGE

3. The Dollop Corporation recently concluded its poll and found that, in the last election, 60% of the respondents voted for Democratic candidates, and 40% of the respondents voted for Republican candidates. The poll also noted that 13% of the respondents voted for third-party Independent candidates.

If the totals in the Dollup poll are correct, it can be inferred that

A. some of the candidates running for office must have been both Democratic and Republican.

B. some of the respondents of the poll must have answered incorrectly.

C. some of those who voted for the candidates of one party also voted for candidates of another party.

D. some of the respondents questioned in the poll did not respond truthfully.

E. not all the respondents questioned in the poll voted.

4. Economist: Because a recessionary economy by definition must also be linked to inflationary Federal Reserve policy, many of the recent editorials calling the present economy recessionary are incorrect.

If the economist's statement is true, which of the following is a necessary assumption in order to justify its conclusion?

A. A recessionary economy is linked to inflationary Federal Reserve policy.

B. Many recent editorials fail to address the inflationary Federal Reserve policy.

C. The present economy is not linked to inflationary Federal Reserve policy.

D. An economy not linked to the inflationary Federal Reserve policy may be recessionary.

E. Many economies that are not recessionary are not linked to inflationary Federal Reserve policy.

5. The following is a letter sent by an auction house to a prospective seller:

We regret to inform you that we cannot accept your fleet of vehicles for auction in our upcoming sale. Due to the limited amount of display space in our showroom—the warehouse can accommodate only 300 vehicles—the auction directors have been obligated to decline many quality fleets for the upcoming auction.

If the letter above is truthful, which of the following can necessarily be deduced?

A. Relatively few of the fleets of vehicles submitted to the auction directors were accepted for auction.

B. The recipient of the letter submitted a quality fleet of vehicles to the auction directors.

C. The recipient of the letter submitted a fleet of vehicles that was not considered to be quality.

D. Only those fleets of vehicles that were considered to be quality were accepted for auction.

E. The quality of the fleet of vehicles was just one consideration in determining which fleets were accepted for auction.

*Questions 6 and 7 are based on the following passage.*

In a conference of casting directors, all agreed that acting talent was rarely a determination for the studios in their selection of stars to headline a particular major motion picture. Studio selection of stars was based on box-office draw. In fact, some of the biggest box-office drawing stars have little or no acting talent. Unfortunately for the studios, however, many of the stars in demand for headlining roles are seldom available.

6. In the above passage, the author makes which of the following arguments?

   A. If a studio determines that a star has acting talent, it ought to consider that star for a headlining role in one of its major motion pictures.

   B. If a studio determines that a star has no acting talent, it ought not consider that star for a headlining role in one of its major motion pictures.

   C. If a studio wants a particular star for a major motion picture, the studio assumes that star will have the ability to act the role.

   D. If a studio signs a star to headline a major motion picture, that star probably has big box-office draw.

   E. If a studio does not sign a star to headline a major motion picture, that star definitely does not have any box-office draw.

7. Which of the following may be deduced from the passage above?

   A. Many stars with big box-office draw are often waiting to be offered work.

   B. Many stars with big box-office draw are consistently working or are otherwise engaged.

   C. Many stars with big box-office draw are also exceedingly fine actors.

   D. Few stars with big box-office draw are also exceedingly fine actors.

   E. The stars with big box-office draw who are available are those who are not good actors.

8. Using a colorless and tasteless chemical called "Burine" in a town's water supply resulted in only one of every six children having extensive cavities, gum disease, or major dental problems.

   Which of the following would be the most relevant information in determining whether "Burine" was responsible for the above-mentioned situation?

   A. What the dental records are of children in another town that also uses "Burine" in its water supply

   B. What happens to the teeth and gums of children when they become adolescents

   C. Whether the children's gum disease and major dental problems are curable or not

GO ON TO THE NEXT PAGE

D. Whether the adults in the town also have similar dental records

E. What the dental records are of children in another town without "Burine" in its water supply

9. Arnold: All of the books in my classic book collection are first editions, and first editions are always valued by expert book collectors.

Roland: That's not true. Mr. Langford is an expert book collector, and he values my signed Robert Frost book of poetry, and it's not a first edition.

Roland's response shows that he has interpreted Arnold's statement to imply that

A. some volumes of Arnold's classic book collection are also signed by their authors.

B. only first editions are valued by expert book collectors.

C. all first editions are valued by expert book collectors.

D. expert book collectors always value signed books of poetry.

E. first editions in a classic collection are more likely to be valued by expert book collectors than signed editions.

10. Studies were conducted in which subjects were asked to indicate which of three lines on a card was the same length as a standard line on another card. In this simple perceptual task, stooges hired by the experimenter gave a clearly incorrect answer. This provided the subject with a dilemma between his perception and his desire to conform to the group. The responses were quite specific: Yielding behavior increased as the number of opposing persons increased up to seven, after which there was little further effect. But when one of the stooges (on instruction from the experimenter) agreed with the subject, yielding behavior sharply declined, even though the majority was still overwhelmingly against him.

Which of the following best expresses the point of the passage above?

A. Stooges should not be allowed to influence subjects' judgment in perception studies.

B. Subjects are rarely certain of their judgment when evaluating the length of lines.

C. Group pressure can be a strong factor on individual judgment in situations requiring perception.

D. As more and more people disagree with a subject, the subject becomes more and more inclined to agree with the group.

E. Ambiguous tasks often cause confusion in the minds of subjects faced with uncertain parameters.

11. The original work on hunger indicated that stomach contractions, as measured by the movements of an inflated balloon in the stomach, were the controlling cue for eating. However, animals without stomachs have normal eating habits. Subsequent work indicated that an "eating center" in the hypothalamus controlled hunger. Other work suggests the presence of specific hungers for materials deficient in a given diet; for example, cows on low-calcium diets eat bones.

In the passage above, the author

A.   argues for one theory over another by citing specific evidence supporting its case.

B.   presents conflicting information without favoring any particular theory.

C.   suggests no important difference among the major findings cited and their implications.

D.   poses a hypothetical premise and proves it with evidence from empirical research.

E.   presents a specific thesis and then uses general supporting information.

12. When Mom cooks, we all eat a delicious dinner. But Mom didn't cook today, so we won't be eating a delicious dinner.

Which of the following is logically most similar to the argument above?

A.   When food is cooked, it always burns. But our food isn't burned, so therefore it wasn't cooked.

B.   When silverware is used at the dining table, we usually have guests. Today we have guests, so we are using the silverware.

C.   When the dog has fleas, he always scratches. But the dog doesn't have fleas, so he won't be scratching.

D.   When a person is fortunate, he or she has great good luck. So a fortunate person will always be lucky.

E.   When a university finishes admitting entering students, the freshman class is complete. Since the freshman class is not complete, the university has not finished admitting entering students.

13. Extrasensory perception (ESP) is a term referring to perception-cognition effects that supposedly circumvent normal sensory channels. The four phenomena considered to be ESP are telepathy (thought transfer), clairvoyance (perception of events not through the senses), psychokinesis (influencing physical events mentally), and precognition of events. Evidence for ESP is largely dependent upon unusual statistical events that require large numbers of trials for weak returns under nonreproducible conditions.

The author of the passage above probably assumes which of the following?

A.   Extrasensory perception may consist of more than the four phenomena mentioned.

B.   Perception-cognition are normally conducted under rigorous controls and specifications.

C.   Much evidence has been gathered from unusual events to support the existence of ESP.

D.   Large numbers of trials have produced evidence that circumvents normal sensory channels.

E.   A basis for scientific proof requires strong results from repeatable, controlled experiments.

GO ON TO THE NEXT PAGE

14. Sociologist: Social roles may either conflict or cooperate within any given person, depending upon the circumstances. They conflict when the behavior patterns demanded by one role cannot be performed while performing the second role. Thus, one cannot easily be a saintly rake or a feminine brute, but given an understanding husband, a woman can be both a loving wife and a loving mother with no conflict between the roles.

The sociologist uses which of the following methods to make his or her point?

A. Applying an individual attribute to a whole

B. Implying contradictions without actually citing them

C. Relying on common-sense notions of social roles

D. Presenting specific examples to clarify a generality

E. Using paradox to highlight an implicit contradiction

15. Jonathan won't drive his car during the holidays, and since he won't, neither will Frances. Additionally, if Frances and Allan both decide not to drive their cars during the holidays, then Judith will no doubt decide to drive her own car, which has steering and brake problems, and consequently is likely to have an accident. Therefore, Judith will likely have an accident.

Which of the following, if true, would allow the author to properly draw the conclusion expressed in the argument above?

A. Judith will not drive her own car.

B. Allan will not drive his own car.

C. Frances will not drive her own car.

D. Frances will drive her own car.

E. Allan will drive his own car.

16. The notion that a court can censor a magazine, broadcaster, or newspaper in advance of publication on the grounds that some other right outweighs the right of free speech is called "prior restraint." Decisions on the issue have made it clear that proponents of prior restraint must justify its imposition in the face of a heavy presumption against its constitutional validity. A 1976 Supreme Court decision unanimously overrode a judge who sought to prohibit pretrial publication of an accused murderer's confession on the grounds that publication would make a fair trial impossible. But the Supreme Court no longer regards First Amendment protection as crucial.

The author of this paragraph uses all of the following EXCEPT:

A. Defining a key term

B. Drawing an analogy

C. Citing an example to clarify a definition

D. Expressing a personal opinion

E. Expressing a conclusion without giving the supporting evidence for reaching it

**17.** Everyone on the tennis team wears Zorfam tennis shoes. Therefore, if you want to be on the tennis team, you should wear Zorfam tennis shoes.

In which of the following is the logical flaw of the same type as in the passage above?

**A.** Every clock in the clock store says three o'clock. Therefore, it must be three o'clock.

**B.** Everyone who completes three papers will pass the course. Therefore, if you want to pass the course, you should write three papers.

**C.** Each apple in this gift basket weighs at least eight ounces. Therefore, the gift basket will be heavy.

**D.** All the houses in this neighborhood are owned by rich people. Therefore, if you want to be rich, you should buy a house in this neighborhood.

**E.** All the mail deliveries are completed before noon. Therefore, if you want your letter to be received in the morning, you should mail it on the preceding day.

**18.** A report of the California Judicial Council deals with anti-female bias in the courts. Women attorneys, witnesses, jurors, defendants, or plaintiffs have less credibility than men. A case involving a $100,000 dispute between two companies lasts 10 days, while in dependency court, a judge may deal with 35 cases a day. These cases, of course, usually involve women and children. But the courts are increasingly aware of gender bias. A first step will be the introduction of gender-neutral language in court rules, documents, and instructions for jurors.

Which of the following is an assumption upon which the argument above depends?

**A.** The number of male judges and male attorneys is far greater than the number of female judges and female attorneys.

**B.** The companies involved in the dispute were not male dominated.

**C.** The language of the courts is not now gender neutral.

**D.** Gender bias is a hypothetical construct with little empirical foundation.

**E.** The courts will undergo significant change in the next several decades.

**19.** All generalizations are false.

Which of the following is structurally most similar to the statement above?

**A.** A man in love is both sad and happy.

**B.** Two birds in the hand are worth two in the bush.

**C.** How can you trust a man with a record of dishonesty?

**D.** Believe me, I never tell the truth.

**E.** All advertising is false advertising.

GO ON TO THE NEXT PAGE

**20.** About 33% of American men between 25 and 50 are overweight. Research has shown that in most cases men between 25 and 50 who are overweight are more subject to heart disease than men who are not overweight.

Which of the following is the most logical conclusion to the passage above?

A. Therefore, 33% of the American men between 25 and 50 should lose weight.

B. Therefore, if 33% of the American men between 25 and 50 were to lose weight, they would reduce their risk of heart disease.

C. Therefore, if the men between 25 and 50 who are overweight were to lose weight, they would reduce their risk of heart disease by 33%.

D. Therefore, if 33% of American men were to lose weight, they would reduce their risk of heart disease.

E. Therefore, if the overweight American men between 25 and 50 were to lose weight, their risk of heart disease would be reduced.

*Questions 21 and 22 are based on the following passage.*

As expected, the worker who tests positive on pre-employment drug screening is more likely to have a higher rate of absence and to be involved in more accidents than a worker who tests negative. But a study of more than 2,500 New England workers had significant results: It found that the absenteeism and accident rates are much lower than the 200% to 300% higher accident rate and 1,500% sick-leave rate that earlier estimates confidently claimed. This new finding has led some scientists to argue that money spent on mandatory drug tests could be better spent on the more serious drug-abuse problem in the criminal population. Opponents insist that the numbers revealed by the study are not "significant" or "substantial." A shortcoming of the study, according to observers, is its failure to consider in any way the possible role of alcohol in addition to drug use in the performance of workers.

**21.** On the basis of the information in the passage, it is reasonable to conclude that the study demonstrates

A. that mandatory preemployment drug screening programs should be established.

B. that mandatory preemployment drug screening programs do not repay their costs.

C. that mandatory preemployment drug screening tests are invasive of privacy and should not be permitted.

D. the greater risk involved in hiring workers who test positive on preemployment drug screening.

E. the need for preemployment screening tests that consider alcohol problems.

**22.** All of the following would help support the case for mandatory drug screening EXCEPT:

A. clarifying the definition of "substantial" numbers.

B. explicating the specific results of the New England study.

C. allowing the study to consider the relevance of alcohol abuse in addition to drug use.

D. providing effective treatments for candidates testing positive on the preemployment screening.

E. finding no statistical difference between those testing positive and those testing negative.

23. The purchase of two large American film production companies by Sony and Matsushita has raised the question of censorship. Both companies are concerned with the image of Japan. Some observers fear that they will censor films that criticize Japan, either as it is now or as it has been—in World War II, for example. They point out that a film like *The Last Emperor* had distribution problems in Japan because of its depiction of the Japanese attack on China. The Japanese companies have replied that the motive for the purchase was solely economic, not nationalistic.

Which of the following, if true, would strengthen the argument against the Japanese companies?

A. A film that is critical of Japan is likely to lose money in Japan.

B. The laws governing freedom of expression in the arts are different in the United States and Japan.

C. A film about World War II could include scenes of Hiroshima.

D. Sony's purchase of a film studio indicates its interest in producing art rather than mere commerce.

E. The hallmark of both Sony and Matsushita is their ability to excel in the world marketplace.

24. Only organically grown produce is sold in McCoy's Market. Vincent Farms raises only organically grown produce. Therefore, all of Vincent Farms' produce was accepted for sale at McCoy's Market.

Which of the following, if added as a premise to the argument above, would make the conclusion valid?

A. All the produce sold in McCoy's Market is organically grown.

B. No organically grown produce is not purchased for sale by McCoy's Market.

C. Vincent Farms is a supplier of produce to McCoy's Market.

D. Organically grown produce may sometimes contain residues of pesticides.

E. McCoy's Market has been known to supply organic produce to many groceries.

25. When baseball slugger Jose Canseco was charged with illegally carrying a concealed weapon in his car, the Egg Commission canceled a proposed television advertisement featuring Canseco. Canseco's agent insists, however, that his endorsement value is unchanged. So long as Jose continues to hit home runs, the agent asserts, no one cares. Still, Canseco has not been asked to appear in any nationwide advertising campaigns. Thus, testimonial advertising _____.

GO ON TO THE NEXT PAGE

Which of the following most logically concludes the final sentence of this passage?

A. with athletes is no longer likely to be used nationwide

B. is an inexpensive and efficient way to make a product known

C. can be jeopardized by the actions of its spokesperson

D. will be useful only so long as an athlete is in the public eye

E. is a poor means of advertising no matter what the product is

26. In a tennis match, it is essential that players keep their eyes on the ball in order to strike it correctly. Therefore, good eyesight is a prerequisite for tennis. Golf, however, is another matter. Since golf is not tennis, good eyesight is not important.

The reasoning in the passage above is flawed because

A. tennis and golf are two completely different sports and, as such, cannot be compared.

B. in tennis, the ball is always moving when being hit, whereas in golf the ball is stationary.

C. what is important in one sport may also be important in a different sport.

D. good eyesight is important in every competitive endeavor, no matter whether it be tennis or golf.

E. there are some excellent golfers who are blind.

IF YOU FINISH BEFORE TIME IS CALLED, CHECK YOUR WORK ON THIS SECTION ONLY. DO NOT WORK ON ANY OTHER SECTION IN THE TEST.

# Section V: Analytical Reasoning

**Time: 35 Minutes**

**24 Questions**

**Directions:** You will be presented with several sets of conditions. A group of questions follows each set of conditions. Choose the best answer to each question, drawing a rough diagram of the conditions when necessary.

*Questions 1 through 7 are based on the following statements.*

A scientist is experimenting with three chemical elements—X, Y, and Z. During his experiments, he records the following information:

> If X reacts with X, the result is Y.
>
> If X reacts with Z, the result is X.
>
> If Y reacts with any element, the result is always Y.
>
> If Z reacts with Z, the result is Z.
>
> The order of the reaction makes no difference.

**1.** Which of the following must be true?

**A.** If X reacts with any element, the result is never X.

**B.** If Z reacts with any element, the result is that element.

**C.** If Y reacts with Y, the result is X.

**D.** If X reacts with any element, the result can be X, Y, or Z.

**E.** If Z reacts with any element, the result cannot be Y.

**2.** If the result of a reaction is Y, then which of the following was true of the reaction?

**A.** Y must have been in the reaction.

**B.** Z must have been in the reaction.

**C.** X could have been in the reaction.

**D.** Y could not have been in the reaction.

**E.** Z could not have been in the reaction.

**3.** If the result of X and Z reacts with the result of Y and Z, then the result is

**A.** X.

**B.** Y.

**C.** Z.

**D.** the result of Z and Z.

**E.** the result of Z and X.

GO ON TO THE NEXT PAGE

4. Which of the following must be FALSE?

   A. Whenever an element reacts with itself, the result is the original element.

   B. If the result is Z, Z had to have been in the reaction.

   C. If the result is Y, Y did not have to have been in the reaction.

   D. Whenever an element reacts with a different element, Z will not be the result.

   E. If the result is X, Z had to have been in the reaction.

5. If the result of a reaction is X, all of the following could have been true EXCEPT:

   A. X was in the reaction.

   B. Y was not in the reaction.

   C. Z was in the reaction.

   D. an element was not reacting with itself.

   E. an element was reacting with itself.

6. If the result of X and X reacts with the result of Z and Z, the result is

   A. X.

   B. Y.

   C. Z.

   D. X or Y.

   E. Y or Z.

7. A new element, W, is introduced. When element W is added to any reaction, the result is W, except when it reacts with Y, the result is Y. If the result of W and Z reacts with the result of W and Y, the result is NOT

   A. X.

   B. Y.

   C. Z.

   D. X or Y.

   E. W, X, or Z.

*Questions 8 through 13 are based on the following statements.*

Twenty books are stacked evenly on four shelves. There are three types of books—science fictions, mysteries, and biographies. There are twice as many mysteries as science fictions. The books are stacked as follows:

   All four science fiction books are on shelf number 2.

   There is at least one mystery on each shelf.

   Shelves numbers 3 and 4 have equal numbers of mystery books.

   No shelf contains only one type of book.

8. Which of the following must be true?

   A. Shelf number 1 contains at least one science fiction book.

   B. Shelf number 2 contains exactly one biography.

   C. Shelf number 3 contains no science fiction books.

   D. Shelf number 3 contains five biographies.

   E. Shelf number 2 contains at least two mystery books.

**9.** Which of the following must be true?

    **A.** No shelf has more than two mysteries.

    **B.** No shelf has more than two biographies.

    **C.** There is never only one mystery on a shelf.

    **D.** There is never only one biography on a shelf.

    **E.** There are always more mysteries than biographies on a given shelf.

**10.** If the books on shelf number 1 and shelf number 4 are combined, it must be true that this combination will contain

    **A.** an equal number of mysteries and biographies.

    **B.** exactly one science fiction.

    **C.** all the biographies.

    **D.** half of all the mysteries.

    **E.** over half of all the biographies.

**11.** All of the following are true EXCEPT:

    **A.** Shelf number 2 contains no biographies.

    **B.** Shelf number 3 contains no science fiction.

    **C.** Shelf number 4 contains equal numbers of each book.

    **D.** Shelf number 1 could contain mostly mysteries.

    **E.** Shelf number 3 could contain three biographies.

**12.** Shelf number 4 must have

    **A.** four mysteries.

    **B.** two different types of books, in the ratio of 3 to 2.

    **C.** two different types of books, in the ratio of 4 to 1.

    **D.** all three different types of books, in the ratio of 2:2:1.

    **E.** four biographies.

**13.** Shelf number 1 must have

    **A.** two different types of books, in the ratio of 3 to 2.

    **B.** two different types of books, in the ratio of 4 to 1.

    **C.** three different types of books, in the ratio of 2:2:1.

    **D.** four mysteries.

    **E.** at least two biographies.

*Questions 14 through 18 are based on the following information.*

A public recreation facility operates throughout all twelve months of the year from January to December, at any time offering only one of four activities—Basketball, Gymnastics, Volleyball, and Weight Training—each activity during two-month periods, as follows:

The first two-month period is January–February, and the remaining five two-month periods follow chronologically.

During any twelve-month period beginning in January, no activity may be offered during four consecutive months.

GO ON TO THE NEXT PAGE

Section V Analytical Reasoning

Basketball may not be offered during the January–February period.

If during January–February Gymnastics is offered, then Weight Training cannot be offered November–December.

Either May–June, November–December, or both these periods must offer Weight Training, which may be offered at other times also.

Each of the four activities must be offered at least once during the year.

14. Which of the following is an acceptable schedule for six two-month periods, beginning in January?

A. Volleyball, Gymnastics, Weight Training, Volleyball, Weight Training, Gymnastics

B. Volleyball, Gymnastics, Weight Training, Basketball, Volleyball, Basketball

C. Volleyball, Basketball, Gymnastics, Weight Training, Volleyball, Basketball

D. Gymnastics, Basketball, Weight Training, Volleyball, Basketball, Weight Training

E. Gymnastics, Basketball, Weight Training, Volleyball, Gymnastics, Gymnastics

15. If Weight Training is offered only during May–June and November–December, which of the following must be true of the year's schedule?

A. Volleyball is offered for exactly four months.

B. Basketball is offered for exactly four months.

C. Volleyball is offered January–February.

D. Gymnastics is offered September–October.

E. Basketball is offered March–April.

16. Which of the following statements is possible?

A. Weight Training is offered May–June, and Gymnastics is offered November–December.

B. Gymnastics is offered January–February, and Weight Training is offered July–August.

C. Weight Training is offered March–April and September–October.

D. Gymnastics is offered January–February and May–June.

E. Basketball is offered May–June and November–December.

17. All of the following schedules are allowable EXCEPT:

A. Volleyball is offered March–April, and Weight Training is offered September–October.

B. Volleyball is offered January–February, and Weight Training is offered March–April.

C. Gymnastics is offered January–February, and Weight Training is offered September–October.

D. Gymnastics is offered January–February, and Weight Training is offered March–April.

E. Basketball is offered March–April, and Gymnastics is offered September–October.

18. Suppose Gymnastics is offered only during January–February and November–December. What else must be true of that year's schedule?

   A. Volleyball or Weight Training is offered during March–April.

   B. Basketball or Volleyball is offered during September–October.

   C. Volleyball is offered immediately before Basketball is offered.

   D. The same activity is not offered May–June and September–October.

   E. Only one activity, besides Gymnastics, is offered a total of four months.

*Questions 19 through 24 are based on the following statements.*

Five boys (Al, Paul, Jim, Sam, and Bob) are being arranged in height order for a photograph. The photographer, after arranging the boys in order, determines the following information:

   Sam is taller than Al.

   Bob is shorter than Jim.

   Bob is taller than Paul.

   Sam is shorter than Jim.

   Paul is shorter than Al.

19. From the information given, which of the following must be the tallest boy?

   A. Al
   B. Bob
   C. Sam
   D. Jim
   E. Paul

20. Which of the following must be true?

   A. Bob is not taller than Sam.
   B. Al is not taller than Jim.
   C. Bob is taller than Al.
   D. Bob is taller than Sam.
   E. Paul is taller than Al.

21. Which of the following CANNOT be true?

   A. Paul is taller than Sam.
   B. Jim is taller than Al.
   C. Al is taller than Bob.
   D. Bob is taller than Sam.
   E. Sam is taller than Bob.

22. If Harold joins the group and he is taller than Bob but shorter than Al, which of the following must be true?

   A. Harold is taller than Sam.
   B. Harold is shorter than Paul.
   C. Al is taller than Sam.
   D. Al is taller than Bob.
   E. Harold is taller than three of the men.

23. If Tom joins the group and is taller than Bob, which of the following must be true about Tom?

   A. Al is taller than Tom.
   B. Tom is taller than Al.
   C. Sam is taller than Tom.
   D. Jim is taller than Tom.
   E. Tom is taller than Paul.

GO ON TO THE NEXT PAGE

**24.** If Ernie joins the group and is the same height as two of the other boys,

    **A.** Sam is the same height as Al.

    **B.** Al and Bob must be the same height.

    **C.** Sam and Bob must be the same height.

    **D.** Bob must be the same height as Ernie.

    **E.** Jim and Sam must be the same height.

IF YOU FINISH BEFORE TIME IS CALLED, CHECK YOUR WORK ON THIS
SECTION ONLY. DO NOT WORK ON ANY OTHER SECTION IN THE TEST.

# Writing Essay

**Time: 30 Minutes**

**Directions:** You are to complete a brief essay on the given topic. You may take no more than 30 minutes to plan and write your essay. After reading the topic carefully, you should probably spend a few minutes planning and organizing your response. YOU MAY NOT WRITE ON A TOPIC OTHER THAN THE GIVEN TOPIC.

The quality of your writing is more important than either the quantity of writing or the point of view you adopt. Your skill in organization, mechanics, and usage is important, although it is expected that your essay will not be flawless because of the time pressure under which you write.

Keep your writing within the lined area of your essay booklet. Write on every line, avoid wide margins, and write carefully and legibly.

> NOTE: On the actual LSAT, the essay topic is at the top of the essay writing page. Scratch paper for organizing and prewriting is provided.

GO ON TO THE NEXT PAGE

Writing Essay

# Essay Topic

Read the following description of Sendak and Krull, candidates for promotion to staff supervisor at the software manufacturing firm of Bytonics, Inc. Then, write an argument for promoting either Sendak or Krull. Use the information in this description and assume that two general policies guide the promotion decisions at Bytonics:

- Promotions are based on a combination of experience and effectiveness on the job.

- Effectiveness on the job is measured by periodic on-site evaluations, evidence of innovative ideas, and reliable completion of assigned tasks.

Sendak earned a master's degree in computer science before joining Bytonics, where she has worked for five years. She was a computer enthusiast long before it was fashionable, designing new software for local businesses while she was still in high school. At Bytonics, she has received an on-site evaluation twice each year, and all but one of the several managers who have observed her work filed positive reports. As the competition among software firms has continued to increase, Sendak has been partly responsible for the strong position of Bytonics. Working overtime often, she has developed a series of new programs for teaching foreign languages to elementary school students. The programs have been adopted and used effectively by a number of schools throughout the country. As well as having created these programs, Sendak has managed to carry out all of her assigned tasks fully and efficiently.

Krull has worked at Bytonics for fifteen years, since her graduation from high school. She began as a messenger and quickly learned the essentials of computer software by persistently asking intelligent questions of the company experts and volunteering for progressively more challenging software tasks. Her thirty on-site evaluations all contain lavish praise; managers note especially her reliability. Any task she is given, no matter how difficult, will be seen to successful completion. Although Krull has not designed any original software as yet, she is a talented critic of others' ideas and has offered perceptive advice that has helped improve a number of new Bytonics products.

# Answers and Complete Explanations For Practice Test 2

## Answer Key for Practice Test 2

| Section I<br>Analytical<br>Reasoning | Section II<br>Logical<br>Reasoning | Section III<br>Reading<br>Comprehension | Section IV<br>Logical<br>Reasoning | Section V<br>Analytical<br>Reasoning |
|---|---|---|---|---|
| 1. E | 1. C | 1. C | 1. C | 1. B |
| 2. B | 2. E | 2. E | 2. C | 2. C |
| 3. C | 3. D | 3. A | 3. C | 3. B |
| 4. D | 4. C | 4. A | 4. C | 4. A |
| 5. A | 5. E | 5. B | 5. E | 5. E |
| 6. D | 6. A | 6. E | 6. D | 6. B |
| 7. E | 7. D | 7. D | 7. B | 7. E |
| 8. C | 8. E | 8. D | 8. E | 8. C |
| 9. E | 9. A | 9. B | 9. B | 9. D |
| 10. C | 10. C | 10. E | 10. C | 10. E |
| 11. C | 11. B | 11. C | 11. B | 11. C |
| 12. E | 12. E | 12. A | 12. C | 12. B |
| 13. E | 13. E | 13. B | 13. E | 13. E |
| 14. A | 14. A | 14. B | 14. D | 14. B |
| 15. D | 15. C | 15. C | 15. B | 15. C |
| 16. D | 16. A | 16. D | 16. B | 16. A |
| 17. D | 17. E | 17. A | 17. D | 17. D |
| 18. B | 18. D | 18. B | 18. C | 18. E |
| 19. E | 19. D | 19. C | 19. D | 19. D |
| 20. E | 20. E | 20. B | 20. E | 20. B |
| 21. E | 21. E | 21. B | 21. D | 21. A |
| 22. A | 22. C | 22. B | 22. E | 22. D |
| 23. D | 23. C | 23. C | 23. A | 23. E |
| 24. E | 24. D | 24. A | 24. B | 24. D |
|  | 25. C | 25. D | 25. C |  |
|  |  | 26. E | 26. C |  |
|  |  | 27. B |  |  |
|  |  | 28. C |  |  |

# How to Score Your Exam

Your score on the actual LSAT is simply the number of questions you answered correctly (minus a small adjustment factor) scaled to a 120–180 scoring range. There is no penalty for incorrect answers other than no credit. The experimental section (in this case, one of the Logical Reasoning sections) would not count toward your score.

# Analyzing Your Test Results

Use the charts on the following pages to carefully analyze your results and spot your strengths and weaknesses. You should complete the entire process of analyzing each subject area and each individual problem for each Practice Test. Then reexamine the results for trends in types of errors (repeated errors) or poor results in specific subject areas. THIS REEXAMINATION AND ANALYSIS IS IMPORTANT TO YOU: IT SHOULD ENABLE YOU TO CONCENTRATE ON YOUR AREAS OF WEAKNESS AND IMPROVE THEM.

## Tally Sheet

Use the Answer Key to mark the number of questions you finished, got right, and got wrong in the following grid.

| | Possible | Completed | Right | Wrong |
|---|---|---|---|---|
| Section I: Analytical Reasoning | 24 | | | |
| Section II: Logical Reasoning | 25 | | | |
| Section III: Reading Comprehension | 28 | | | |
| Section IV: Logical Reasoning | 26 | | | |
| Section V: Analytical Reasoning | 24 | | | |
| OVERALL TOTALS | 127 | | | |

## Analysis Sheet for Problems Missed

One of the most important parts of test preparation is analyzing why you missed a problem so that you can reduce the number of future mistakes. Now that you have taken Practice Test 2 and corrected your answers, carefully tally your mistakes by marking them in the proper column.

## Reason for Mistake

|  | Total Missed | Simple Mistake | Misread Problem | Lack of Knowledge |
|---|---|---|---|---|
| Section I: Analytical Reasoning |  |  |  |  |
| Section II: Logical Reasoning |  |  |  |  |
| Section III: Reading Comprehension |  |  |  |  |
| Section IV: Logical Reasoning |  |  |  |  |
| Section V: Analytical Reasoning |  |  |  |  |
| OVERALL TOTALS |  |  |  |  |

Reviewing this data should help you determine WHY you are missing certain problems. Now that you have pinpointed the type of error, take the next practice test and focus on avoiding your most common type of error.

# Section I: Analytical Reasoning

From the information given, you can construct the following diagram:

1. **E.** U can receive but cannot send messages.

2. **B.** A message may be relayed from R to Q by using station T.

3. **C.** S can relay a message to Q only by going through first R and then T, thus requiring two relays, not one.

4. **D.** If T is destroyed, there will be no way of getting a message to Q.

5. **A.** One may get a message from Q to U by going through first R and then S. None of the other choices can be done with exactly two relays.

6. **D.** Beginning at T, a message may be relayed three times before going through another station twice: T to Q to R to S to U.

**7. E.** V can get a message to W: V to T to Q to R to S to U to W. U can get a message to Q: U to W to S to R to T to Q. R can get a message to W: R to S to U to W. No station can get a message to V.

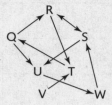

From the information given for questions 8 through 13, you can construct the following chart:

```
                    D?
    A                            E
    1   2          3         4   5
    E                            A
              B    ?    C
```

**8. C.** If the Danish yacht is third, the order will be

<u>A/E</u>   <u>B</u>   <u>D</u>   <u>C</u>   <u>A/E</u>

Belgium will finish second.

**9. E.** The order will be E B C D A.

**10. C.** If the Danish yacht finishes second twice, then Belgium must finish second four times (32 points), and the other two times would finish third (12 points) for a total of 44 points.

**11. C.** England can finish only first or fifth. If England has 36 points, it must have three first-place finishes (30 points) and three fifth-place finishes (6 points). Therefore, Australia must also have three first-place finishes and three last-place finishes, for a total of 36 points. None of the other options *must* be true, although some *may*.

**12. E.** England could be only as low as 28, since it will have four fifth-place and two first-place finishes; Belgium could be only as low as 36. Either Canada or Denmark could finish fourth in all six races, for a total of 24 points.

**13. E.** If Finland finishes behind both Canada and Denmark, it also finishes behind Belgium and whoever finishes first. Therefore, Finland finishes ahead of only one yacht, or fifth of six yachts.

```
              D    B    C    F
              B    D    C    F
    A/E       B    C    D    F    A/E
     1        2    3    4    5     6
```

From the information given for questions 14 through 19, you can draw either of the following charts:

| Men | Women |
|---|---|
| B C D | A E F G |

| Nat | Soc |
|---|---|
| A B C | D E F G |

| Instr | Prof |
|---|---|
| A D E G | B C F |

|   | M | W | N | S | I | P |
|---|---|---|---|---|---|---|
| A |   | X | X |   | X |   |
| B | X |   | X |   |   | X |
| C | X |   | X |   |   | X |
| D | X |   |   | X | X |   |
| E |   | X |   | X | X |   |
| F |   | X |   | X |   | X |
| G |   | X |   | X | X |   |

**14. A.** If D and B are chosen, the other two *must* be A and F so that natural scientists equal social scientists and instructors equal professors.

**15. D.** If A and D are chosen, the other members will be B and F or C and F. Thus, F *must* be on the committee with either B or C.

**16. D.** If F is chosen, the committee will consist of either ADBF or ADCF. Therefore, both A and D must be chosen. Of the choices given, choice D, D, is correct.

**17. D.** D and E cannot serve on the committee together. The other pairs can serve together as follows: choice A, AB with DF, choice B, AC with DF, choice C, CD with AF, and choice E, EG with BC.

**18. B.** The only possible committee will be EGBC.

**19. E.** E cannot be used with A.

For questions 20 through 24, you can construct the following chart:

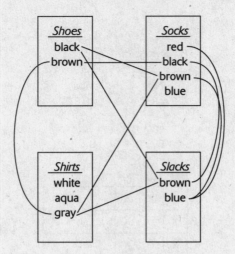

20. **E.** If Sam wears black shoes, he will *not* wear brown slacks. Therefore, he must wear blue slacks. If he wears blue slacks, he *cannot* wear red socks.

21. **E.** Since black does not go well with brown, B and D are incorrect, because each of these creates a black-brown combination.

22. **A.** Blue slacks cannot be worn with red socks.

23. **D.** Sam could wear a white shirt, brown slacks, and blue socks. The only general statement is that black does not go with brown.

24. **E.** A complete and accurate list of the possible colors he could wear could not include red or brown, so choices C and D can be eliminated. Choices A and B are accurate, but they are not complete because they are missing blue. Each of the colors in choice E is a possibility.

# Section II: Logical Reasoning

1. **C.** The transitional word *nevertheless* establishes a juxtaposition of the phrases immediately before and after it. Therefore, A and B are incorrect. Choice D may be a good answer, but C is better, because it addresses a concern initially introduced in the paragraph and brings the passage full circle.

2. **E.** Only C and E describe situations in which a media event precedes a real-life event. In C, the medium is not an artistic one; in E television may be regarded as an art form.

3. **D.** Choices B and E are contradicted by the passage, and the passage does not support the probability of A or C. Choice D is reasonable, plausible, and probable, given the information in the passage.

4. **C.** The student's qualification shows that he or she doubts whether the Congressman's statement is absolutely true, but the response is not so pronounced as to suggest any of the other choices.

5. **E.** The passage restricts its attention to salaries, and its details clearly indicate that federal pay is significantly high, thus possibly supporting the conclusion in E.

6. **A.** This statement is consistent with the comparison between federal and private workers established in the passage. Choice D contradicts information in the passage, C is irrelevant, and B and E are not mentioned in the passage.

7. **D.** The argument presupposes that television can be used to inform the public (*provide air time to all candidates to debate the issues*). Choices B, C, and E are each irrelevant to the argument.

8. **E.** This choice weakens the point made by the final observation. Each of the other choices either strengthens points made by the observation or is irrelevant.

9. **A.** Only this choice necessarily introduces a contrasting statement, one that would probably take issue with the points of the argument. C and D might possibly begin critical, contrasting statements but may have other uses as well.

10. **C.** Geographic location and employment status are irrelevant issues, so A and B should be eliminated. D and E are too general and vague. Only C makes explicit the point of the author's argument, that interpretation of the Texas law is arrogant and unsound.

11. **B.** By describing the special relief programs as a *flood,* the author gives the programs a negative connotation and suggests disapproval.

12. **E.** The researcher concluded that women could be just as capable as men in math but that they develop other abilities because of social pressures. Thus, the researcher assumes that women do conform to social expectations.

13. **E.** Choices A and B are irrelevant to the argument, and D is an illogical criticism. E is a logical conclusion that poses a significant problem.

14. **A.** All the other choices are much less relevant than the issue of how efficiently and effectively the program helps students to achieve competency.

15. **C.** Each of the other choices requires assumptions and conclusions not supported or implied by the argument. The stress in the argument on reduced funds leads logically to the conclusion that further spending is unwise.

16. **A.** Bacon advocates retaining dignity without intruding upon liberty. The author implies that retaining dignity is impossible without intruding upon another's liberty by stating that intruding upon liberty is impossible. B, C, D contradict the author's argument, and E presents an irrelevant issue.

author discusses liberty and dignity in absolute terms.

han Swift is comparing laws to a cobweb, noting that little insects get caught insects can break on through. He thus is indicating that the legal system is inequitable: that the small will get caught (sentenced) while those with more power can avoid sentencing.

19. **D.** The passage sets up the thesis that sometimes individuals yield to others' interests. Choices A and E are unsubstantiated or not mentioned in the passage; C does not fit the structure of the sentence; B could possibly be the correct answer, but D more nearly completes the thought of the passage and is neatly juxtaposed with the first part of the incomplete sentence.

Section **II** Logical Reasoning

**20. E.** From the letter, we cannot validly conclude if the score of the candidate was above or below 1000; all it says is that "we were not even able to accept all those with SAT scores of 1000 or above. . . ." Choices A and B can be eliminated. Choice C can be eliminated because we cannot conclude that none of the students selected had scores below 1000. Choice D can be eliminated because we have no idea how many students with scores at or above 1000 were rejected. Choice E is the only one that can be validly concluded from the information given.

**21. E.** You want to find the statement that is a logical continuation of the facts given in the passage. The best strategy is to read through each choice and evaluate whether it *must* be so or not, eliminating those that are irrelevant, or contradictions, or merely possible. Choice E is the only answer that *has* to be true. The passage states that houses connected to city sewage must follow the Verdex Code, while houses connected to a septic tank must follow the Stipex Code. Therefore, the Stipex Code does not apply to houses connected to city sewage systems.

**22. C.** Choices A, B, and E present information that supports the value of sleep, and D dissociates advanced capabilities from the mind, thus damaging the author's mind/mindlessness distinction.

**23. C.** Only choice C asserts the positive value of sleep and thus weakens the author's stance in favor of decreased sleep.

**24. D.** The commercial either explicitly states or implies all but D. It makes no reference to how long it will take to fall asleep or how quickly the drug works. It does, however, claim to provide a restful, good night's sleep, with added energy and no aftereffects the next morning.

**25. C.** The method of caffeine intake helps to safely limit the amount of caffeine that any person can ingest over a short period of time. For foods such as coffee, one can drink only so much before becoming full from the liquid. Pills, however, can be taken in any quantity without subsequent discomfort, and this can lead to possible problems.

# Section III: Reading Comprehension

**1. C.** The sixth paragraph states that *depending upon the complexity and the amount of the claim, one arbitrator may suffice*. The number of arbitrators has no bearing, however, on the objectivity of the given industry.

**2. E.** The first sentence of the passage states that an arbitration award is *final and binding*.

**3. A.** Since an arbitration award is rendered within 30 days after the hearing and cannot be postponed through seemingly endless appeals, an AIDS patient (with a shorter-than-normal life expectancy) would be the best candidate for arbitration.

**4. A.** In a survey of some 200 construction arbitrations in 1995, the author notes that almost half were settled or withdrawn before the hearing stage, which is not unlike disputes that are to be litigated in the courts.

**5. B.** If 81% require only one hearing, it can be inferred that the remaining 19% require more than one hearing.

**6. E.** The author distinguishes between arbitration and compromise by indicating that in arbitration an *expert* determines what is fair using expert and independent evaluation. Hence, a party may expect any degree of reward (nothing, or more, or less than the claim). However, a compromise would most probably *split the difference*, or award a settlement somewhere between the two parties' claims.

**7. D.** Unlike a court of law, an arbitrator need not have knowledge of the laws of compensation; rather, an arbitrator should be objective and have expertise and competence in the given industry.

**8. D.** Choices A and C do not mention Africa. The passage deals only briefly with the West B and does not deal with the control of juvenile delinquency. Choice D summarizes clearly the central concerns of the passage.

**9. B.** The second paragraph of the passage explicitly states that maladjusted behavior of minors should not be termed juvenile delinquency.

**10. E.** According to the third paragraph of the passage, the *exact lower and upper age limits differ from country to country.*

**11. C.** Tanzania and Kenya are cited after a reference to *most of the East African countries.*

**12. A.** The sixth paragraph points to the very large percentage of Africans below 15 and below 25. Although the passage does mention *lack of parental control,* it does not mention an *impressionable age,* choice C.

**13. B.** The passage cites *lack of parental control* as one possible cause.

**14. B.** The last paragraph of the passage points to the lack of *medico-psychosocial resources* in Africa.

**15. C.** This situation establishes a relationship between price and quantity that parallels the paragraph 2 explanation of the law of demand. This section discusses *the consumer's desire to get the "best buy,"* and goes on to say that *if the price of good A increases, the individual will tend to substitute another good and purchase less of good A.* Since the appearance of a lower-priced breakfast drink makes orange juice more *expensive,* in relation, the law of demand as so described would prevail.

**16. D.** The third paragraph distinguishes *individual demand* and *market demand*; the former is exercised by a single person, whereas the latter is exerted by a *group* of individuals. With this distinction in mind, we may conclude that a group of individuals constitutes a market. Choice B contradicts the paragraph. Choices A, C, and E might be true under certain conditions, but those conditions are not specified in the question or in the passage.

**17. A.** Initially, the passage emphasizes a distinction between *demand* and *quantity demanded,* concluding that *demand shifts when there is a change in income, expectations, taste, and so forth, such that a different quantity of the good is demanded at the* same *price.* This statement fits A precisely. All other choices include or allow for a *changing* price.

**18. B.** The fourth paragraph states, *there is a positive correlation between quantity supplied and product price.* Since that means that quantity and price are related, any choice (in this case, all choices except B) with a relational connotation does not tell us what the two items are *not.*

**Section III Reading Comprehension**

**19. C.** The passage says that *demand shifts when there is a change in income, expectations, taste, and so forth, such that a different quantity of the good is demanded at the same price*. Choices A, D, and E all involve a *changing* price, and B would reduce income so that demand would *decrease*.

**20. B.** The issues of supply and demand are the essential themes running throughout the entire passage.

**21. B.** Although prices are discussed, illegal price fixing in particular is never addressed by the passage.

**22. B.** The author uses *qua* in the midst of stressing the human tendency to *compare* the characteristics of inanimate objects to human characteristics.

**23. C.** Each of the paragraphs is enclosed in quotation marks, and the phrase *to quote his own words* in the first paragraph clearly indicates that the author is recording a viewpoint other than his or her own.

**24. A.** The bulk of the speaker's argument creates the case that presumably unconscious entities—the vapour engine, the potato, the oyster—do possess a sort of consciousness if looked at from an unconventional point of view.

**25. D.** The main argument of the passage, that presumably unconscious things do possess a sort of consciousness, is summarized in the first sentence of the fourth paragraph; the opposite case (no consciousness) is also summarized here, but the summary of the main argument is nevertheless present.

**26. E.** In this paragraph, the speaker implies this belief with the rhetorical question *Is not everything interwoven with everything?*

**27. B.** When discussing potatoes and oysters in the third paragraph, the speaker points out that we suppose that such creatures do not have emotions because they make no sounds, thus implying that they may indeed have emotions that are invisible to our limited, conventional human perception.

**28. C.** In the third paragraph (lines 42–78), the author stresses the human tendency to understand other creatures *qua* mankind and implies the limitations of such understanding with several phrases, notably *but mankind is not everybody*.

# Section IV: Logical Reasoning

**1. C.** Dr. Maizels was not able to locate any specific physical ailment causing the patient's pain, and so he concludes that there must not be a physical reason for the patient's pain. His reasoning therefore assumes that another physician will concur with his finding. However, this does not necessarily have to be so; another physician's examination could, in fact, prove otherwise.

**2. C.** The passage gives two attributes (perforated, gummed) for a particular group. It then cites an individual with those attributes, concluding that the individual therefore most likely belongs to the group. C is the only choice that parallels this reasoning.

3. **C.** Since the poll does not state that respondents voted for only one party's candidates, the most reasonable inference that can be made is that some of the voters questioned must have voted for candidates of more than one party. This would explain why the percentage appears to total more than 100%.

4. **C.** The passage states that by definition a recessionary economy must be linked to inflationary Federal Reserve policy. Since it says that recent editorials are incorrect in calling the present economy recessionary for the above reason, the economist must be making the assumption that the present economy is not linked to inflationary Federal Reserve policy.

5. **E.** Although choices B and D are both possible, neither can necessarily be deduced. Only choice E is a deduction that can be made. Since, for example, a fleet of vehicles numbering 320 could not be accommodated in the showroom regardless of its quality, another consideration in determining acceptance (besides quality) is fleet size.

6. **D.** The operative criterion for choosing a star to headline a major motion picture is simple box-office draw. All other criteria (for example, acting talent) is irrelevant to the choice. Choice E is not necessarily true, because more than one box-office drawing star may be considered for a role with only one chosen. Those not chosen still have box-office draw.

7. **B.** The final phrase (*the stars in demand for headlining roles are seldom available*) indicates that many stars with big box-office draw are either consistently working or otherwise engaged.

8. **E.** Although choices B and C would be somewhat relevant, choice E is by far the most relevant in determining if the *Burine* was responsible. Choice E involves a control group: It measures the effect of water *without* Burine on a population of children to see if there is any difference between those using Burine and those not using it.

9. **B.** Roland's response indicates that he thought Arnold's statement meant that only first editions are valued by expert book collectors. Choice C is what Arnold meant, but B is how Roland interpreted it.

10. **C.** Although choice D is partially true, it is correct only up to seven, after which it is no longer correct. Only choice C accurately expresses the point of the passage: that group pressure can alter a subject's judgment on simply perceptual tasks.

11. **B.** Three distinct and opposing theories are presented, but the author takes no position favoring any one of them.

12. **C.** The fallacious logic confuses a sufficient condition: *When Mom cooks, we eat a delicious dinner,* with a necessary condition: *Only when Mom cooks, we eat a delicious dinner.* Note that it isn't necessary for *Mom* to do the cooking in order for us to eat a delicious dinner; someone else could do the cooking. In the same regard, just because the dog doesn't have fleas doesn't mean the dog couldn't scratch for another reason.

13. **E.** The final sentence repudiates the evidence supporting ESP by stating that the weak results generated from a large number of trials were not conducted under reproducible conditions. Therefore, the author assumes that one basis for scientific proof requires strong results from reproducible conditions.

14. **D.** By using two examples (*saintly rake* and *feminine brute*), the sociologist not only provides actual instances of contradictions to prove the point, but also offers specific examples to clarify the generality expressed in the first two sentences.

15. **B.** The first sentence makes it clear that neither Jonathan nor Frances will drive their cars during the holidays. However, nothing in the passage assures that Allan will also decide not to drive his car during the holidays (. . . *if Frances and Allan both . . .*), and therefore we cannot conclusively deduce that Judith will drive her own car. Only by knowing that Allan will not drive his own car do we then have all the pieces in place to conclude that Judith will decide to drive her own car and therefore likely have an accident.

16. **B.** The passage does not use analogy, but it does employ the other techniques.

17. **D.** The passage mistakes an element that a particular population has in common for a cause. In choice D, the owning of a house (common element) is misunderstood as a cause, like the tennis shoes in the passage. Notice that there is no precise pattern agreement between any of the answer choices and the passage.

18. **C.** The 10 days that the companies have on the court calendar are contrasted with the brief time given to cases that usually involve women. If gender-neutral language is to be introduced, the language now cannot be neutral.

19. **D.** The statement is self-contradictory, since it is a generalization but asserts that all generalizations are false. Similarly, it is contradictory to believe a self-admitted liar.

20. **E.** The question refers to a percentage of overweight American men, not just to American men or to overweight men.

21. **D.** The study supports the modest claim of choice D but does not demonstrate whether or not mandatory testing should be established.

22. **E.** All but choice E would assist the case for mandatory testing.

23. **A.** If profit is the motive, profit in this case would justify censorship.

24. **B.** If no organically grown produce is not purchased by McCoy's, and Vincent Farms has only organically grown produce, all its produce would be accepted for sale by McCoy's.

25. **C.** The passage suggests that the negative actions of a spokesperson in his or her own personal life can affect the public to such an extent that the endorsement of a product can be jeopardized.

26. **C.** Because two sports may differ, the reader may not therefore conclude that what is important for one is not necessarily important for the other. The same quality may be important for several endeavors, however different those endeavors may be. The conclusion of the passage incorrectly assumes that good eyesight is a prerequisite *only* for tennis.

# Section V: Analytical Reasoning

To help answer questions 1 through 7, you may have constructed the following chart:

|   | X | Y | Z |
|---|---|---|---|
| X | Y | Y | X |
| Y | Y | Y | Y |
| Z | X | Y | Z |

1. **B.** From the chart, notice that whenever Z reacts with an element, the result is the other element.

2. **C.** Y can result from a reaction with any one of the elements.

3. **B.** The result of X and Y is X. The result of Y and Z is Y. When X reacts with Y, the result is Y.

4. **A.** When X reacts with X, the result is not X, but Y. All the other statements are true.

5. **E.** If the result of a reaction was X, then the two elements that reacted can be only X with Z. Therefore, all the statements are true except choice E.

6. **B.** The result of X and X is Y. The result of Z and Z is Z. Thus, the result of Y and Z is Y.

7. **E.** Since Y is involved in the reaction, the result must be Y; therefore, it is not W, X, or Z. Although answers A and C contain two of these letters, neither answer is as complete as E. You could have expanded the chart like this:

|   | X | Y | Z | W |
|---|---|---|---|---|
| X | Y | Y | X | W |
| Y | Y | Y | Y | Y |
| Z | X | Y | Z | W |
| W | W | Y | W | W |

From the information given for questions 8 through 13, you could have constructed the following charts, which may be helpful in enabling you to answer. (Note that the circled books must be positioned as shown.)

```
1. B B M M (M)        1. B B B B (M)
2. (S S S  M)    or   2. (S S S  M)
3. B B B M  M         3. B B M M  M
4. B B B M (M)        4. B B M M (M)
```

8. **C.** From the given information, all the science fiction books are on shelf number 2. Thus, none can be on shelf number 3.

9. **D.** There is never only one biography on a shelf.

10. **E.** Shelves 1 and 4 together contain over half of the biographies and no science fiction.

11. **C.** There is no possible way that shelf number 4 could contain equal numbers of each book. Since five books are on a shelf, they cannot be evenly divided.

12. **B.** Shelf number 4 must contain either three biographies and two mysteries or three mysteries and two biographies. Either way, the ratio is 3 to 2.

13. **E.** Shelf number 1 has either four biographies and one mystery or two biographies and three mysteries.

From the information given for questions 14 through 18, you can draw the following diagram:

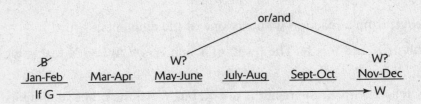

14. **B.** Choice A does not contain Basketball. Choice C does not have Weight Training either May–June, November–December, or both. Choice D has Gymnastics during January–February and also Weight Training in November–December, which is not allowed by the facts. And choice E has Gymnastics in two consecutive spots. Only choice B is acceptable.

15. **C.** If Weight Training is offered only May–June and November–December, then Weight Training is not also offered January–February. From the facts, since Weight Training is offered November–December, then Gymnastics cannot be offered January–February. We know also from the facts that Basketball is not offered January–February. This leaves only Volleyball for January–February.

16. **A.** Choice B is not possible: If Gymnastics is offered January–February, then Weight Training cannot be offered November–December, which means Weight Training must be offered May–June, which with July–August would be four consecutive months, which is not allowed. Choice C is not possible because with the addition of either May–June or November–December, that would make four consecutive months for Weight Training. Choices D and E are each not possible because each would not allow for Weight Training to be offered during either May–June or November–December. Only A is possible.

17. **D.** If Gymnastics is offered January–February, then Weight Training cannot be offered November–December, which means Weight Training must be offered May–June. But with Weight Training offered March–April (from choice D), this would make four consecutive months of offering Weight Training, which is not allowed.

18. **E.** If Gymnastics is offered January–February and November–December, then Weight Training must be offered during May–June. That leaves three open two-month slots for the remaining two activities, which means that only one of three activities (Weight Training, Volleyball, or Basketball) will be offered for two slots, or a total of four months.

For questions 19 through 24, using a visual display will help place the boys in some order.

Tallest

J
- - - - - -
S      ↑
       B?
A      ↓
- - - - - -
P

Shortest

Notice that Bob cannot be placed definitively. This is not necessary to answer the questions.

**19. D.** From the diagram, Jim is obviously the tallest.

**20. B.** From the chart, we can see that only B must be true. Choices A, C, and D could be true, but that is not what the question asks. Choice E is false.

**21. A.** Choice B is true, and choices C, D, and E each could be true. Only choice A cannot be true.

**22. D.** If Harold joins the group and is taller than Bob but shorter than Al, then the order of all six boys becomes definitively determined:

J
S
A
H
B
P

Thus, only D will be true: Al is taller than Bob.

**23. E.** Tom may be taller than Bob, but this information does not allow us to place Tom in relation to either Sam or Al. Tom could be shorter or taller than Jim, but Tom must be taller than Paul.

**24. D.** If Ernie joins the group and is the same height as two of the boys, Ernie must be the same height as *either* Bob and Al or Bob and Sam. Therefore, Ernie must be at least the same height as Bob.

# Practice Test 3

Section I:     Logical Reasoning—35 minutes; 24 questions

Section II:    Reading Comprehension—35 minutes; 28 questions

Section III:   Logical Reasoning—35 minutes; 26 questions

Section IV:    Analytical Reasoning—35 minutes; 24 questions

Section V:     Reading Comprehension—35 minutes; 27 questions

               Writing Essay—30 minutes

# Answer Sheet For Practice Test 3

(Remove This Sheet and Use It to Mark Your Answers)

## Section I

1 Ⓐ Ⓑ Ⓒ Ⓓ Ⓔ
2 Ⓐ Ⓑ Ⓒ Ⓓ Ⓔ
3 Ⓐ Ⓑ Ⓒ Ⓓ Ⓔ
4 Ⓐ Ⓑ Ⓒ Ⓓ Ⓔ
5 Ⓐ Ⓑ Ⓒ Ⓓ Ⓔ
6 Ⓐ Ⓑ Ⓒ Ⓓ Ⓔ
7 Ⓐ Ⓑ Ⓒ Ⓓ Ⓔ
8 Ⓐ Ⓑ Ⓒ Ⓓ Ⓔ
9 Ⓐ Ⓑ Ⓒ Ⓓ Ⓔ
10 Ⓐ Ⓑ Ⓒ Ⓓ Ⓔ
11 Ⓐ Ⓑ Ⓒ Ⓓ Ⓔ
12 Ⓐ Ⓑ Ⓒ Ⓓ Ⓔ
13 Ⓐ Ⓑ Ⓒ Ⓓ Ⓔ
14 Ⓐ Ⓑ Ⓒ Ⓓ Ⓔ
15 Ⓐ Ⓑ Ⓒ Ⓓ Ⓔ
16 Ⓐ Ⓑ Ⓒ Ⓓ Ⓔ
17 Ⓐ Ⓑ Ⓒ Ⓓ Ⓔ
18 Ⓐ Ⓑ Ⓒ Ⓓ Ⓔ
19 Ⓐ Ⓑ Ⓒ Ⓓ Ⓔ
20 Ⓐ Ⓑ Ⓒ Ⓓ Ⓔ
21 Ⓐ Ⓑ Ⓒ Ⓓ Ⓔ
22 Ⓐ Ⓑ Ⓒ Ⓓ Ⓔ
23 Ⓐ Ⓑ Ⓒ Ⓓ Ⓔ
24 Ⓐ Ⓑ Ⓒ Ⓓ Ⓔ

## Section II

1 Ⓐ Ⓑ Ⓒ Ⓓ Ⓔ
2 Ⓐ Ⓑ Ⓒ Ⓓ Ⓔ
3 Ⓐ Ⓑ Ⓒ Ⓓ Ⓔ
4 Ⓐ Ⓑ Ⓒ Ⓓ Ⓔ
5 Ⓐ Ⓑ Ⓒ Ⓓ Ⓔ
6 Ⓐ Ⓑ Ⓒ Ⓓ Ⓔ
7 Ⓐ Ⓑ Ⓒ Ⓓ Ⓔ
8 Ⓐ Ⓑ Ⓒ Ⓓ Ⓔ
9 Ⓐ Ⓑ Ⓒ Ⓓ Ⓔ
10 Ⓐ Ⓑ Ⓒ Ⓓ Ⓔ
11 Ⓐ Ⓑ Ⓒ Ⓓ Ⓔ
12 Ⓐ Ⓑ Ⓒ Ⓓ Ⓔ
13 Ⓐ Ⓑ Ⓒ Ⓓ Ⓔ
14 Ⓐ Ⓑ Ⓒ Ⓓ Ⓔ
15 Ⓐ Ⓑ Ⓒ Ⓓ Ⓔ
16 Ⓐ Ⓑ Ⓒ Ⓓ Ⓔ
17 Ⓐ Ⓑ Ⓒ Ⓓ Ⓔ
18 Ⓐ Ⓑ Ⓒ Ⓓ Ⓔ
19 Ⓐ Ⓑ Ⓒ Ⓓ Ⓔ
20 Ⓐ Ⓑ Ⓒ Ⓓ Ⓔ
21 Ⓐ Ⓑ Ⓒ Ⓓ Ⓔ
22 Ⓐ Ⓑ Ⓒ Ⓓ Ⓔ
23 Ⓐ Ⓑ Ⓒ Ⓓ Ⓔ
24 Ⓐ Ⓑ Ⓒ Ⓓ Ⓔ
25 Ⓐ Ⓑ Ⓒ Ⓓ Ⓔ
26 Ⓐ Ⓑ Ⓒ Ⓓ Ⓔ
27 Ⓐ Ⓑ Ⓒ Ⓓ Ⓔ
28 Ⓐ Ⓑ Ⓒ Ⓓ Ⓔ

## Section III

1 Ⓐ Ⓑ Ⓒ Ⓓ Ⓔ
2 Ⓐ Ⓑ Ⓒ Ⓓ Ⓔ
3 Ⓐ Ⓑ Ⓒ Ⓓ Ⓔ
4 Ⓐ Ⓑ Ⓒ Ⓓ Ⓔ
5 Ⓐ Ⓑ Ⓒ Ⓓ Ⓔ
6 Ⓐ Ⓑ Ⓒ Ⓓ Ⓔ
7 Ⓐ Ⓑ Ⓒ Ⓓ Ⓔ
8 Ⓐ Ⓑ Ⓒ Ⓓ Ⓔ
9 Ⓐ Ⓑ Ⓒ Ⓓ Ⓔ
10 Ⓐ Ⓑ Ⓒ Ⓓ Ⓔ
11 Ⓐ Ⓑ Ⓒ Ⓓ Ⓔ
12 Ⓐ Ⓑ Ⓒ Ⓓ Ⓔ
13 Ⓐ Ⓑ Ⓒ Ⓓ Ⓔ
14 Ⓐ Ⓑ Ⓒ Ⓓ Ⓔ
15 Ⓐ Ⓑ Ⓒ Ⓓ Ⓔ
16 Ⓐ Ⓑ Ⓒ Ⓓ Ⓔ
17 Ⓐ Ⓑ Ⓒ Ⓓ Ⓔ
18 Ⓐ Ⓑ Ⓒ Ⓓ Ⓔ
19 Ⓐ Ⓑ Ⓒ Ⓓ Ⓔ
20 Ⓐ Ⓑ Ⓒ Ⓓ Ⓔ
21 Ⓐ Ⓑ Ⓒ Ⓓ Ⓔ
22 Ⓐ Ⓑ Ⓒ Ⓓ Ⓔ
23 Ⓐ Ⓑ Ⓒ Ⓓ Ⓔ
24 Ⓐ Ⓑ Ⓒ Ⓓ Ⓔ
25 Ⓐ Ⓑ Ⓒ Ⓓ Ⓔ
26 Ⓐ Ⓑ Ⓒ Ⓓ Ⓔ

CUT HERE

## Section IV

1 Ⓐ Ⓑ Ⓒ Ⓓ Ⓔ
2 Ⓐ Ⓑ Ⓒ Ⓓ Ⓔ
3 Ⓐ Ⓑ Ⓒ Ⓓ Ⓔ
4 Ⓐ Ⓑ Ⓒ Ⓓ Ⓔ
5 Ⓐ Ⓑ Ⓒ Ⓓ Ⓔ
6 Ⓐ Ⓑ Ⓒ Ⓓ Ⓔ
7 Ⓐ Ⓑ Ⓒ Ⓓ Ⓔ
8 Ⓐ Ⓑ Ⓒ Ⓓ Ⓔ
9 Ⓐ Ⓑ Ⓒ Ⓓ Ⓔ
10 Ⓐ Ⓑ Ⓒ Ⓓ Ⓔ
11 Ⓐ Ⓑ Ⓒ Ⓓ Ⓔ
12 Ⓐ Ⓑ Ⓒ Ⓓ Ⓔ
13 Ⓐ Ⓑ Ⓒ Ⓓ Ⓔ
14 Ⓐ Ⓑ Ⓒ Ⓓ Ⓔ
15 Ⓐ Ⓑ Ⓒ Ⓓ Ⓔ
16 Ⓐ Ⓑ Ⓒ Ⓓ Ⓔ
17 Ⓐ Ⓑ Ⓒ Ⓓ Ⓔ
18 Ⓐ Ⓑ Ⓒ Ⓓ Ⓔ
19 Ⓐ Ⓑ Ⓒ Ⓓ Ⓔ
20 Ⓐ Ⓑ Ⓒ Ⓓ Ⓔ
21 Ⓐ Ⓑ Ⓒ Ⓓ Ⓔ
22 Ⓐ Ⓑ Ⓒ Ⓓ Ⓔ
23 Ⓐ Ⓑ Ⓒ Ⓓ Ⓔ
24 Ⓐ Ⓑ Ⓒ Ⓓ Ⓔ

## Section V

1 Ⓐ Ⓑ Ⓒ Ⓓ Ⓔ
2 Ⓐ Ⓑ Ⓒ Ⓓ Ⓔ
3 Ⓐ Ⓑ Ⓒ Ⓓ Ⓔ
4 Ⓐ Ⓑ Ⓒ Ⓓ Ⓔ
5 Ⓐ Ⓑ Ⓒ Ⓓ Ⓔ
6 Ⓐ Ⓑ Ⓒ Ⓓ Ⓔ
7 Ⓐ Ⓑ Ⓒ Ⓓ Ⓔ
8 Ⓐ Ⓑ Ⓒ Ⓓ Ⓔ
9 Ⓐ Ⓑ Ⓒ Ⓓ Ⓔ
10 Ⓐ Ⓑ Ⓒ Ⓓ Ⓔ
11 Ⓐ Ⓑ Ⓒ Ⓓ Ⓔ
12 Ⓐ Ⓑ Ⓒ Ⓓ Ⓔ
13 Ⓐ Ⓑ Ⓒ Ⓓ Ⓔ
14 Ⓐ Ⓑ Ⓒ Ⓓ Ⓔ
15 Ⓐ Ⓑ Ⓒ Ⓓ Ⓔ
16 Ⓐ Ⓑ Ⓒ Ⓓ Ⓔ
17 Ⓐ Ⓑ Ⓒ Ⓓ Ⓔ
18 Ⓐ Ⓑ Ⓒ Ⓓ Ⓔ
19 Ⓐ Ⓑ Ⓒ Ⓓ Ⓔ
20 Ⓐ Ⓑ Ⓒ Ⓓ Ⓔ
21 Ⓐ Ⓑ Ⓒ Ⓓ Ⓔ
22 Ⓐ Ⓑ Ⓒ Ⓓ Ⓔ
23 Ⓐ Ⓑ Ⓒ Ⓓ Ⓔ
24 Ⓐ Ⓑ Ⓒ Ⓓ Ⓔ
25 Ⓐ Ⓑ Ⓒ Ⓓ Ⓔ
26 Ⓐ Ⓑ Ⓒ Ⓓ Ⓔ
27 Ⓐ Ⓑ Ⓒ Ⓓ Ⓔ

# Section I: Logical Reasoning

Time: 35 Minutes

24 Questions

**Directions:** You will be presented with brief passages or statements and will be required to evaluate their reasoning. In each case, select the best answer choice, even though more than one choice may present a possible answer. Choices that are unreasonable or incompatible with common-sense standards should be eliminated.

*Questions 1 and 2 are based on the following passage.*

The new vehicle inspection program is needed to protect the quality of the state's air, for us and for our children. Auto exhausts are a leading contributor to coughing, wheezing, choking, and pollution. The state's long-term interests in the health of its citizens and in this area as a place to live, work, and conduct business depend on clean air.

1. Which of the following, if true, would most <u>seriously</u> weaken the argument above?

   A. Since smog devices were made mandatory automotive equipment by the existing inspection program three years ago, pollution has decreased dramatically and continues to decrease.

   B. Pollution problems are increasing in other states as well as in this one.

   C. Sometimes, coughing, wheezing, and choking are caused by phenomena other than pollution.

   D. Vehicle inspectors are not always careful.

   E. The state should not impose its interests upon the citizenry but should instead allow public health to be regulated by private enterprise.

2. Which of the following is an unstated assumption made by the author?

   A. Working and conducting business may be different activities.

   B. The state has been interested in the health of its citizens even before this inspection program was proposed.

   C. Exhaust emissions contribute to pollution.

   D. The new inspection program will be effective.

   E. Our ancestors did not suffer from air pollution.

GO ON TO THE NEXT PAGE

**3.** Dietician: We doubt that the latest government report will scare Americans away from ham, bacon, sausages, hot dogs, bologna, and salami or that it will empty out the bars or cause a run on natural food supplies. If a diet were to be mandated from Washington, Americans probably would order the exact opposite course. Therefore, the diet that does make sense is to eat a balanced and varied diet composed of foods from all food groups and containing a reasonable calorie intake.

Which of the following is more directly implied by the passage above?

**A.** Vitamins and exercise are necessary to combat disease.

**B.** A government report warned of the risks of meat and alcoholic beverages.

**C.** A recent report made unorthodox suggestions for a more nutritional diet.

**D.** Eating a balanced and varied diet will not prevent disease.

**E.** Washington should not mandate any particular diet because individuals vary in their nutritional needs.

**4.** In his first message to Congress, Harry Truman said, "The responsibility of the United States is to serve and not dominate the world."

Which of the following is one basic assumption underlying Truman's statement?

**A.** The United States is capable of dominating the world.

**B.** The United States chooses to serve rather than dominate the world.

**C.** World domination is a virtue.

**D.** One must be decisive when facing a legislative body for the first time.

**E.** The United States, preceding Truman's administration, had been irresponsible.

**5.** Without sign ordinances, everyone with the price of a can of spray paint can suddenly decide to publicly create their own personal Picassos, and soon the entire town would start to look like something out of *Alice in Wonderland*. Therefore, we need sign ordinances.

All of the following are assumptions underlying the argument in the passage EXCEPT:

**A.** Spray paint can be used to create graffiti.

**B.** The town looking like *Alice in Wonderland* is undesirable.

**C.** Sign ordinances are effective.

**D.** No other effective means of deterring graffiti presently exist.

**E.** Sign ordinances are rarely if ever effective.

**6.** Speaker: One need not look very far to find abundant examples of incivility and brutality in the most genteel corners of American society.

Questioner: Then why don't we step up law enforcement in the slums of our cities?

The question reveals which of the following misunderstandings?

A. The misunderstanding that incivility and brutality have become more abundant

B. The misunderstanding that law enforcement is related to the problems of incivility and brutality

C. Misunderstanding of the speaker's position relative to incivility and brutality

D. Misunderstanding of the meaning of the word *genteel*

E. Misunderstanding of the meaning of the words *incivility* and *brutality*

7. Experience shows that for every burglar shot by a homeowner, there are many more fatal accidents involving small children, family slayings that could have been avoided but for the handy presence of a gun, and thefts of handguns by the criminals they are intended to protect against.

Which of the following facts, if true, would most seriously weaken the above contention?

A. Criminals tend to sell the handguns they steal during the commission of a burglary.

B. Burglars are also capable of causing fatal accidents.

C. Every burglar shot by a homeowner is stopped from committing scores of further burglaries and injuring scores of other citizens.

D. The number of burglars shot by homeowners is larger than the number of burglars shot by renters.

E. Not all fatal accidents involve guns.

*Questions 8 and 9 are based on the following passage.*

Voters on June 8 approved a $495 million bond issue for a state prison construction that is an obvious priority. Now, the legislature has voted to put five more general obligation bond issues on the November ballot, adding another $1.5 billion to the state's long-term debt. Those on the November menu include $500 million for building and remodeling public schools, $450 million to extend the veterans' home loan program, $200 million to subsidize low-interest mortgages for first-time home buyers, $85 million to acquire land for environmental protection, and $280 million to help counties expand or remodel their jails.

8. Which of the following statements is a point to which the author is most probably leading?

A. Two of these bond issues are certainly more important than the others.

B. We must face the obvious conclusion that prison construction is much less important than the improvement of public education and social programs for lawful citizens.

C. The cost of these bond issues is, on the face of it, negligible.

D. The voters cannot be expected to help make financial decisions for the state because most voters are suffering from their own severe financial problems.

E. These five bond proposals are quite enough, and between now and November, voters will have to study them carefully to make sure that five are not too many.

GO ON TO THE NEXT PAGE

9. Which of the following facts would most strongly weaken an argument for approval of the five new bond issues?

   A. Environmental protection is not an overriding concern of the constituency.

   B. The state's long-term debt cannot lawfully exceed $1.5 billion.

   C. Improvements in education, the environment, criminal prosecution, and the real estate market are favored by the voters.

   D. Similar bond proposals in other states have not been successful.

   E. Two bills related to the housing of criminals are quite enough.

10. Famous painter James Whistler said, "Industry in art is necessity—not a virtue—and any evidence of the same, in the production, is a blemish, not a quality."

    Whistler is arguing that

    A. of necessity, art becomes industrialized.

    B. the qualities of art are its virtues.

    C. blemished paintings are the work of overindustrious artists.

    D. the product reflects the means of production.

    E. the artist must work hard, but the art should look easy.

11. Deliberations of our governing bodies are held in public in order to allow public scrutiny of each body's actions and take to task those actions which citizens feel are not, for whatever reason, in their best interests.

    With which of the following statements would the author of the above passage probably agree?

    A. Deliberations of our governing bodies should be held in public.

    B. Public scrutiny usually results in the criticism of our governing bodies.

    C. The best interests of the public usually do not coincide with the motives of our governing bodies.

    D. No government decisions ought to be kept from the public.

    E. Citizens in other countries are not cared for by the government.

*Questions 12 and 13 are based on the following passage.*

Recent studies indicate that more violent crimes are committed during hot weather than during cold weather. Thus, if we could control the weather, the violent crime rate would drop.

12. Which of the following is an assumption necessary for the reasoning in the passage above to be valid?

    A. There is no relationship between weather conditions and crime rate.

    B. The relationship between weather conditions and crime rate is not controllable.

C. The relationship between weather conditions and crime rate is coincidental.

D. The relationship between weather conditions and crime rate is controllable.

E. The relationship between weather conditions and crime rate is causal.

13. The argument would be strengthened if it pointed out that

A. the annual crime statistics for New York are higher than those for Los Angeles.

B. in laboratory tests, increased heat alone accounted for increased aggressive behavior between members of the test group.

C. poor socioeconomic conditions, more uncomfortable in hot weather than in cold, are the direct causes of increased crime.

D. weather control will be possible in the near future.

E. more people leave their doors and windows open during hot weather.

14. The state's empty $4 million governor's mansion on the banks of the Capitol River may be sort of a suburban Taj Mahal, as the governor once said. But why shouldn't the state unload it?

Which of the following is one of the author's basic assumptions?

A. The governor's mansion is out of place in the suburbs.

B. The reader is aware of the state's intention to "unload" the governor's mansion.

C. No one has yet lived in the governor's mansion.

D. The state is trying to sell the governor's mansion.

E. The governor was correct.

15. All triangles are two-dimensional.

All squares are two-dimensional.

All triangles are squares.

This logic would be valid if

A. only squares are two-dimensional.

B. only triangles are two-dimensional.

C. some triangles are two-dimensional.

D. some squares are two-dimensional.

E. some squares are three-dimensional.

*Questions 16 and 17 are based on the following passage.*

There was a time, not so long ago, when major public figures in the United States were glad to merely have the opportunity to speak before prestigious national organizations such as the American Bar Association. In that time, expenses might or might not have been reimbursed, and if an honorarium was offered, many public figures would ask that it be given to a charity.

**16.** The above passage most logically precedes which of the following statements?

  **A.** Now public officials can command five-figure fees for speaking.

  **B.** Now honoraria are rarely offered, and speakers often appear for no compensation.

  **C.** The American Bar Association has been involved in various controversies over the years.

  **D.** There was also a time, very long ago, when national organizations had no use for public speakers.

  **E.** Some charities manage their money well, while others do not.

**17.** Which of the following, if true, would most seriously weaken the author's implied point in the above statement?

  **A.** Charities rarely receive the honoraria offered to speakers.

  **B.** Prestigious national organizations have decreased sharply in number since 1975.

  **C.** Present economic problems make it impossible for many national organizations to reimburse their speakers.

  **D.** Very few public figures request compensation for their speeches these days.

  **E.** Today, charities request money from public figures rather than waiting until it is offered.

**18.** It is never easy to draw a line between what ought to be mandated by law and what should remain optional in public safety, including the way automobiles are designed and the way they are driven. The issue of over-regulation in our society often turns on deciding where common sense leaves off and the law should step in.

The statement above follows logically from which of the following statements?

  **A.** Historically, parents have lacked sufficient concern for the safety of small children in automobiles and have resisted legislative efforts to mandate the use of special "kiddie seats."

  **B.** Those who manufacture and market car seats for small children strongly supported legislation that would make the use of such seats mandatory.

  **C.** Common sense tells most American parents that the chances for an auto accident to occur are slim and that their children are relatively safe most of the time.

  **D.** Parents were taking an increasing interest in protective car seats for their small children at the same time that Congress was considering a bill mandating a special "kiddie seat" restraint for children.

  **E.** Because automobiles are private property, the government has no right to regulate their design or use.

*Questions 19 and 20 are based on the following passage.*

We have nothing to fear but fear itself? Nonsense. Even the bravest of us may become terrified in the face of any number of gravely threatening situations.

19. To accept this author's argument, we must agree that becoming afraid is

A. an occasional trait of the fearless.

B. fearful.

C. a common and acceptable human quality.

D. nonsense.

E. allowable only in gravely threatening situations.

20. The author's argument might be weakened by pointing out that

A. a less fearful attitude may minimize the threat of a situation.

B. fear promotes more accurate responses to threatening situations.

C. any blanket generalization is highly vulnerable to criticism.

D. who we fear is more important than what we fear.

E. brave people often admit that they have been afraid.

21. When Louis Pasteur said, "Chance favors the prepared mind," the famous French scientist most nearly meant

A. take a chance only if you're prepared.

B. pasteurization was a chance that Pasteur prepared for.

C. being prepared will be favorable to those who take chances.

D. happenstance will be more beneficial to those who are prepared.

E. we all have a chance to be prepared.

22. Which of the following most logically completes the passage at the blank below?

Filmmakers tend to highlight their emotional points with visuals, rather than dialogue. Words tend to be the tools of playwrights. Images are the stuff that films are made of. Nevertheless, many successful films have been made from stage plays and contain little else than one location or one stage set. It would seem, then, that films _____.

A. are not necessarily a filmmaker's medium

B. are not limited to any one particular style

C. are solely built upon visual and eye-catching scenes

D. are better made by playwrights and novelists

E. perhaps are better understood by literary critics

GO ON TO THE NEXT PAGE

**23.** It really isn't necessary to eat a balanced diet of meat, breads, vegetables, and dairy products. After all, with the wide variety of vitamin/mineral supplements on the market today, one can simply eat the foods one likes the most and take the supplements to balance one's diet and provide the missing nutrients.

Which of the following supports the conclusion in the passage above.

**A.** Excess vitamin intake can lead to many health problems that can range from minor infections to serious diseases.

**B.** The four food groups—meats, dairy products, breads, and vegetables—are essential to maintaining a nutritional diet and a healthy body.

**C.** Studies have shown that three meals a day and the proper proportions of the four food groups are required in order to insure a strong immune system resistant to diseases.

**D.** Of the four food groups, each one provides certain nutrients that when combined help to build a strong, healthy body.

**E.** In order to maintain a healthy diet, only the vitamins and minerals derived from foods are required; other elements are not necessary.

**24.** A variety of portable camcorders are now available that reproduce lifelike video and audio for playback on home televisions. Tapes used by these camcorders are available on two formats: VHS-C and Hi8mm. VHS-C tapes can be played in standard VHS video recorders through the use of an included adapter, but Hi8mm tapes require purchasing cables and installing them. The Hi8mm camcorders produce higher quality images than VHS-C. Therefore, sales of the VHS-C are likely to be considerably greater than those of the Hi8mm format.

The argument above logically depends on which of the following assumptions?

**A.** VHS-C camcorders are superior to Hi8mm camcorders in all respects, providing excellent overall performance.

**B.** Due to their easy portability and capacity for reproducing pictures and sound, VHS-C camcorders are an ideal choice for people who wish to capture those once-in-a-lifetime moments.

**C.** The cost and inconvenience of additional cables required for playback by the Hi8mm format outweighs the customer's desire for picture clarity.

**D.** In recent years, manufacturers have reduced both the size and the weight of VHS-C and Hi8mm camcorders, making them handheld marvels weighing a little over a pound.

**E.** Both Hi8mm and VHS-C camcorders are widely available in most electronics and department stores.

IF YOU FINISH BEFORE TIME IS CALLED, CHECK YOUR WORK ON THIS SECTION ONLY. DO NOT WORK ON ANY OTHER SECTION IN THE TEST.

# Section II: Reading Comprehension

**Time: 35 Minutes**

**28 Questions**

**Directions:** Each passage in this group is followed by questions based on its content. After reading a passage, choose the best answer to each question and blacken the corresponding space on the answer sheet. Answer all questions following a passage on the basis of what is *stated* or *implied* in that passage. You may refer back to the passage.

*Questions 1 through 7 are based on the following passage.*

Masses of newcomers convert to new religions. The upsurgence of nontraditional religious sects may actually be a comment on the current social climate.
(5) Few would doubt the lost prominence of traditional religious values. Sex is more acceptable, drugs are more understandable, and greed is a part of life. In contrast, many of the new religious sects
(10) strictly regulate sex, alcohol, drugs, and money. For some, joining may be considered novel rebellion, for it acts as a nonsecular experience and isolates the member from a sinfully oriented society.
(15) Within this view, the newcomers are saved from degradation within the permissive, immoral environment.

Another reason for the mass conversions lies in the need for community.
(20) Urban society consists of a pattern of temporary associations. Instead of homogeneous neighborhoods, communities are diverse and ever changing, and close interpersonal contact is missing.
(25) With the rising divorce rate, even the traditional family support structure is eroding, thereby reducing family cohesion. Many individual children sense an unfulfilled need for dependable relation-
(30) ships characterized by deep affection. It is understandable why a warm,

communal, religious sect attracts converts. The sect acts as a surrogate family distinctively noting close bonds of com-
(35) panionship. With the strict rules on sex, alcohol, drugs, and money, the members know what to expect in this tightly knit group. The instable characteristics of the larger society no longer exist, and in-
(40) stead, the members experience an assured community relationship. This stability gives certainty to life and fills the communal void.

Still, another reason for the mass con-
(45) version is that some converts may be residual members of the 1960s counterculture. Out of the political ferment of the prior era, a new consciousness developed. Success was no longer defined to
(50) these counterculture members in monetary terms. Peace, harmony, and societal associations were key elements, and the members were content with their status. After the Vietnam War, the movement
(55) lost its momentum as the former flower children entered the social mainstream. For those remaining in the counterculture, anomie developed. The stability of their social environment was dying, and
(60) those who would not accept traditional norms sought refuge within religious sects. In these settings, no pressure existed to enter the greater society. The conversion process, although considered
(65) brainwashing by many, was a welcome

GO ON TO THE NEXT PAGE

relief to these members. For them, a lost counterculture was reborn in a new form, and once again, peace, harmony, and societal association existed in its (70) purest state.

One such religious association is the Unification Church. This church claims up to two million members worldwide, with its headquarters in Tarrytown, New (75) York. Under the direction of Reverend Sun Myung Moon, the church has attained remarkable growth in its relatively brief existence, but it has mainly been the center of controversy as many (80) view the followers as merely brainwashed victims.

The membership is predominantly white, young, and unmarried, with almost half attending school immediately (85) prior to joining but few continuing thereafter. A sizeable proportion has a prior history of emotional problems and drug abuse. This obvious disequilibration in many members' subjective state (90) may make them less resistant to conversion. Nevertheless, research indicates a direct relationship between the religious experience and significant psychological improvement. A reported reduction (95) in neurotic distress and in the overall suicide risks certainly suggests a stabilizing in psychological status. Logically, the conversion to strict religious rules reduces autonomy by lowering the (100) decision-making process. For those with a prior history of anxiety, the acceptance of the church's guidance diminishes frustrations as the church makes all significant decisions. The member loves (105) the church. It can do no wrong, and as with medieval faith, a trust element reduces worry and makes the member thankful to be saved. By analogy, psychotherapy ameliorates the problem (110) though the treatment may be difficult. Likewise, the conversion may be disruptive, but psychological improvements do occur as the member experiences greater satisfaction with life. Although the over-(115) all well-being may be significantly below the population as a whole, the church members have still made remarkable improvements by relieving prior internal turmoil.

(120) These results are difficult to accept. Parents, for example, are caught between their allegiance to society and their children's repudiation of it. It is hard to believe church members vol-(125) untarily selected "deviant" lifestyles. Consequently, the conversion process is viewed by many in brainwashing terminology.

1. According to the author, religious conversion may serve to accomplish all of the following EXCEPT:

   A. reducing anxiety and worry.

   B. relieving internal turmoil.

   C. diminishing tendencies toward suicide.

   D. increasing personal autonomy.

   E. enhancing trust in institutions.

2. The author of the passage considers mass conversion to new religions in large part as

   A. a current but soon-to-be-reversed social trend.

   B. a response to deteriorating community values.

   C. a deprogramming of coercive ideology.

   D. an involuntary surrendering of intellectual freedom.

   E. salvation from immoral degradation.

3. The author of the passage makes which of the following assumptions?

   A. The divorce rate will likely continue to climb.

   B. The values of the 1960s counterculture were doomed to fail.

   C. Consistent expectations are an important psychological requisite.

   D. Psychological equilibrium enhances an individual's tendency to conversion.

   E. Deviant behavior is unacceptable to all members of society.

4. According to the passage, the author suggests that after the early 1970s, former flower children

   A. more vociferously repudiated mainstream values.

   B. dissolved their associations with religious sects.

   C. questioned the brainwashing of religious sects.

   D. manifested no change in neurotic distress.

   E. became more socially alienated.

5. With which of the following statements about voluntary conversion would the author of the passage most probably agree?

   A. No one would ever voluntarily surrender intellectual freedom and flexibility to follow strict religious beliefs.

   B. Those who submit to religious regimentation must have been coercively persuaded to do so.

   C. People have been voluntarily joining totalistic movements for centuries.

   D. Nontraditional religions prey on unsuspecting individuals to maintain their memberships.

   E. Emotional equilibrium increases voluntary conversion to nontraditional religious sects.

6. Which of the following would be the most appropriate title for this passage?

   A. The Function of Conversion

   B. Brainwashing and Society

   C. Conversion: A Cause for Psychological Instability

   D. Involuntary Conversion

   E. Flower Children and the Counterculture

7. The primary purpose of the passage is to

   A. expose the untoward and dangerous results of conversion.

   B. indicate outrage at the number of unwitting victims of mass conversion.

   C. argue that involuntary conversion should be registered.

   D. increase public awareness of deceptive conversion activities.

   E. present possible causes for recent mass conversion.

Section II Reading Comprehension

GO ON TO THE NEXT PAGE

*Questions 8 through 14 are based on the following passage.*

The imposition of rent control to reg-ulate rapidly rising rents has met with a great deal of controversy. Proponents ar-gue that rent is an inflexible cost. As
(5) such, if rents increase substantially, es-pecially over the short term, the tenant must either pay the increase or move. If housing shortages exist, the tenant has no alternative but to pay the higher rent.
(10) Families are forced to restructure their budgetary priorities, thereby postponing the purchase of anything but essential consumer goods and services. Family diets and appropriate medical care may
(15) be adversely affected. Because of the strong social approval associated with adequate housing, the government has from time to time attempted to regulate its cost through rent control.
(20) The economy is presently character-ized by deep-seated and chronic prob-lems. One consequence of this economic hardship is that fewer and fewer families are able to afford home ownership.
(25) Accordingly, renting is no longer consid-ered a short-term, temporary housing situation. Under these circumstances, proponents of rent regulation contend that rent ceilings are required as a means
(30) of long-term financial relief in the face of this economic burden. This rationale must, of course, be reconciled with the fact that rent control has traditionally been imposed as a short-term measure
(35) in response to an emergency housing shortage.

Although rent-control controversy has primarily focused on opposition between tenants and landlords, other
(40) conflicts have arisen that deserve con-sideration. If it can be demonstrated that rent control tends to reduce apartment construction, it becomes a conflict be-tween present renters and future renters.

(45) To the extent that rent control encour-ages the conversion of apartments to condominiums, it also represents a con-flict between renters and potential home buyers.
(50) The purpose of almost all rent-control ordinances is to protect tenants from in-ordinate rent increases in a time of a limited rental housing stock. If the rent-control community has little available
(55) land for further development, a rent-control ordinance with moderate fea-tures can be justified on a long-term basis. In this situation, rent control can be further justified because the loss of
(60) consumer's surplus is minimized. On the other hand, if the community wishes to stem the tide of rising rents while at the same time provide investors with in-centives to construct much needed
(65) apartment units, the justification for rent control on even a long-term basis cannot be easily made. The elastic supply curve for rental housing implies that rent con-trol would produce a tremendous soci-
(70) etal loss in terms of consumer's surplus. Moreover, even a slightly restrictive or-dinance may well serve to negate the purpose of maintaining investment in-centives. Short-term rent control cannot
(75) be recommended under any circum-stances simply because it has the effect of any temporary price freeze. Specifically, it creates a pent-up desire on the part of landlords to raise rents ex-
(80) orbitantly after decontrol takes place. Also, rent control ordinances with highly restrictive features cannot be justified.

There is no question that rent control
(85) is an interference in the free market. Such interference, however, has been justified in the societal interest for a wide spectrum of publicly provided goods and services. Local decision mak-
(90) ers and legislative bodies in a growing number of communities have begun to

view rent control as a necessary compo-
nent of housing and land-use policy.
Long-term, moderate rent control can be
(95) justified in communities where construction is not taking place as a result of
physical and/or policy constraints. The
decision by a locality to impose rent
control should be based upon a critical
(100) examination of many complex and inter-
active variables. It is incumbent on the
judiciary to require such an examination
and to realize that rent control in one
community may be appropriate while
(105) being inappropriate in another. The
courts should be flexible in this regard
and not use narrow grounds upon which
to rule on the validity of a quite significant public policy issue. As a single
(110) measure of validity, the housing emergency and associated vacancy rate are
limiting and archaic. In an era of growth
controls, conservation of scarce resources, and high inflation, rent control
(115) can be an appropriate and necessary policy choice.

**8.** Which of the following best describes
the position of the author of this
passage on the imposing of rent
control?

   **A.** Rent control unjustly violates the
property rights of property owners.

   **B.** Short-term rent control should be
imposed after careful study of the
economic situation.

   **C.** Long-term rent control can
frequently be justified.

   **D.** Rent is an inflexible cost.

   **E.** Rent-control disincentives must be
equaled by other investment
incentives.

**9.** According to the passage, the rent-
control issue may logically be regarded
as a conflict between all of the
following EXCEPT:

   **A.** tenants and landlords.

   **B.** present renters and future renters.

   **C.** renters and potential home buyers.

   **D.** new apartment construction and
conversion to condominiums.

   **E.** long-term solutions and short-term
tax credits.

**10.** The purpose of most rent-control
ordinances is to

   **A.** encourage housing construction.

   **B.** prevent unfair rent increases.

   **C.** encourage home buying rather than
renting.

   **D.** prevent landlord profits.

   **E.** terminate a shortage of rental
housing.

**11.** Supporters of the case for rent control
are likely to use all of the following
arguments EXCEPT:

   **A.** Rent control encourages the rate of
conversion of rental property to
condominiums.

   **B.** Many landlords are greedy for high
profits.

   **C.** The burden of large rent increases
falls most heavily on those with
low incomes.

GO ON TO THE NEXT PAGE

**D.** Without controls, a tenant who cannot pay increased rent must pay moving costs.

**E.** Rents are more likely to rise when rental properties are in short supply and renters are abundant.

**12.** Rent control will probably be unnecessary at a time of

**A.** high unemployment.

**B.** an oversupply of renters.

**C.** an oversupply of rental housing.

**D.** declining stock prices.

**E.** high single-unit home construction.

**13.** Under which of the following situations would the author of the passage be most likely to support rent control?

**A.** A community eager to encourage new housing construction

**B.** A community eager to encourage its population growth

**C.** A community with no additional land for new rental housing

**D.** A community with many vacancies in rental housing

**E.** A community with a decreasing population of renters

**14.** Opponents of rent control are likely to use all of the following arguments EXCEPT:

**A.** Rent control is an interference in the market.

**B.** Decontrol is usually followed by much higher rents.

**C.** Rent control depresses the construction of new rental housing.

**D.** In cities with little available building land, rent control minimizes the loss of consumer's surplus.

**E.** Rent control deprives an owner of the free use of his or her property.

*Questions 15 through 21 are based on the following passage.*

By now, the dangers to our lives and health because of exposure to radioactive elements are a matter of common knowledge. The events at nuclear facili-
(5) ties around the country, especially Three Mile Island, have virtually destroyed the myth of the failsafe attributes of nuclear power plants that had been indoctrinated into trusting Americans by the Nuclear
(10) Regulatory Commission.

The logical query becomes one of why the federal government insists on implementing this clear and present danger by allowing an ineffective federal
(15) agency to be the last word on the issue of maintenance and operation of nuclear generating plants. Further, why does the federal government refuse to allow a state to preserve and promote the wel-
(20) fare of the people of that state by virtue of reasonable and prudent legislation?

In response to the first query, the federal government would probably state that the Nuclear Regulatory
(25) Commission is not ineffective. However, the Three Mile Island accident has brought to the public forum information that shows federal standards of management, inspection, maintenance, and
(30) safety to be woefully inadequate. Indeed a recent report indicates that only 1%–5% of safety related activities are inspected by the NRC and that inspectors can never be sure if and when an in-
(35) stallation is safe. In fact, the NRC has recently withdrawn its support for its

own sweeping study completed in 1975, which had indicated that plants were safe and that the chances of an accident
(40) were a million to one.

In addition, the NRC had dismissed the possibility of an accident at a nuclear plant; therefore, they had no require-ment for protection against the conse-
(45) quences of such an accident.

Taking into consideration the lack of federal standards, the lack of protections against the possibility of a nuclear disas-ter, and the lack of a demonstrated tech-
(50) nology for nuclear waste disposal, one may reasonably conclude that ineffec-tive is a euphemism when describing the NRC.

In response to the second query, it
(55) must be noted that the courts have held that the preemption in this area was not expressed in the Atomic Energy Act, but rather has been found by implication. Granted, preemption may rightfully be
(60) found by implication. The argument for not finding preemption, however, be-comes more credible when the preemp-tion is not found to have been expressed by Congress, ergo raising genuine tri-
(65) able issues.

Clearly, we are faced with a dilemma, the states' serious concern for human lives as opposed to the federal govern-ment's dogmatic development of the nu-
(70) clear industry.

Perhaps a reasonable solution to this conundrum is for the courts in the future to keep in mind that the foremost issue is survival of the human species.
(75) Perhaps the courts should recall that the original drafters of the Constitution prefaced that document with a pream-ble, which articulates the concern for the general welfare of all the citizens, and
(80) that the Constitution was drafted to in-sure that the general welfare would be promoted and preserved, not to threaten life and health.

15. The author's argument in the passage reflects

A. an enumeration of the dangers to life and health by the unsafe operation of nuclear generating plants.

B. a balanced approach to the consideration of federal standards for nuclear generating plants.

C. a lack of tolerance for the courts' inability to enforce nuclear safety regulations.

D. a strong criticism of the federal government in its efforts to maintain safe nuclear power plants.

E. the idea that safety standards ought to be controlled by state rather than federal agencies.

16. The phrase "federal agency" in lines 14–15 refers to

A. the Atomic Energy Commission.

B. the central branch of government.

C. Washington D.C.

D. the Nuclear Regulatory Commission.

E. Three Mile Island.

17. The author assumes all of the following about nuclear power plants EXCEPT:

A. At one time, they were considered by American citizens to be safe.

B. They cannot be managed by government agencies so that the health and safety of citizens are protected.

GO ON TO THE NEXT PAGE

C. They are not as carefully inspected by federal agencies as they ought to be.

D. Formerly there were no requirements for protection against an accident at nuclear power sites.

E. A technology for effective nuclear waste disposal has yet to be developed.

18. With which of the following statements is the author of the passage most likely to agree?

A. A major cause of the deterioration of our nation's air and water is the negligence of the Environmental Protection Agency, a federal regulatory body.

B. The space shuttle disaster could have been avoided by a more thorough investigation of the private agencies providing equipment and expertise.

C. Annual deficits of the United States Postal Service are best attributed to the rising cost of transportation.

D. Residents of Three Mile Island ought to petition the federal government for more federal safety regulations.

E. A nuclear disaster can best be avoided by maintaining the current level of inspection and management.

19. The author suggests that when the federal government places a priority upon the development of nuclear industry, it fails to do which of the following?

A. Preempt the rights of the states to protect their citizenry

B. Determine whether nuclear power will in fact be an effective means of providing energy

C. Acknowledge a demonstrated technology for nuclear waste disposal

D. Concern itself with an important goal addressed by the nation's founding fathers

E. Solve the dilemma between states' rights and federal power

20. The author argues that the federal government

A. consistently required protection against a nuclear accident.

B. failed to complete a study indicating that power plants are safe.

C. neglected to provide a means for safe disposal of nuclear waste.

D. effectively maintained and operated all nuclear plants.

E. instituted rigorous nuclear inspection-training programs.

**21.** Which of the following can be inferred from the information about preemption and the courts?

    **A.** Any argument for preemption must be based upon implied, rather than stated, directives.

    **B.** Due to preemption issues, Congress will rescind the Atomic Energy Act.

    **C.** The courts may not hold preemption in the area of nuclear power.

    **D.** Preemption is not rightfully expressed by Congress, except in extraordinary circumstances.

    **E.** Preemption is not an issue whose resolution is to be determined in any way by the courts.

*Questions 22 through 28 are based on the following passage.*

The term *euthanasia* is derived from the Greek word meaning a "good, or peaceful, death." Like abortion, euthanasia has received ever-increasing support,
(5) particularly during the last two decades, and its proponents demand profound changes in our individual, social, and moral attitudes toward death.

As a framework for the discussion of
(10) euthanasia in social education, it should be emphasized that two contemporary developments have resulted in forcing the subject of euthanasia to the forefront of social morality and ethics in modern
(15) societies. First, advanced technology has reached the level whereby the medical profession possesses a much wider range of choices between life and death. Second is the ever-increasing demands
(20) of the individual to maintain and exercise his rights over matters affecting his mental health, physical health, and his right to live or die.

With regard to the former, in techno-
(25) logically advanced societies, mere biological existence can be prolonged indefinitely by new drugs, and by artificial life support mechanisms. Sophisticated apparatus, new drugs, and
(30) the artificial transplantation of vital organs can give a new lease on life to persons who, in many instances, would rather die. From the standpoint of human rights, the depressing evidence con-
(35) cerning needless human suffering continues to prompt the idea that people, like animals, have the legal and moral right to a merciful death, or euthanasia.

Like abortion, the concept of legaliz-
(40) ing the right to a merciful death has raised many significant moral, social, legal, and medical questions. The proposals to legalize voluntary euthanasia, under stringent conditions, have resulted
(45) in considerable criticism from organized Christianity. This is not surprising, since the sacredness of human life and personality is a fundamental tenet of the Christian faith. A basic concept for stu-
(50) dent awareness is that much of the criticism of euthanasia from organized religion, as well as other segments of the society, involves both the relativity of the term and the negative precedent
(55) that legalized euthanasia could set for humanity.

Euthanasia, or mercy killing, is an idea that conjures up nearly as much fear as death itself among many. Indeed,
(60) it is one thing to translate the Greek word into "the good death"; it is another to be specific about such a benign term. Such questions arise as: Is it something you do to yourself: suicide? Is it
(65) something that others do to you: murder? Could it be used as an excuse for genocide: the mass killing of the innocent, young or old, who happen to be a

GO ON TO THE NEXT PAGE

(70) "political," "economic," or "racial" bur-den on a particular society? The racial theories and mass extermination prac-tices of the Nazi period in Germany con-tinue to haunt the Western world and reinforce the fear of any legislation that (75) could result in a repetition of this tragic era in contemporary history.

In its literal connotation, euthanasia, in the voluntary sense, reflects none of these social tragedies. Its legal and moral (80) interpretation means that any individual who is incurably sick or miserably se-nile, whose condition is hopeless, and who desires to die, should be enabled to do so; and that he should be enabled to (85) do so without his incurring, or his family incurring, or those who provide or ad-minister the means of death incurring, any legal penalty or moral stigma whatsoever.

**22.** The author implies that this essay's audience comprises which of the following groups?

   **A.** Students

   **B.** Physicians

   **C.** Proponents of euthanasia

   **D.** Critics of euthanasia

   **E.** The terminally ill

**23.** According to the passage, the translation of euthanasia into "the good death" (line 61) is inadequate because

   **A.** death is never good.

   **B.** of the Greek tendency to oversimplify.

   **C.** that translation does not indicate many possible connotations of the term.

   **D.** it is implicitly associated with abortion.

   **E.** as societies become more advanced, euthanasia significantly changes its meaning.

**24.** According to the passage, one of the factors that has established euthanasia as an important social issue is

   **A.** a change in American lifestyles.

   **B.** its recognized relationship to capital punishment.

   **C.** a militant Christian movement against it.

   **D.** the threat of mass extermination.

   **E.** the number of individuals who insist upon making their own health decisions.

**25.** Which of the following can be most directly inferred from the author's attitude expressed in the passage?

   **A.** Euthanasia should be legalized.

   **B.** Suicide can be considered a type of euthanasia.

   **C.** Those who attempt suicide should be punished.

   **D.** Moral and legal issues clearly define the difference between suicide and euthanasia.

   **E.** The relationship between suicide and euthanasia remains ambiguous.

26. The primary purpose of this passage is to

 A. argue for the social acceptance of euthanasia.

 B. argue against the social acceptance of euthanasia.

 C. summarize attitudes, questions, and definitions related to euthanasia.

 D. summarize the moral arguments for and against euthanasia.

 E. stress the rights of the individual.

27. In the final paragraph, the author implies his or her support of

 A. a strengthened national insurance plan.

 B. a more efficient hospital and hospice system.

 C. the elimination of crimes of violence.

 D. the prosecution of doctors who assist suicide.

 E. the right of individuals to decide their own fate.

28. It can be inferred from the passage that euthanasia is a less important social issue in which of the following contexts?

 A. A society that is not technologically advanced

 B. A society that respects the rights of the individual

 C. A society whose hospitals contain artificial life-supporting mechanisms

 D. A Christian society

 E. A society in which euthanasia carries a legal penalty

Section ■ Reading Comprehension

IF YOU FINISH BEFORE TIME IS CALLED, CHECK YOUR WORK ON THIS SECTION ONLY. DO NOT WORK ON ANY OTHER SECTION IN THE TEST.

# Section III: Logical Reasoning

**Time: 35 Minutes**

**26 Questions**

**Directions:** You will be presented with brief passages or statements and will be required to evaluate their reasoning. In each case, select the best answer choice, even though more than one choice may present a possible answer. Choices that are unreasonable or incompatible with common-sense standards should be eliminated.

1. The water quality of Lake Tahoe—the largest, deepest, high mountain lake in North America—is steadily diminishing. Protecting its delicate ecological balance is essential.

   Which of the following arguments most closely resembles the argument above?

   A. The ability of many famous artists of the 1950s is steadily diminishing. Encouraging their continued productivity is essential.

   B. Erosion has taken its toll on Mt. Rushmore, defacing the historical monument. Appropriating money for its repair and restoration must be given priority.

   C. The quality of life in our older cities has ceased to be a concern to many legislators.

   D. The water quality of Lake Erie has been a diminishing concern of both Americans and Canadians over the past decade.

   E. The Grand Canyon, a deep natural excavation and a national monument, has steadily diminished in its appeal to tourists. Protecting its waning popularity is essential.

2. In parts of the world where the life spans are short, forty may be regarded as an advanced age. People who live longer are believed to possess special powers. These elders are sometimes treated with a deference based on fear rather than love.

   The final statement in the passage above is based on which of the following assumptions?

   A. Deference is normally accorded based on love.

   B. Few elders are treated with deference.

   C. People who live shorter lives have no special powers.

   D. People with special powers are not loved.

   E. A deference based on fear is stronger than one based on love.

3. The fish Alpha Splendes usually lives in a lake where there are sufficient dissolved alkalis. Lake Huron contains dissolved alkalis, soda, and potash. There are no Alpha Splendes in Lake Huron.

    Which of the following can be inferred from the above passage?

    A.  Therefore, Alpha Splendes needs alkalies other than soda and potash.

    B.  Therefore, there may not be sufficient dissolved alkalis in the lake.

    C.  Therefore, there will be no Alpha Splendes living in this lake.

    D.  Therefore, Lake Huron contains no dissolved alkalis.

    E.  Therefore, Alpha Splendes will never live in Lake Huron.

4. The evolution of the various forms of life from biochemical mass must not be considered a linear progression. Rather, the fossil record suggests an analogy between evolution and a bush whose branches go every which way. Like branches, some evolutionary lines simply end, and others branch again. Many biologists believe the pattern to have been as follows: Bacteria emerged first, and from them branched viruses, red algae, blue-green algae, and green flagellates. From the latter branched green algae, from which higher plants evolved, and colorless rhizoflagellates, from which diatoms, molds, sponges, and protozoa evolved. From ciliated protozoa (ciliophora) evolved mulinucleate (syncytial) flatworms. These branched into five lines, one of

which leads to the echinoderms and chordates. The remaining lines lead to most of the other phyla of the animal kingdom.

Which of the following best expresses the analogy between evolution and a bush?

A.  Species is to evolution as bush is to branching.

B.  Species is to branching as bush is to evolution.

C.  Evolution is to species as bush is to branch viruses.

D.  Evolution is to species as bush is to branches.

E.  Evolution is to species as branches is to bush.

5. Many overweight people first succeed at dieting and then relapse to former eating patterns, gaining back all the weight they had lost. When this cycle repeats over and over, it is called "yo-yo dieting." At one time, research showed that yo-yo dieting was harmful to health, even more harmful than being chronically overweight. However, one well-designed study found that yo-yo dieting, while not beneficial, is better than maintaining an unhealthy level of obesity.

Which of the following, if true, most plausibly accounts for the new finding?

A.  Yo-yo dieting increases the risk for heart disease.

B.  People who are consistent yo-yo dieters eat healthier than those who maintain obesity.

GO ON TO THE NEXT PAGE

Section III Logical Reasoning

C. The body is under stress whenever weight is gained or lost.

D. People who want to lose weight should exercise as well as eat healthier foods.

E. A person's weight is determined more by genetic factors than by what he or she eats.

6. The addictive nature of spicy foods made from hot peppers has a simple explanation. Because hot peppers aggravate the tissues inside the mouth, the brain releases endorphins, a protein that is released after any injury to the body. These endorphins produce feelings of well-being. Therefore, people who eat hot peppers begin to associate feelings of well-being with eating spicy foods and thereby become addicted.

Which of the following statements, if true, provides the best support for the argument in the passage?

A. Peppers that are not spicy also have an addictive quality.

B. The penchant for spicy foods appears to be culturally determined.

C. Some people have almost no tolerance for spicy foods.

D. The release of endorphins is the basis of acupuncture.

E. Endorphins are chemically similar to opium-derived narcotics.

7. Science writer: The term "articulation disorder" refers to the difficulty of an individual using the speech sounds of the language spoken around him. No communication dysfunction is more familiar to the speech pathologist than the problem of misarticulation. Articulation disorders represent over two-thirds of the speech clinician's caseload; a rather sizeable percentage when one considers that voice, rhythm, and language disorders also fall under this professional's purview.

The science writer implies that one of the factors contributing to the importance of articulation disorders is

A. the speech clinician's practice of treating nonserious disorders.

B. the lack of organic causes of such disorders.

C. the tendency of many children to "outgrow" the disorder.

D. the high incidence of such disorders.

E. the stress placed on such disorders by hospital administrators.

*Questions 8 and 9 are based on the following passage.*

It is evident that the methods of science have been highly successful. Psychologist B.F. Skinner believes that the method of science should be applied to the field of human affairs. We are all controlled by the world, part of which is constructed by man. Is this control to occur by accident, by tyrants, or by ourselves? A scientific society should reject accidental manipulation. He asserts that a specific plan is needed to promote fully the development of human beings and society. We cannot make wise decisions if we continue to pretend that we are not controlled.

As Skinner points out, the possibility of behavioral control is offensive to many people. We have traditionally regarded man as a free agent whose behavior occurs by virtue of spontaneous inner changes. We are reluctant to abandon the internal "will" which makes prediction and control of behavior impossible.

8. According to the passage, Skinner would probably agree with each of the following statements EXCEPT:

A. Rats and pigeons are appropriate animals for behavioristic study.

B. These behaviors we normally exhibit are not the only ones we are capable of.

C. The concept of behavioral control has popular appeal.

D. Inner causes of behavior are more difficult to observe than outer ones.

E. Positive reinforcement will affect learning in school.

9. The author implies that Skinner feels that the scientific procedure he advocates might be effective as

A. a means of enhancing our future.

B. an explanation of the causes of dictatorship.

C. a means for replacing teachers with computers.

D. a way of identifying characteristics common to rats, pigeons, and humans.

E. a way to understand the human mind.

10. On a swimming team:

All freestyle swimmers are Olympic winners.

No blue-eyed swimmer is an Olympic winner.

All Olympic winners go on to lucrative professional careers.

If all of the above are true, which of the following must also be true about the swimming team?

A. All those who go on to professional careers are freestyle swimmers.

B. Only freestyle swimmers go on to professional careers.

C. Some blue-eyed swimmers go on to lucrative professional careers.

D. No blue-eyed swimmer is a freestyle swimmer.

E. Only blue-eyed swimmers don't go on to lucrative careers.

11. Dear Sir or Madam:

Up until last Sunday, I was very pleased with the Stanford Brand Auto Polisher that I purchased at your store several years ago. Unfortunately, as I was using it on my $20,000 sports car, the waxing head flew off and smashed my windshield. In addition, when the head dislodged, the underworkings caused a large scratch on the front fender, which will cost an additional $300 to fix. I herewith enclose damage costs, as well as request replacement costs for the Standford Brand Auto Polisher, which is under warranty. (I will send you a copy of the twelve-month guarantee form that I filled out upon purchase.)

I look forward to hearing from you.

Sincerely,

P.R. Knockridge

GO ON TO THE NEXT PAGE

Which of the following is an essential condition that the writer of the letter fails to realize?

A. Knockridge's letter should have been dated.

B. Stanford Brand products, and not the store, will provide the replacements or damage costs.

C. The twelve-month guarantee is no longer valid.

D. A copy of the warranty should have been included.

E. Estimates of the damage should have been included.

*Questions 12 and 13 are based on the following passage.*

Every speech intended to persuade either argues for a proposition or argues against a proposition. Any speech that argues for a proposition either presents all the facts or presents a few of the facts, and any speech that argues against a proposition either presents all of the facts or presents a few of the facts. No speech that presents either all the facts, a few of the facts, or just one fact is uninformative.

12. If the statements made in the passage above are true, it follows that

A. every speech presents either all of the facts or a few of the facts.

B. every speech intended to persuade presents many of the facts of the argument.

C. every uninformative speech presents none of the facts.

D. some uninformative speeches present either all the facts or a few of the facts.

E. some speeches intended to persuade present neither all the facts nor a few of the facts.

13. Which of the following statements represents a valid conclusion based upon the passage above?

A. No speech intended to persuade presents some of the facts.

B. No informative speech both intends to persuade and contains a few of the facts.

C. No informative speech both argues against a proposition and contains all the facts.

D. No informative speech is intended to persuade.

E. No speech is both intended to persuade and uninformative.

14. A child learns about the ways of the society in which he was born from his playgroup. He will later transfer the experience gained in the primary group to the society at large. Very often, patterns of authority are consistent throughout a culture, from parental to political to spiritual.

Which of the following would be the most logical continuation of the passage above?

A. Thus, one may learn relationships between primary groups.

B. Thus, one cannot generalize from one group to the next.

C. Thus, one may learn what is held to be of value in a society.

D. Thus, one may determine the ways of society at a young age.

E. Thus, one realizes that depriving the child does not change his social behavior.

15. Because cigarette smokers usually have a bad cough and Butch has a bad cough, it follows that Butch is probably a cigarette smoker.

Which of the following most closely parallels the reasoning used in the argument above?

A. Because nonsmokers don't get emphysema and Bud doesn't have emphysema, it follows that Bud is probably not a smoker.

B. Because weightlifters usually have large muscles and Bill is a weightlifter, it follows that Bill has large muscles.

C. Because diamonds usually have little color and this gem has little color, it follows that this gem is probably a diamond.

D. Because people with short hair usually get more haircuts and Al has short hair, it follows that Al recently got a haircut.

E. Because coughing spreads germs and Sam is coughing, Sam is spreading germs.

16. The dance tonight is a ball, and my child's toy is a ball. Therefore, in addition to the fact that they are called by the same name, there is a way in which the dance and my child's toy are like each other.

Which of the following would explain why the conclusion of the argument does not logically follow from the premises stated in the passage?

A. The dance tonight may not in fact be a ball.

B. The dance tonight and my child's toy are not each a ball in the same sense of the word.

C. Something that is neither a dance nor a toy may nonetheless be a ball.

D. A ball cannot be anything except a specific kind of dance or a general type of toy.

E. A child's toy and a kind of dance may be related in ways other than just their nomenclature.

17. Philosophy instructor: Socrates believed that virtue is the outcome of knowledge and that evil is fundamentally ignorance. This is an early instance of the belief that the intellectual or rational is dominant in man and morally superior.

Socrates' point of view, as described by the instructor, implies which of the following conclusions about evil people?

A. They are ignorant.

B. They are unable to achieve complete self-knowledge.

GO ON TO THE NEXT PAGE

C. They are inherently virtuous but incapable of showing it.

D. They are often either ignorant or irrational.

E. They often dominate those who are morally superior.

*Questions 18 and 19 are based on the following passage.*

Skinner established himself as one of the country's leading behaviorists with the publication of his *Behavior of Organisms* in 1938. Although obviously influenced by Watson's behaviorism, Skinner's system appears to follow primarily from the work of Pavlov and Thorndike. Unlike some other followers of Watson, who studied behavior in order to understand the "workings of the mind," Skinner restricted himself to the study of overt or measurable behavior. Without denying either mental or physiological processes, he found that a study of behavior does not depend on conclusions about what is going on _____.

18. Which of the following is the best completion for the final sentence in the passage above?

A. outside the organism

B. outside the brain

C. inside the organism

D. inside the nervous system

E. outside the nervous system

19. Which of the following can be concluded from the information given in the passage above?

A. Some followers of Watson's behaviorism seek to understand the "workings of the mind."

B. Followers of Pavlov seek to understand the "workings of the mind."

C. The work of Thorndike varies from the work of Pavlov.

D. The work of Pavlov and Watson varies from the work of Thorndike.

E. Watson's behaviorism did not influence Skinner.

*Questions 20 and 21 are based on the following passage.*

All acts have consequences. Given this fact, we may wish to play it safe by never doing anything.

20. The speaker implies that

A. we may prefer to live safely.

B. all acts have consequences.

C. consequentiality is not safe.

D. doing nothing has lesser consequences.

E. not doing anything is not an act.

21. What conclusion about consequences must we accept if we accept the speaker's statement?

A. Consequences are significant only for active people.

B. All consequences are dangerous.

# AGGREGATE MATERIALS

**NEW & USED EQUIPMENT & SUPPLIES**

www.aggmat.com

TOLL FREE (866) 558-0822 • FAX (918) 748-8838

III

1 E
2 B
3 C
4 B
5 E X
6 A
7 E
8 B
9 E X
10 E
11 E X
12 C X
13 D X
14 B X
15 C
16 D
17 E
18 E ?
19 D X
20 C ?
21 B ?
22 C
23 D
24 D
25 D ?
26 B X

IV

1 D ?
2 D ?
3 C ?
4 A
5 A
6 B X
7 A
8 D
9 E
10 D X
11 C X
12 B X
13 D
14 D
15 A
16 E
17 A X
18 B X
19 B
20 C
21 D
22 A
23 E
24 D
25 D X
26 C X

C.  There are some acts that do not produce consequences.

D.  Consequences have moral force.

E.  Inaction has moral force.

**22.** In some societies, when death approaches, the dying person is moved out of the living quarters as a precaution against spiritual pollution. A corpse may be washed and dressed, perhaps painted and decorated, before being disposed of. In some cultures, corpses are placed where animals and the natural elements can get rid of the soft body parts. In India, bodies are usually cremated. The body may be buried in a seated or fetal position, facing camp or eastward, and so forth. Burial may be directly in the ground or in a coffin, tree trunk, large basket, or pottery urn. Some peoples practice an initial interment of a year or so followed by a disinterment, the bones being collected at this time and placed elsewhere.

At least one form of burial mentioned in the passage suggests a symbolic connection between

A.  mother and father.

B.  birth and death.

C.  infanticide and genocide.

D.  embalming and cremation.

E.  civilization and primitivism.

*Questions 23 and 24 are based on the following passage.*

In most economies, the government plays a role in the market system. Governments enforce the "rules of the game," impose taxes, and may control prices through price ceilings or price supports. These actions necessarily may create shortages or surpluses. In most developed and interdependent economies, the necessity of the government's playing some role in the economy seldom is disputed.

**23.** The final sentence in the passage suggests that

A.  interdependence goes in hand with development.

B.  there are underdeveloped countries whose attitude toward government control may be hostile.

C.  disputes over government control usually come from an illiterate populace.

D.  price supports are necessary.

E.  economic success is a sophisticated achievement.

**24.** The author of the passage would probably agree that

A.  economic surpluses are always good.

B.  market shortages are a necessary evil.

C.  higher prices strengthen the economy.

D.  price ceilings add to the shortages.

E.  surpluses are not usually created intentionally.

Section III Logical Reasoning

GO ON TO THE NEXT PAGE

*Questions 25 and 26 are based on the following information.*

A family of nine consists of three girls, three boys, two blue-eyed parents, and one grandparent. Four of the six children have blue eyes. Five of the six children have freckles.

25. Which of the following can be deduced from the information given in the passage above?

   A.  All four of the blue-eyed children have freckles.

   B.  At least one girl has no freckles.

   C.  None of the girls has blue eyes.

   D.  At least two of the girls have freckles.

   E.  The grandparent has blue eyes.

26. From the information given, all of the following must be true EXCEPT

   A.  one of the children does not have freckles.

   B.  more adults have blue eyes than brown eyes.

   C.  all of the boys could have blue eyes.

   D.  at least three children have blue eyes and freckles.

   E.  at least three children have brown eyes.

IF YOU FINISH BEFORE TIME IS CALLED, CHECK YOUR WORK ON THIS SECTION ONLY. DO NOT WORK ON ANY OTHER SECTION IN THE TEST.

# Section IV: Analytical Reasoning

Time: 35 Minutes

24 Questions

**Directions:** You will be presented with several sets of conditions. A group of questions follows each set of conditions. Choose the best answer to each question, drawing a rough diagram when necessary.

*Questions 1 through 6 are based on the following statements.*

> Liz, Jenni, Jolie, and Rick have an English final on Friday, and they all would like to study together at least once before the test.
>
> Liz can study only on Monday, Tuesday, and Wednesday nights and Thursday afternoon and night.
>
> Jenni can study only on Monday, Wednesday, and Thursday nights and Tuesday afternoon and night.
>
> Jolie can study only on Wednesday and Thursday nights, Tuesday afternoon, and Monday afternoon and night.
>
> Rick can study the afternoons and nights of Tuesday, Wednesday, and Thursday and on Monday afternoon.

1. If the group is to study twice, the days could be

    A. Monday and Wednesday.

    B. Tuesday and Thursday.

    C. Wednesday and Thursday.

    D. Monday and Friday.

    E. Tuesday and Wednesday.

2. If three students tried to study together when all four couldn't,

    A. this would be possible only at two different times.

    B. it would have to be on Wednesday night.

    C. Rick could not attend the three-person groups.

    D. this could be accomplished on Monday and Tuesday only.

    E. this would not be possible.

3. If Liz decided to study every night, she would

    A. never be able to study with Rick.

    B. never be able to study with Jolie.

    C. have at least two study partners each night.

    D. have to study alone on Monday night.

    E. study with only Jenni on Thursday night.

GO ON TO THE NEXT PAGE

4. If the test were moved up one day to Thursday morning, which of the following must be true?

   A. The complete group would not be able to study together.

   B. Liz could study in the afternoon.

   C. Rick and Jolie would not be able to study together.

   D. Jolie and Jenni could study together three times.

   E. Liz could study at four different times.

5. Dan wants to join the study group. If the larger study group is to be able to study all together, Dan will have to be available on

   A. Wednesday night.

   B. Thursday afternoon.

   C. Tuesday night.

   D. Monday night.

   E. Wednesday afternoon.

6. How many of the students are available to study at a time when no other student is available to study?

   A. 0

   B. 1

   C. 2

   D. 3

   E. 4

*Questions 7 through 13 are based on the following statements.*

Two women, Amy and Carla, and two men, Bernard and Doug, are doctors. One is a dentist, one a surgeon, one an optometrist, and one a general practitioner. They are seated around a square table with one person on each side.

Bernard is across from the dentist.

Doug is not across from the surgeon.

The optometrist is on Amy's immediate left.

Carla is the general practitioner.

The surgeon and general practitioner are married to each other.

The general practitioner is not on Carla's immediate left.

The general practitioner is across from the optometrist.

7. Which of the following must be true?

   A. Bernard is the dentist.

   B. The surgeon and general practitioner are women.

   C. Carla is across from Amy.

   D. The dentist is across from the surgeon.

   E. Doug is the surgeon.

8. Which of the following must be true?

    A.   Two women sit next to each other.

    B.   Two men sit next to each other.

    C.   No two men sit next to each other.

    D.   Two women sit across from each other.

    E.   A man sits next to two women.

9. Which of the following must be true?

    A.   The dentist is across from the optometrist.

    B.   The surgeon sits across from the general practitioner.

    C.   Doug is the optometrist.

    D.   The surgeon sits across from a man.

    E.   Carla is the dentist.

10. Which of the following must be true?

    A.   Doug is the general practitioner.

    B.   Bernard is the surgeon.

    C.   Carla is the dentist.

    D.   Amy is the optometrist.

    E.   Doug is the dentist.

11. If the surgeon and the optometrist switch seats, which of the following would no longer be true?

    A.   Each man sits next to a woman.

    B.   Doug sits next to Bernard.

    C.   Each man sits opposite a woman.

    D.   Carla sits next to Amy.

    E.   Bernard sits next to Carla.

12. If Bernard and Amy switch seats,

    A.   Carla sits across from Amy.

    B.   Doug sits across from Bernard.

    C.   Bernard sits across from Amy.

    D.   Carla sits next to Doug.

    E.   Amy sits next to Bernard.

13. If both men leave the table, the

    A.   optometrist and dentist remain.

    B.   surgeon and optometrist remain.

    C.   surgeon and general practitioner remain.

    D.   general practitioner and dentist remain.

    E.   general practitioner and optometrist remain.

*Questions 14 through 18 are based on the following statements.*

The mythical countries of Bongo and Congo are flat, exactly square shaped, and lie next to each other in an east-west direction, though not necessarily in that order. Their common border spans the width of both countries.

   The capital city of one of the countries is "A." It lies due east from the other capital, "B."

   "C" is the border city of Congo, on the Bongo boundary.

   "D" is the harbor city of Bongo for ships coming from the west.

GO ON TO THE NEXT PAGE

"E" is the easternmost city of Bongo.

"F" is 27 miles due west of Congo's capital city, in Congo.

The main highway, Bongo-Congo 1, goes from "B" eastward to the coastal city of "G."

**14.** Going east to west, a traveler would encounter cities in which order?

A. G, A, E, C, F

B. A, F, C, B, E

C. D, B, E, C, F

D. G, A, F, C, E

E. C, B, E, F, A

**15.** When the sun rises, the first city to see it is

A. G.

B. F.

C. B.

D. E.

E. D.

**16.** When the sun sets, the last city to see it is

A. G.

B. F.

C. B.

D. E.

E. D.

**17.** Which of the following must be true?

A. A is to the west of E.

B. C is the last Bongo city encountered on the way to Congo.

C. B is to the east of A.

D. A is the capital city of Congo.

E. B is the capital city of Congo.

**18.** Which statement is true of city "E"?

A. It is the easternmost city of the easternmost country.

B. It is the westernmost city of the westernmost country.

C. It is the easternmost city of the westernmost country.

D. It is the westernmost city of the easternmost country.

E. It is due west of Bongo's capital city.

*Questions 19 through 24 are based on the following information.*

Four members of a class—Barton, William, Dustin, and Patricia—each participate in at least one after-school activity, either together or alone. The activities available are Crew, Debate Team, Newspaper, Drama, and Service. Each time a student participates in a club, his or her class receives one credit toward a class honors award. Here are the known facts:

Service and Debate are held the same time on the same days, so participating in one precludes participating in the other.

One of the four students becomes captain of the debate team, and one becomes editor of the newspaper.

Dustin joins only Drama and is the only student of the four to participate in that activity.

William joins Service.

Patricia participates in Crew.

Patricia and Barton do not join Newspaper.

Patricia declines to participate in any activity with William.

19. Given the preceding facts, what is the greatest total number of class credits that can be earned by these four students?

A. 4
B. 5
C. 6
D. 7
E. 18

20. What are the fewest number of class credits this group of four can earn?

A. 4
B. 5
C. 6
D. 7
E. 8

21. Which of the following must be true?

A. Patricia joins Debate.
B. William joins Newspaper.
C. Dustin joins Debate.
D. Barton joins Service.
E. Barton joins Debate.

22. If Barton participates in Service, which of the following must be true?

A. Only one of the four participates in Crew.
B. Patricia participates in only one activity.
C. Patricia participates in Debate.
D. William participates in Crew.
E. Barton participates in Crew.

23. If Barton participates in exactly two activities, which of the following must be true?

A. Barton participates with Patricia in exactly one activity.
B. Barton participates with William in exactly one activity.
C. William participates in Crew.
D. Barton participates in Debate.
E. Barton participates in Crew.

GO ON TO THE NEXT PAGE

**24.** Suppose the schedule is changed so that Service and Debate are not held at the same time and thus do not preclude each other. If all other conditions remain the same, what is the greatest number of class credits this group of four could earn?

   **A.** 7

   **B.** 8

   **C.** 9

   **D.** 10

   **E.** 11

IF YOU FINISH BEFORE TIME IS CALLED, CHECK YOUR WORK ON THIS SECTION ONLY. DO NOT WORK ON ANY OTHER SECTION IN THE TEST.

# Section V: Reading Comprehension

**Time: 35 Minutes**

**27 Questions**

**Directions:** Each passage in this group is followed by questions based on its content. After reading a passage, choose the best answer to each question and blacken the corresponding space on the answer sheet. Answer all questions following a passage on the basis of what is *stated* or *implied* in that passage. You may refer back to the passage.

*Questions 1 through 7 are based on the following passage.*

Aliens have been entering the United States illegally at a phenomenal rate in recent years, and a substantial segment of this influx may be children. This mi-
(5) gration has brought with it the unique problem of determining what benefits are constitutionally due to these children. The constitutionality of legislation affecting such children may depend
(10) largely on what standard of scrutiny under the equal protection clause to which legislation affecting undocumented children is subjected.

Equal protection analysis was initially
(15) confined to two levels of inquiry. The Supreme Court has traditionally upheld the constitutionality of a statute if the legislation bears a rational relation to a legitimate state interest. This method of
(20) evaluating legislation is extremely deferential to the state, and its application usually results in validation of the legislation since there is almost always a modicum of rationality in a statute.
(25) The Supreme Court has opted for a more stringent level of scrutiny when state legislation infringes on fundamental rights or burdens a suspect class. Under the "strict scrutiny" standard, the
(30) legislation must bear a "necessary relation to a *compelling* state interest." In

contrast to the deferential rational basis test, strict scrutiny has proven largely fatal to legislation, as it demands that the
(35) classification be absolutely necessary to promote the asserted state interest and that no more reasonable means of achieving the state goal be available.

In response to the unyielding rigidity
(40) of the two-tier system, a middle level of scrutiny has emerged. The most common formulation of this intermediate test requires that the state show a substantial relation to an important govern-
(45) mental interest. Intermediate scrutiny has been triggered in two circumstances: ". . . if important, though not necessarily 'fundamental' or preferred 'interests are at stake'. . ." or ". . . if sensitive, al-
(50) though not necessarily suspect, criteria of classifications are employed." The question heretofore unanswered is this: Do undocumented children qualify as either a sensitive or suspect class that
(55) would automatically invoke heightened scrutiny?

In a controversial Texas case, the Supreme Court struck down a Texas statute that withheld from local school
(60) districts any state funds for the education of children not legally admitted to the United States and authorized local school districts to deny enrollment to those children. The Supreme Court has

GO ON TO THE NEXT PAGE

(65) to date recognized three suspect classes: race, national origin, and alienage. But the Court makes clear that illegal alienage is not to be accorded the same status as alienage and "reject[s] the claim that

(70) 'illegal aliens' are a 'suspect class.'" Suspect classes must, by the Court's previous definition, "suffer from 'an immutable characteristic determined solely by accident of birth.'"

(75)     Analysis of the opinion in the Texas case mitigates against the possibility that illegal alien children are for all purposes a sensitive class that will trigger immediate scrutiny. The loose analogy

(80) the Court draws between the plight of illegitimate children and undocumented children does not compel the conclusion that the latter should be accorded sensitive status. Nor can undocumented chil-

(85) dren be deemed a sensitive class by the mere fact that intermediate review was triggered because the presence of the potentially important right of education makes that conclusion impossible.

(90) However, the Texas case may depict a new scheme under which conjunction of right and class is looked at in determining the applicability of middle level review. If future cases bear out the validity

(95) of this formula, the question whether undocumented children or any class is a sensitive one may well become moot. Suffice it to say that at this time, the Court's decisions make it impossible to

(100) proclaim with any certitude that the class of illegal alien children is a pure sensitive class, but clearly it is of sufficient sensitivity to warrant the application of middle level review when the

(105) legislation affecting undocumented children simultaneously impinges upon a right of above marginal importance.

1. In the past, a state that wished to have validated a law that threatened the equal protection of a suspect class would

   A. have to submit the law to two levels of inquiry.

   B. be likely to be successful if the law were subjected to strict scrutiny.

   C. be obligated to demonstrate a compelling state interest if the law is strictly scrutinized.

   D. be obliged to demonstrate a compelling state interest if the law is subject to the deferential rational basis criterion.

   E. probably be examined under the deferential rational basis criterion.

2. In the past, laws infringing on the equal protection rights of a suspect class were likely to be overturned because they must be

   A. both reasonable and legitimate.

   B. related to an important state need.

   C. both reasonable and related to compelling state interests.

   D. absolutely necessary to what may be regarded as state interests.

   E. the most reasonable means of achieving a compelling state interest.

3. Which of the following would be more likely than children of illegal aliens to be regarded by the courts as a suspect class whose constitutional rights are threatened?

   A. Children of Japanese parentage

   B. Children of Mormon parentage

   C. Children of Moslem parentage

   D. Children of Jewish parentage

   E. Children of Communist parentage

4. Moving in order from the most relaxed to the most stringent, the adjectives now applied to describe the "relation" of the state governments' interest are

   A. rational-necessary-substantial.

   B. rational-substantial-necessary.

   C. rational-compelling-necessary.

   D. necessary-substantial-compelling.

   E. necessary-compelling-substantial.

5. In the Texas case discussed in the fifth and sixth paragraphs, the important right of children that had been threatened was

   A. citizenship.

   B. education.

   C. speedy trial.

   D. legitimacy.

   E. medical services.

6. According to the passage, the decision in favor of the children of illegal aliens in the Texas case demonstrates that

   A. alienage and illegal alienage are not the same.

   B. the children of illegal aliens will be regarded as a suspect class in constitutional rights cases.

   C. the nature of the denied right may determine the nature of the review by the courts.

   D. the states do not have the right to deny any children entrance to schools.

   E. local school districts must subsidize the enrollment of the children of illegal aliens in their schools.

7. Which of the following best states the central idea of the passage?

   A. When an important right is threatened, illegal aliens will be protected by the intermediate scrutiny of the courts.

   B. There are now three levels of court scrutiny.

   C. A landmark Supreme Court decision has protected the rights of illegal aliens that state laws in Texas had threatened.

   D. The important rights of children of illegal aliens may now be subject to intermediate scrutiny by the courts.

   E. The three classes most closely protected by the courts are recognized by race, national origin, or allegiance.

Section V Reading Comprehension

GO ON TO THE NEXT PAGE

*Questions 8 through 14 are based on the following passage.*

For centuries, death was defined as occurring when there was a total stoppage of blood circulation and respiration. Not surprisingly, physicians and (5) laymen concluded, when "a person's heart stopped beating and he stopped breathing, he was dead." The inability of medical science to reestablish the heart and lungs after the cessation of activity (10) was ample justification for its definition of death.

The availability and widespread use of cardiopulmonary resuscitation (CPR) has necessitated a redefinition of death. (15) There is a growing trend to define death as an irreversible loss of brain function. All body elements require oxygen, but the brain requires more than any other tissue. The probability of damage after (20) oxygen flow to the brain has ceased depends upon the speed of application of CPR. If the oxygen flow is reestablished within four minutes, brain damage is unlikely. If reestablishment is delayed (25) from four to ten minutes, brain damage is probable. Should the brain lack oxygen for over ten minutes, brain damage is almost certain. Although a debate still continues within the medical profession (30) as to the specific criteria to be utilized to determine brain death, brain death has become the accepted medical standard.

There are nineteen states that have enacted legislation focusing on the cessa- (35) tion of brain function as a statutory definition of death. In 1970, Kansas was the first state to adopt brain death as part of its death statute. The statute provided for alternative definitions of death—one (40) based on brain death, the other based on the absence of spontaneous cardiac and respiratory function. Maryland, New Mexico, and Virginia modeled their statutes after the Kansas law. The

(45) remaining fifteen states have passed legislation within the last few years. These statutes differ from the previous ones in that there is no provision for the determination of death based on respira- (50) tory and cardiac cessation, the sole criterion for defining death being the absence of brain function.

The problem of distinguishing ordinary and extraordinary levels of care has (55) not been simple. The first noted distinction was phrased as follows:

Ordinary means are all medicines, treatments, and operations which offer a reasonable hope of benefit and which can (60) be obtained and used without excessive expense, pain, or other inconvenience.

Extraordinary means are all medicines, treatments, and operations which cannot be obtained or used without ex- (65) cessive expense, pain, or other inconvenience or which, if used, would not offer a reasonable hope of benefit.

Reasonable hope of benefit is no longer an applicable standard. The value (70) of life is not to be equated with quality of life. It is fundamental to the human condition to seek life and to retain it, no matter how heavy the burden. In a recent case, the Court held that a mentally re- (75) tarded person has a right to experience life to his greatest potential, that the patient's ultimate mental capabilities should not enter into a physician's decision regarding treatment.

(80) Also, the excessive pain standard is no longer applicable. No doctor can subjectively assess what treatment or diagnostic procedure causes a person excessive pain, as each person has a dif- (85) ferent tolerance level. In addition, pain can be managed with analgesics. Then too, treatments such as chemotherapy and setting a broken leg can cause excruciating pain but are deemed to be (90) within the ordinary standard of medical care. Diagnostic procedures such as

arterial blood gases and angiograms can cause excruciating pain but are also re-garded as within the ordinary standard (95) of medical care.

A physician is responsible for provid-ing reasonable and ordinary care accord-ing to present standards of the medical profession in the treatment of patients. A (100) doctor, however, has no duty to provide extraordinary care, and such services may be withheld at any time. As medical science advances, our definition of the physician's standard of care changes to (105) incorporate newly acquired skills and knowledge.

CPR has traditionally been included within the extraordinary standard of care. Changes in distinguishing extraordinary-(110) ordinary care, CPR advances in medical skill, and the attendant redefinition of death have transformed CPR into an ordi-nary standard of medical care. This means that when a physician writes DNR (115) (Do Not Resuscitate), ONTR (Order Not to Resuscitate), or similar meaning phrases informing trained personnel not to perform CPR, he may now have breached his duty.

**8.** Cardiopulmonary resuscitation undermines the nineteenth-century definition of death because it

    **A.** restores the flow of oxygen to the brain.

    **B.** may enable a patient to be moved to a hospital before brain damage can occur.

    **C.** restores the flow of oxygen to the heart.

    **D.** may enable a patient to avoid brain damage if it is performed immediately.

    **E.** restores the operation of the heart and lungs.

**9.** Compared to older legal definitions of death, the most recently adopted ones are likely to use

    **A.** only heart cessation as a criterion.

    **B.** both heart and breath cessation as criteria.

    **C.** only cessation of brain function as a criterion.

    **D.** both cessation of heart and brain function as criteria.

    **E.** cessation of heart, breath, and brain function as criteria.

**10.** According to the passage, the use of brain death as the standard to determine death

    **A.** has replaced the use of heartbeat and breathing.

    **B.** is the accepted legal rather than medical norm.

    **C.** is the universal criterion in hospitals.

    **D.** still varies from state to state.

    **E.** is the determination of the doctor, not the courts

**11.** We can infer from the passage that a blind and deaf patient in a life-threatening situation would, according to the courts, be

    **A.** entitled to the same care as sighted and hearing patients.

    **B.** entitled to extraordinary levels of care.

    **C.** allowed to refuse even ordinary levels of care.

GO ON TO THE NEXT PAGE

Section **V** Reading Comprehension

D. allowed to refuse extraordinary levels of care.

E. protected against subjection to excessive pain.

**12.** The passage alludes to chemotherapy and angiograms in order to

A. illustrate the advances of modern treatment of diseases.

B. illustrate medical procedures that may be very painful.

C. cite examples of ordinary medical care.

D. cite examples of extraordinary care.

E. cite specific examples of diagnostic medical procedures.

**13.** The final paragraph of the passage (lines 107–119) asserts that a physician ordering trained personnel not to perform CPR

A. may have forbidden extraordinary care.

B. is operating within his or her rights as a doctor.

C. may do so if the patient is suffering excessive pain.

D. may have failed to provide for ordinary care.

E. has failed to provide for ordinary care.

**14.** The central point of the passage is that

A. CPR is no longer an extraordinary standard of care.

B. CPR is no longer an ordinary standard of care.

C. legal definitions of death have failed to keep pace with medical ones.

D. legal decisions can affect medical practices.

E. the distinction between ordinary and extraordinary levels of care is no longer meaningful.

*Questions 15 through 21 are based on the following passage.*

Each year, thousands of representation elections are conducted all over the nation by the National Labor Relations Board. An entire area of very specialized
(5) law has developed regarding the conduct of campaigns in NLRB elections.

No labor attorney, no matter how extensive his experience and expertise, can come up with a campaign program
(10) during an NLRB election which will guarantee the employer a victory. The final decision on the question of unionization rests in the subjective minds of the employees, each with varying back-
(15) grounds, moods, desires, and motivations. No matter the confidence that the employer has in his employees not to let him down, he must recognize the possibility that he will lose the election, and
(20) should make plans in that event.

When faced with an election loss, the employer has two options. His first one is to accept the results of the election and to sit down with the union and at-
(25) tempt to negotiate a contract. The law requires him to bargain in good faith with the union over wages, hours, and other terms and conditions of employment. He could get off fairly easy, nego-
(30) tiating with the union a contract he can live with. However, he might not be so lucky. The union might present him with demands which he feels are excessive,

(35) and upon his refusal to agree to these, might lead his employees out on strike, with all of the consequences.

The other alternative available to an employer faced with a loss in an NLRB election is to file objections to the elec-
(40) tion and to pursue these objections administratively through the NLRB and finally to the courts. By filing objections to the election and pursuing his appeal to the courts, such right as is given to
(45) him by law, the employer can delay the day when he must bargain with the union, sometimes by as much as two to three years, given current circuit court backlogs.

(50) Given the short time in which an employer has to prepare his objections after an election, he should be familiar with all of the possible types of election objections at the beginning of the cam-
(55) paign. Then, during the course of the election campaign, he can observe with a heightened alertness. If the election is lost, he is able to move quickly and accurately. It is nearly impossible to get
(60) the Board to take notice of election objectives which are submitted or allegedly discovered after the five-day period. Later objections convey the impression of being fabricated, whereas
(65) objections filed right on the heels of the election do not.

Several cases have held that elections should be set aside which were won by the unions on the basis of last minute
(70) misrepresentation by the unions about wage rates and fringe benefits in unionized plants. In one case, a bargaining order was denied enforcement on the grounds that during the election cam-
(75) paign, the union sent out letters misinforming employees of the employer's profits. In another case, an election was set aside where the union made an election eve address over the radio, in
(80) which it implied that a management representative who had earlier made an antiunion radio address, privately wanted the employees to vote for the union. It has also been held that the use of cam-
(85) paign literature which conceals the true identity of the sponsor may be grounds for setting an election aside.

Another ground for setting aside an election is undue supervisory influence
(90) upon employees in favor of the union. The theory behind this objection is that supervisors normally have great control over the lives of employees who work under them. They can assign daily tasks
(95) to employees and can make, or choose not to make, recommendations and reports which lead to employee advancement. If the supervisor is pressuring the employees to vote for the union, then a
(100) certain type of coercion is present, and it cannot be said that the employees, in voting for the union, have truly expressed their feelings.

After the votes are counted, and the
(105) employer has lost an NLRB election, he has a very limited time in which to act if he intends to file objections to the election and ultimately refuse to bargain and take the matter to the Court of
(110) Appeals. It is therefore important that the employer first, be aware of the type of conduct on the part of unions and the NLRB itself which has in the past led to elections being set aside and second, be
(115) alert for any evidence during the course of the election campaign and the voting process of such conduct. Then, in the unfortunate event that the employer loses his NLRB election, he will be in a
(120) position to move quickly and accurately.

GO ON TO THE NEXT PAGE

15. The use of words and phrases like, "let him down" (line 17), "fairly easy" (line 29), and "lucky" (line 32) reveal the

   A. misguided confidence of employers.

   B. untrustworthiness of employees.

   C. antiunion bias of the author.

   D. bias of the author against employers.

   E. uncertainty of election results.

16. The author regards the employer's straightforward acceptance of an NLRB election and bargaining with the union as

   A. the only possible response.

   B. an option the author highly recommends.

   C. certain to precipitate a strike.

   D. the only way to avoid a strike.

   E. an option about which the author has reservations.

17. The passage suggests that even an unsuccessful objection to an NLRB election can be used to

   A. reverse an election result.

   B. delay bargaining with a union.

   C. eliminate bargaining with a union altogether.

   D. require a new election.

   E. encourage union acceptance of a contract.

18. An employer who has not appealed an NLRB election and refuses to bargain in good faith with a union that has won the election is

   A. breaking the law.

   B. entitled to take his or her case to the circuit court.

   C. entitled to delay bargaining for up to three years.

   D. establishing grounds for a union action.

   E. effectively admitting culpability in the dispute.

19. The reasons given in the sixth and seventh paragraphs (lines 67–103) for setting aside elections are based on the assumption that the election

   A. was won by the union.

   B. was won by the employer.

   C. was won by means of misrepresentation.

   D. was won by means of improper influence.

   E. had no clear winner in its results.

20. The passage cites all of the following as grounds for an election challenge EXCEPT:

   A. undue supervisorial influences.

   B. misinformation about employer finances.

   C. extensive use of campaign literature.

   D. misrepresentation of fringe benefits.

   E. misrepresentation of wages.

**21.** Which of the following best states the central idea of the passage?

A. Both unions and employers should study the NLRB election procedures before an election to avoid irregularities.

B. An employer should challenge an NLRB election if the employer wishes to delay bargaining.

C. Employers should hire a well-trained labor lawyer before any NLRB election takes place.

D. An employer should know about and watch for established grounds for appealing the outcome of an NLRB election.

E. With careful preparation, an employer should be able to win an NLRB election.

*Questions 22 through 27 are based on the following passage.*

Much debate has occurred concerning the causes and effects of acid rain. The leading theory posits that the two facets of its causation are weather patterns and
(5) human activity. The burning of sulfur-containing coal by industry and utilities and smelting and refining activities, primarily in the Midwest, produce the gases sulfur dioxide ($SO_2$) and various
(10) oxides of nitrogen (collectively $No_x$). The amount of such emissions has been estimated between tens and hundreds of millions of tons annually. These industrial gases are carried into the atmos-
(15) phere where part of the mass may be oxidized further to sulfur trioxide ($SO_3$) and sulfates ($HSO_4-$ and $SO_4=$) and higher oxides of nitrogen. Once airborne, these combined pollutants are
(20) carried by prevailing winds over northeastern states where they combine with atmospheric water and fall to earth in ordinary rainstorms. The magnitude of controlling the problem is appreciated
(25) by recognizing that emission and injection into the atmosphere occur in State A, further oxidation may occur over State B, while precipitation and final harmful effects occur in State C,
(30) 1,000 or more miles distant.

It is beyond question that airborne pollutants can be transported great distances. Industrial pollution has been detected on the Greenland ice cap,
(35) thousands of miles from industrial sites. Nor is it seriously debatable that the increased acidity of precipitation is due to human activities. Rain and snow have shown a detectable and significant in-
(40) crease in acidity over the last 200 years, being transformed from "pure" precipitation to an acid one. This rise in acidity parallels the rise in industrial activity and the use of coal as a major fuel, be-
(45) ginning with the Industrial Revolution.

Although the phenomenon of acid rain has come under scrutiny only relatively recently, a number of presently identifiable effects and potential conse-
(50) quences have received attention. When acidic components remain suspended in air long enough for inhalation, as in the case of fogs or aerosols, terrestrial mammalian respiratory problems arise. In
(55) those aquatic systems which lack much buffering capacity, fish are affected by a drop in pH, resulting in lowered disease resistance and failure to reproduce. Thus, a disruption in the food chain be-
(60) gins. One effect on plants is the actual leaching of nutrients from within the plants themselves by direct acid rain action. The combined effects portend a decrease in forest productivity as well as a
(65) like effect on cultivated grain crops.

Human endeavors are likewise the direct victims of such pollution. Acid rain

GO ON TO THE NEXT PAGE

has been blamed for the decomposition of marble structures such as the (70) Parthenon in Athens, hitherto relatively unscathed by normal weathering in 25 centuries. Thus, in a relatively few decades, man's industrial activity has risen to the point of threatening serious (75) harm to his own well being as well as that of plant and animal ecosystems. Further, a decline in fossil fuel use in the next 30 years is not likely.

There are three fundamental obsta- (80) cles to effective control of acid rain: the bifurcated territorial nature of the emission/precipitation phenomena, the federalist character of government within the United States, and contempo- (85) rary political defects.

Acid rain would seem to present an archetype situation ripe for interstate compact utilization. The emitting states must admit that industries within their (90) borders are causing serious harm to other states, with long-term irremedia-ble effects. The downwind states must likewise concede that it is impractical to demand of vital industries that they ei- (95) ther stop polluting immediately or shut down, without those states providing incentives.

22. From details of this passage, we can infer that acid rain in Europe

   A.  is not a problem.

   B.  is not so harmful as it is in the United States.

   C.  has been controlled by laws.

   D.  is a problem in the industrial north but not in Mediterranean countries.

   E.  is as great a problem as it is in the United States.

23. According to the passage, a predictable effect of acid rain is the

   A.  decline in the productivity of cultivated grain crops.

   B.  increase in the insect population.

   C.  increase in cardiac disease in humans.

   D.  increase in richness of the forest soils.

   E.  decline in the annual rainfall.

24. Which of the following, according to the passage, would most directly reduce the incidence of acid rain?

   A.  Increase in the height of industrial chimneys in the Midwest

   B.  Decrease in the use of solar and water power to create electricity

   C.  Use of nuclear energy to replace use of fossil fuels

   D.  Reliance upon wind power in lieu of nuclear power

   E.  Increase in research to discover new waste-storage technologies

25. The reference to the continued use of fossil fuel in the last sentence of the fourth paragraph (lines 77–78) is intended to

   A.  make logical the transition to the next paragraph.

   B.  remind the reader that the primary cause of acid rain will not go away.

   C.  fix the blame for acid rain upon the users of fossil fuels.

   D.  encourage the development of other sources of energy.

   E.  show why the disadvantages of acid rain are balanced by the advantages to humans.

**26.** Of the "three fundamental obstacles to effective control of acid rain" listed in lines 80–85, the author deals

   A.   equally with all three.

   B.   mostly with the first.

   C.   mostly with the second.

   D.   mostly with the third.

   E.   more with the second and third than with the first.

**27.** In lines 81–82, the phrase, "bifurcated territorial nature of the emission/precipitation phenomena" refers to

   A.   the two houses of the federal legislature.

   B.   pollution in one state becomes acid rain in another.

   C.   states that possess heavy industry are more willing to pass strict environmental laws.

   D.   states without heavy industry are more likely to pass strict environmental laws.

   E.   no two states have the same environmental problems.

IF YOU FINISH BEFORE TIME IS CALLED, CHECK YOUR WORK ON THIS SECTION ONLY. DO NOT WORK ON ANY OTHER SECTION IN THE TEST.

# Writing Essay

Time: 30 Minutes

**Directions:** You are to complete a brief essay on the given topic. You may take no more than 30 minutes to plan and write your essay. After reading the topic carefully, you should probably spend a few minutes planning and organizing your response. YOU MAY NOT WRITE ON A TOPIC OTHER THAN THE GIVEN TOPIC.

The quality of your writing is more important than either the quantity of writing or the point of view you adopt. Your skill in organization, mechanics, and usage is important, although it is expected that your essay will not be flawless because of the time pressure under which you write.

Keep your writing within the lined area of your essay booklet. Write on every line, avoid wide margins, and write carefully and legibly.

NOTE: On the actual LSAT, the essay topic is at the top of the essay writing page. Scratch paper for organizing and prewriting is provided.

## Essay Topic

Members of the Edgemeer City Council must decide whether to support Proposition Q or Proposition R, initiatives on the November ballot. Proposition Q would permit exploration and drilling for oil in those areas close to the city's beaches that geologists have determined are rich in oil and natural gas. Proposition R would prohibit drilling in the waters adjacent to the city's beaches. Write an argument in support of one of the two propositions based on the following information. Two considerations influence your conclusions:

- The schools, the police, and the fire departments of the city are seriously in need of additional funding.

- The second largest source of city income is from its tourist business that depends chiefly on the luxury hotels that line the city's beaches.

Proponents of Proposition Q point out that passage of the bill could lead to tripling the funds available for the city's schools and police and fire departments within five years. The proposition will not permit drilling on the beaches, only in the waters off shore. Environmental experts have carefully studied the areas to be affected and insist there is no danger to the environment. By providing shelter for smaller animals, oil platforms have been shown to increase the amount of marine life. New sources of locally produced oil and gas will reduce the nation's dependence on foreign oil.

Proponents of Proposition R argue that passage of the bill will protect the city's beaches from pollution and preserve the tourist industry on which the city depends. Seepage from off shore wells or an oil spill, they argue, could wipe out the marine life and destroy the city's most dependable source of revenue. In addition, oil drilling off shore will reduce property values in beach-front areas and thus lessen the tax income of the city.

# Answers and Complete Explanations For Practice Test 3

## Answers for Practice Test 3

| Section I | Section II | Section III | Section IV | Section V |
|-----------|------------|-------------|------------|-----------|
| Logical Reasoning | Reading Comprehension | Logical Reasoning | Analytical Reasoning | Reading Comprehension |
| 1. A | 1. D | 1. B | 1. C | 1. C |
| 2. D | 2. B | 2. A | 2. D | 2. E |
| 3. B | 3. C | 3. B | 3. C | 3. A |
| 4. A | 4. E | 4. D | 4. D | 4. B |
| 5. E | 5. C | 5. B | 5. A | 5. B |
| 6. D | 6. A | 6. E | 6. B | 6. C |
| 7. C | 7. E | 7. D | 7. D | 7. D |
| 8. E | 8. C | 8. C | 8. A | 8. E |
| 9. B | 9. E | 9. A | 9. C | 9. C |
| 10. E | 10. B | 10. D | 10. B | 10. D |
| 11. A | 11. A | 11. C | 11. E | 11. A |
| 12. E | 12. C | 12. C | 12. C | 12. B |
| 13. B | 13. C | 13. E | 13. D | 13. D |
| 14. B | 14. D | 14. D | 14. D | 14. A |
| 15. A | 15. D | 15. C | 15. A | 15. C |
| 16. A | 16. D | 16. B | 16. E | 16. E |
| 17. D | 17. B | 17. A | 17. D | 17. B |
| 18. D | 18. A | 18. C | 18. C | 18. A |
| 19. C | 19. D | 19. A | 19. D | 19. A |
| 20. A | 20. C | 20. E | 20. B | 20. C |
| 21. D | 21. A | 21. B | 21. B | 21. D |
| 22. B | 22. A | 22. B | 22. C | 22. E |
| 23. E | 23. C | 23. B | 23. E | 23. A |
| 24. C | 24. E | 24. B | 24. B | 24. C |
|  | 25. E | 25. D |  | 25. B |
|  | 26. C | 26. E |  | 26. B |
|  | 27. E |  |  | 27. B |
|  | 28. A |  |  |  |

# How To Score Your Exam

Your score on the actual LSAT is simply the number of questions you answered correctly (minus a small adjustment factor) scaled to a 120–180 scoring range. There is no penalty for incorrect answers other than no credit. The experimental section (in this case, one of the Reading Comprehension sections) would not count toward your score.

# Analyzing Your Test Results

Use the charts on the following pages to carefully analyze your results and spot your strengths and weaknesses. You should complete the entire process of analyzing each subject area and each individual problem for each Practice Test. Then examine these results for trends in types of errors (repeated errors) or poor results in specific subject areas. THIS REEXAMINATION AND ANALYSIS IS IMPORTANT TO YOU: IT SHOULD ENABLE YOU TO RECOGNIZE YOUR AREAS OF WEAKNESS AND IMPROVE THEM.

## Tally Sheet

Use the Answer Key to mark the number of questions you finished, got right, and got wrong in the following grid.

| | Possible | Completed | Right | Wrong |
|---|---|---|---|---|
| Section I:<br>Logical Reasoning | 24 | | | |
| Section II:<br>Reading Comprehension | 28 | | | |
| Section III:<br>Logical Reasoning | 26 | | | |
| Section IV:<br>Analytical Reasoning | 24 | | | |
| Section V:<br>Reading Comprehension | 27 | | | |
| OVERALL TOTALS | 129 | | | |

## Analysis Sheet for Problems Missed

One of the most important parts of test preparation is analyzing why you missed a problem so that you can reduce the number of future mistakes. Now that you have taken Practice Test 3 and corrected your answers, carefully tally your mistakes by marking them in the proper column.

## Reason for Mistake

| | Total Missed | Simple Mistake | Misread Problem | Lack of Knowledge |
|---|---|---|---|---|
| Section I: Logical Reasoning | | | | |
| Section II: Reading Comprehension | | | | |
| Section III: Logical Reasoning | | | | |
| Section IV: Analytical Reasoning | | | | |
| Section V: Reading Comprehension | | | | |
| OVERALL TOTALS | | | | |

Reviewing the above data should help you determine WHY you are missing certain problems. Now that you have pinpointed the type of error, focus on avoiding your most common type of error.

# Section I: Logical Reasoning

1. **A.** The argument for further supervision of vehicle use is most weakened by the statement that present safeguards are already doing the job. C and D slightly weaken the argument but do not address the overall position of the author.

2. **D.** In order to argue for a new inspection program, the author must assume that that particular program, if enacted, will be effective. C, the only other choice related to the points of the argument, expresses stated information rather than an unstated assumption.

3. **B.** Since the dietician doubts that Americans will stop eating meats or visiting bars, one may infer that he or she is referring to the latest government report warning of the risks of meat and alcoholic beverages.

4. **A.** Truman's statement is not warranted unless one assumes the U.S. capability to dominate the world; that assumed capability makes the choice between serving and dominating possible and is thus a basic assumption.

5. **E.** All of the statements except E are assumptions of the author essential to the argument. The author assumes spray paint to be the medium that graffiti painters use and implicitly abhors the possibility of a town looking like *Alice in Wonderland*. In addition, his or her desire for sign ordinances assumes that they work and are effective in deterring spray painting.

6. **D.** The questioner understands the speaker to be referring to a problem restricted to the slums and so does not understand that *genteel* refers to upper-class situations.

7. **C.** This choice most directly addresses the argument of the passage. The passage argues that for every burglar shot, there are scores of slayings of the innocent; C argues that for every burglar shot, there are scores of prevented slayings.

8. **E.** By listing high costs, the author is probably leading to the conclusion that the state's debt is being strained, a conclusion expressed in E. C contradicts the author's emphasis on high costs. A, B, and D are neither expressed nor implied by the passage; their choice would rely on extraneous assumptions.

9. **B.** This fact indicates that the passage of all the bond measures, which would take the debt over $2.5 billion, is illegal.

10. **E.** Whistler is saying that constant effort (industry) is necessary but that artwork (production) should not evidence that effort.

11. **A.** By describing in very positive terms the effects of public deliberations, the author suggests the opinion that such deliberations *should* be public.

12. **E.** The only correct choice is E; it is argued that hot weather *causes* crime. This is not mere coincidence, and the statement does not state that we *can* control the weather.

13. **B.** The argument posits an exclusive relationship between hot weather and crime. A, C, and E contradict such an exclusive relationship. D is irrelevant to the relationship, and B provides evidence supporting and strengthening the heat-crime relationship.

14. **B.** The author's final question necessarily rests on the assumption that the reader is aware of the state's intention; the author omits information expressing or explaining this intention.

15. **A.** Diagrams can sometimes be helpful:

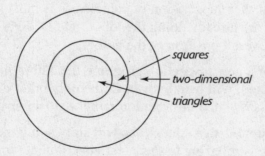

If only squares are two-dimensional and since triangles are two-dimensional, then triangles would have to be squares.

16. **A.** The passage stresses a past condition, implying a contrast with a present condition; only A, B, and E refer to present conditions, and only A refers to a *contrasting* present condition.

17. **D.** The author's implied point is that the time has passed when speakers appeared for little or no compensation. D weakens this point by suggesting that this time has *not* passed.

18. **D.** Only choice D states specifically the problem that is addressed in the initial statement, implicitly raising the question concerning the relationship between private action and public law. The examples it presents lead to the generalization that this relationship, or conflict, is difficult to resolve. None of the other choices is better because each of them

resolves the conflict one way or another, so each is inconsistent with the illogical conclusion of the initial passage.

19. **C.** By agreeing that fear is acceptable, we can also agree that fearing fear is nonsense. D, the only other choice that corresponds at all with the argument of the passage, is a weak choice because the author is arguing that fearing fear itself is acceptable.

20. **A.** Choices B and E support the author's argument by stressing further the importance of fear. C could either support or weaken the argument, depending upon whether it is taken to refer to the blanket generalization that the author attacks or to the further generalization that the author presents. D is irrelevant to the argument, which does not stress the importance of the source of fear.

21. **D.** *Chance favors the prepared mind* means that those who are *prepared* will be favored by chance—that is, will be able to take advantage of and most benefit from chance occurrences.

22. **B.** The passage juxtaposes visual images with words. Although films tend to be more visual, some successful films have been built primarily on the words of the playwright and don't include exciting visual images. Therefore, C is incorrect. D and E are assumptions unsupported by the passage. Choice A may be partially correct; however, B most logically completes the main thrust of the passage—that is, that films may be solidly built on something other than visual images and thus manifest a different style.

23. **E.** If a vitamin/mineral supplement can maintain one's health by making up for the deficiencies resulting from eating an unbalanced diet, then they must provide everything needed that food provides. This choice suggests that food and/or vitamin/minerals supplements are capable of providing the nutrients necessary for survival and that no other elements are needed to maintain a healthy body. This is the only choice that in any way supports the argument in the passage.

24. **C.** Although consumers would likely prefer to have higher picture clarity, the expenses and inconvenience of purchasing extra cables for playback exceed the value the consumer places on quality pictures. Because of these added costs of 8mm format, the consumer is likely to forego picture clarity in favor of the lower price of VHS-C and the convenience of easy playback.

# Section II: Reading Comprehension

1. **D.** According to the author, conversion to strict religious rules reduces personal autonomy by *lowering the decision-making process*.

2. **B.** The author cites as the reasons for mass conversions the need for community, residual effects of the 1960s counterculture, and (in the first paragraph) a rebellion against a *sinfully oriented society*. The word *involuntary* makes choice D incorrect; choice E is wrong, because the *author* does not envision mass conversion as salvation, though its adherents may in fact do so.

3. **C.** The passage views conversion to a cult as a means to resolve the unfulfilled need that many have for strict rules and relationships, which modern urban society appears less able to provide.

4. **E.** The author notes that while many flower children entered the mainstream, some remained, becoming even more uncertain and alienated *(anomie)*.

5. **C.** The author views conversion to religious sects as a means for an individual to fulfill important unrealized social and psychological needs, and thus would probably agree that such voluntary conversion has been going on for centuries.

6. **A.** Of the choices, *The Function of Conversion* is the most appropriate title. Choices B and D are off the mark *(involuntary* is incorrect). C is reversed; it should read, *Psychological Instability: A Cause for Conversion*. E is far too specific.

7. **E.** The primary focus of the passage is exploring the reasons mass conversions occur.

8. **C.** The author favors long-term rent control in certain instances. He or she would not agree with choices A, B, or E. Although D is true, it is not a position concerning the imposing of rent control.

9. **E.** The third paragraph of the passage lists all conflicts as relevant except choice E. Short-term tax credits were never an issue.

10. **B.** The first sentence of the fourth paragraph asserts this purpose of most rent-control ordinances.

11. **A.** Supporters of rent control can use choices B, C, D, and E. That rent controls lead to condominium conversions and thus to an even smaller supply of rental units would not support a case for rent control.

12. **C.** If there is an oversupply of available units, the landlords are more likely to lower the rental rates to obtain tenants than to raise them. Consequently, rent controls are less necessary.

13. **C.** If there is no possibility of building new rental housing, the price of the available housing is likely to rise and rent control may be appropriate. A community wishing to control population growth does not encourage new housing. New housing is generally discouraged by rent control.

14. **D.** Choices A, B, C, and E are all points opponents of rent control are likely to make.

15. **D.** Throughout the passage, the author continually criticizes the federal government and, in particular, the Nuclear Regulatory Commission, a federal agency, for ineffectiveness in maintaining and operating safe nuclear power plants.

16. **D.** The ineffective federal agency referred to is the Nuclear Regulatory Commission.

17. **B.** Although the author harshly criticizes federal government for its ineffective regulation of nuclear power plants, the author never assumes that such plants cannot be managed safely.

18. **A.** As the passage presents a harsh criticism of the federal government in its failure to protect people from the dangers of nuclear pollution, it is likely that the author may also take the federal government to task in its failure to protect the environment from the dangers of chemical pollution. Choice D is incorrect, as there is no reason to believe that additional federal safety regulations will be more effective than the current federal safety standards.

19. **D.** In the final paragraph, the author points out that the writers of our Constitution prefaced it with a preamble, articulating their concern for the general welfare of all citizens.

20. **C.** Choice C was a failing of the federal government, according to the author of the passage. The author cites a 1975 study that the NRC did, in fact, complete and from which it later withdrew its support.

21. **A.** Only choice A is correct. The courts have held that preemption was not explicitly expressed *but may rightfully be found by implication.*

22. **A.** The phrase *A basic concept for student awareness . . .* implies that the author is writing for an audience of students.

23. **C.** In the fifth paragraph, the author calls this translation into question by suggesting the many possible meanings of *euthanasia.*

24. **E.** In the second paragraph, the author discusses two developments that have contributed to the importance of euthanasia; choice E reiterates the second development discussed. Each of the other choices mentions a subject touched upon in the passage, but none of these subjects is connected so explicitly with the importance of euthanasia as a social issue.

25. **E.** Although the essay offers implied and expressed arguments for and against the legality of euthanasia, the author remains indefinite about whether it should be legalized or whether practitioners should be punished. Lines 63–64 suggest that suicide can be considered a type of euthanasia, but that possibility is rejected in the following paragraph defining the term literally; the relationship between suicide and euthanasia remains ambiguous.

26. **C.** The passage is a general summary that contains arguments but which of itself does not constitute one; therefore, A and B are weak choices. D and E are both too narrow, stressing secondary rather than primary purposes of the passage.

27. **E.** Although the author may approve of several of these ideas, the last paragraph implies only support of individuals' right to choose for themselves. Notice the use of phrases like *incurably sick* and *miserably senile.*

28. **A.** The passage asserts that the growing importance of euthanasia as a social and moral issue has partially resulted from the growth of advanced technology and coincident medical advances. Therefore, we may infer that euthanasia has not become as important an issue in less advanced regions.

# Section III: Logical Reasoning

1. **B.** The argument mentions the reduced quality of a nationally prominent outdoor attraction and advocates its protection. Only B makes a similar argument about a similar phenomenon.

2. **A.** The final statement that elders believed to possess special powers are *sometimes treated with a deference based on fear rather than love* assumes that deference is normally accorded based on love.

3. **B.** The only reasonable inference from the argument would be that the alkalies in Lake Huron may be insufficient to support Alpha Splendes.

**4. D.** *Evolution* is to *species* in the same way as *bush* is to *branches*. Just as the branches of a bush reach out every which way in varying lengths, the results of evolution (forms of life, species) have developed in irregular "branches." This is the main point of the paragraph.

**5. B.** In this question you need to find a statement that explains why yo-yo dieting is better for you than just being constantly overweight. Two of the choices are irrelevant, D and E. Two of the choices argue against this conclusion, A and C. This leaves you with B. Choice B states that yo-yo dieters eat healthier foods than do those who just stay overweight. This healthier food may lead to greater health benefits in the end.

**6. E.** The only statement that strengthens the argument is E: that endorphins are chemically similar to certain narcotics. This statement supports the argument that people can become addicted to an endorphin rush, just as people can become addicted to narcotics.

**7. D.** The science writer implies the importance of articulation disorders by mentioning how heavily they contribute to a clinician's caseload.

**8. C.** In the second paragraph, we read of his recognition that behaviorism is offensive to many people—that it does *not* have popular appeal.

**9. A.** The passage discusses the possible application of Skinner's theory to the field of human affairs and in promoting the development of humankind.

**10. D.** Since no blue-eyed swimmer is an Olympic winner, then no blue-eyed swimmer may be a freestyle swimmer, since *all* freestyle swimmers are Olympic winners. Choices B and E are false because they exclude other possibilities which may, in fact, exist.

**11. C.** All of the other choices may be conditions that the writer fails to realize. However, only C is the crucial condition: since the product was purchased *several years ago*, the twelve-month warranty is no longer valid.

**12. C.** If no speech that presents one or more facts is uninformative, any and every uninformative speech must present no facts.

**13. E.** Since all speeches intended to persuade contain few or all facts, such a speech cannot be uninformative, since an uninformative speech is *factless*.

**14. D.** The passage presumes that certain consistent patterns exist within a culture, from playgroup to society at large, from parental authority to political authority. In such a way, children are able to learn the ways of society. Choice C is not correct because the passage deals with authority, not with what is held to be of value.

**15. C.** The direct connection between cigarette smoking and coughing made in the passage is not an exclusive connection that would warrant the conclusion that because Butch has a bad cough, he's probably a cigarette smoker. Butch could have a cold. In the same way, just because diamonds have little color, we cannot conclude that a gem with little color is probably a diamond (it could be, for instance, clear glass). There is a presumption of exclusivity in both instances. Choice C is a stronger answer than A because the form of the argument is precisely the same in C and the original. Also, A is an absolute (*don't*) and C uses the word *usually* as does the original.

**16. B.** The same word may have more than one meaning, each of which may be completely different from the others. In this case, the word *ball* means two different things.

**17. A.** This question draws from a simple, explicit statement: *Socrates believed . . . that evil is fundamentally ignorance.* Each of the other choices is an unwarranted complication or extension of this statement.

**18. C.** As the passage states, Skinner cared about only *overt* or measurable behavior, not any response only *within* the organism.

**19. A.** The passage explicitly states that some followers of Watson studied behavior to understand the *workings of the mind.*

**20. E.** Choices A and B are not implied; they are explicitly stated. C is vague; the meaning of *consequentiality* is not clear. D is incorrect because the author is arguing that doing nothing has no consequences. Choice E is correct. This author says that doing nothing keeps us safe from consequences; this could be true only in light of the implication that doing nothing is not an act.

**21. B.** According to the author, the alternative to experiencing consequences is playing it *safe.* This can mean only that consequences are dangerous.

**22. B.** Burial in the fetal position is mentioned, so a connection is suggested between the fetus (unborn child) and the corpse, between birth and death.

**23. B.** The last sentence says that it is developed or interdependent economies that acquiesce to the idea that government must control economy to some extent. This leaves underdeveloped countries unspoken for and raises the possibility that they might not acquiesce to government control.

**24. B.** The paragraph states that government action may create shortages or surpluses.

**25. D.** From the information given, if five of the six children have freckles and if three of the six children are girls, at least two of the girls have freckles.

**26. E.** Since four children have blue eyes, only two children can have brown eyes to give a total of six children.

# Section IV: Analytical Reasoning

Questions 1 through 6 are most easily solved by first making a simple chart from the information given:

|       | Mon. | Tues. | Wed. | Thurs. |
|-------|------|-------|------|--------|
| Liz   | N    | N     | N    | AN     |
| Jenni | N    | AN    | N    | N      |
| Jolie | AN   | A     | N    | N      |
| Rick  | A    | AN    | AN   | AN     |

**1. C.** By referring to the chart, you can see that the conditions are met on only Wednesday and Thursday.

**2. D.** Since they could all study together only Wednesday and Thursday, Monday and Tuesday are the only possible days. Choice A is incorrect because they could study together more than twice on the two days.

**3. C.** The chart makes it clear that Liz could have at least two study partners each night.

**4. D.** This is true because Jolie and Jennie could study together Monday, Tuesday, and Wednesday.

**5. A.** Since the four could study together on Wednesday night and Thursday night, Dan would have to be available on one of those two nights. The only choice given is Wednesday night A.

**6. B.** On Wednesday afternoon, only Rick is available to study.

Questions 7 through 13 are more easily answered after constructing a simple diagram and filling in the places. Notice that you could answer some of the questions without the diagram. From the first statement, place Bernard across from the dentist.

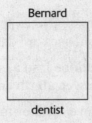

(Bernard is now obviously not the dentist.)

From the seventh statement, you could tentatively place the general practitioner and the optometrist.

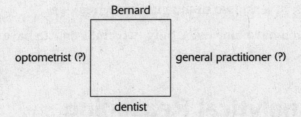

The fourth statement tells you that Carla is the general practitioner. Now you can deduce that Bernard must be the surgeon, and since Doug is not across from the surgeon (second statement), then Doug must be the optometrist.

The final placement can be made from the third statement, because Amy must be the dentist, and the optometrist (Doug) must be on Amy's left.

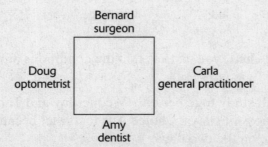

7. **D.** Since the seventh statement tells you that the general practitioner is across from the optometrist, the dentist must be across from the surgeon. This question could have been answered easily from the diagram.

8. **A.** Amy and Carla sit next to each other.

9. **C.** It is evident by referring to the diagram that Doug is the optometrist.

10. **B.** Once again, this is evident from the diagram. You could have eliminated A, C, and D easily from the third and fourth statements.

11. **E.** If the two men switch seats, Carla will now sit next to Doug, not next to Bernard.

12. **C.** If Bernard and Amy switch seats, they still sit across from each other.

13. **D.** If the two men leave the table, Carla (the general practitioner) and Amy (the dentist) remain at the table.

Questions 14 to 18 are not difficult to solve if you construct an accurate map. It is important to realize that as one moves to the left, one is going west, and moving right means going east. When traveling to the west, a person will come across the eastern border first. The map should look something like this:

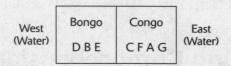

West (Water) | Bongo — D B E | Congo — C F A G | East (Water)

14. **D.** Traveling east to west, the cities would be reached in this order: G, A, F, C, E.

15. **A.** The sun rises in the east. The first city to see it would be the easternmost city, "G."

16. **E.** The sun sets in the west. The last city to see it would be the westernmost city, "D."

17. **D.** As the map shows, "B" is the capital of Bongo and "A" is the capital of Congo. City "C" is a Congo city, not a Bongo city.

18. **C.** City "E" is the city on the eastern border of Bongo, the westernmost country.

From the information given for questions 19 through 24, you can draw the following chart:

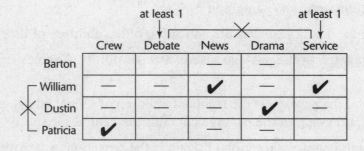

|  | Crew | Debate | News | Drama | Service |
|---|---|---|---|---|---|
| Barton |  |  | — | — |  |
| William | — | — | ✔ | — | ✔ |
| Dustin | — | — | — | ✔ | — |
| Patricia | ✔ |  | — | — |  |

Notice that since one of the four becomes editor of the newspaper, that student must be William.

19. **D.** Four credits have already been earned. Barton can join at most only two more groups: Crew and either Debate or Service (see the first fact). William cannot join Crew because Patricia won't participate with him, and Patricia can join one more: either Debate or Service, but not both (see the first fact). With the four clubs already joined, that gives a total of seven possible credits.

20. **B.** From the chart we can see that the four students have already earned four credits. But since one credit must be earned by Barton (because each students joins at least one club), the minimum total is five.

21. **B.** Although other choices may be possible, only choice B (William joins Newspaper) must occur. From the facts, one of the four becomes editor of the newspaper, and from the chart, that student must be William because the others do not join Newspaper.

22. **C.** If Barton participates in Service, then she cannot also participate in Debate (see the first fact). That leaves only Patricia, who becomes captain of the debate team.

23. **E.** If Barton participates in exactly two activities, the two will be either Crew and Debate or Crew and Service. In either case, Barton will participate in Crew.

24. **B.** In addition to the four activities already chosen in the chart, Barton could join Crew, Debate, and Service, and Patricia could also join Debate (but not Service because William is in Service—see the last fact). That totals eight class credits.

# Section V: Reading Comprehension

1. **C.** The third paragraph of the passage defines the criteria that would be applied in the past to a law threatening a suspect class.

2. **E.** Although choice D is tempting for its use of *absolutely necessary*, the phrase *what may be regarded as* is not strong enough to describe a *compelling state interest*.

3. **A.** The recognized suspect classes are race, national origin, and alienage. Religion or politics is not an issue.

4. **B.** To answer this question, you must consult the passage, not your own definitions of these adjectives. The three definitions are *rational relation to a legitimate interest* (paragraph 2), *substantial relation to an important interest* (paragraph 4), and *necessary relation to a compelling interest* (paragraph 3).

5. **B.** The issue in the Texas case was the education of the children of illegal aliens.

6. **C.** The last paragraph of the passage asserts this possibility. Choices B, D, and E are untrue.

7. **D.** The subject of the passage is the rights of children of illegal aliens, not rights of illegal aliens. The last paragraph of the passage contains the central idea.

8. **E.** The nineteenth-century definition of death is the cessation of heartbeat and breath. CPR restores both of these functions after they have stopped. The other choices describe CPR accurately but do not deal with the nineteenth-century definition of death.

**9. C.** The third paragraph cites absence of brain function as the only criterion in the most recent definitions of death.

**10. D.** Paragraph three makes clear that some states have not adopted new legal definitions of death and some use brain, heart, and breath cessation as criteria.

**11. A.** The fourth paragraph describes a decision of the Court denying that the *quality* of life may be equated with the *value*. The passage offers no information from which we can infer choices C and D and contradicts choices B and E.

**12. B.** The passage refers to these procedures in the fifth paragraph as examples of potentially very painful treatments.

**13. D.** Since CPR may now be regarded as commonplace, to deny it may be to deny ordinary care. Notice that the passage uses *may*.

**14. A.** The passage denies choice B, and choice E overstates. Choices C and D are true, but the central subject of the passage is CPR and the last paragraph makes its main point.

**15. C.** The author reveals anti-union, pro-employer sympathies throughout the passage as well as in these phrases.

**16. E.** The employer can either bargain or challenge the election.

**17. B.** The fourth paragraph discusses how a challenge can delay bargaining for as long as three years.

**18. A.** According to the third paragraph, the law requires an employer who has lost an NLRB election to bargain with the union if he or she does not appeal the results of the election.

**19. A.** The assumption in these paragraphs is a union victory in the NLRB election. Choices C and D are both true, but would be the best answer only if they were combined.

**20. C.** The passage refers to misleading campaign literature that conceals a sponsor but not to campaign literature of itself.

**21. D.** Although choice A is probably true and B and C are probably ideas the author supports, the bests choice here is D.

**22. E.** The passage refers to the damage to the Parthenon in Athens by acid rain and says nothing to justify any of the optimistic inferences of choices A, B, and C.

**23. A.** The third paragraph mentions the decline in the productivity of cultivated grain crops.

**24. C.** The reduction of the burning of fossil fuels should lead to a reduction of acid rain. A higher chimney would simply disperse the pollutants at a higher point above the ground.

**25. B.** Choices A and E are simply untrue, while C and D do not explain the effect of the sentence.

**26. B.** The passage does not deal explicitly with what effects government or contemporary political defects have on effective control of acid rain.

**27. B.** This awkward phrase simply means that pollution in one state becomes acid rain in another.

# Final Preparation: "The Final Touches"

1. Before the day of the exam, become familiar with the testing center location and nearby parking facilities.

2. You should spend the last week of preparation primarily on reviewing strategies, techniques, and directions for each area.

3. Don't *cram* the night before the exam.

4. Bring the proper materials to the test—identification, admission ticket, three or four sharpened Number 2 pencils, a watch, and a good eraser. Bring a sweater or jacket in case the test room is air-conditioned.

5. Start off crisply, working the ones you know first, and then coming back and trying the others (the "plus-minus" strategy, page 5).

6. If you cannot work a problem, at least take an educated guess.

7. Mark in reading passages, underline key words, write out information, draw diagrams, take advantage of being permitted to write in the test booklet.

8. Use the "elimination" strategy (page 6).

9. Make sure that you are answering *what is being asked* and that your answer is reasonable.

# Notes

# CliffsNotes

## LITERATURE NOTES

Absalom, Absalom!
The Aeneid
Agamemnon
Alice in Wonderland
All the King's Men
All the Pretty Horses
All Quiet on the Western Front
All's Well & Merry Wives
American Poets of the 20th Century
American Tragedy
Animal Farm
Anna Karenina
Anthem
Antony and Cleopatra
Aristotle's Ethics
As I Lay Dying
The Assistant
As You Like It
Atlas Shrugged
Autobiography of Ben Franklin
Autobiography of Malcolm X
The Awakening
Babbit
Bartleby & Benito Cereno
The Bean Trees
The Bear
The Bell Jar
Beloved
Beowulf
The Bible
Billy Budd & Typee
Black Boy
Black Like Me
Bleak House
Bless Me, Ultima
The Bluest Eye & Sula
Brave New World
The Brothers Karamazov
The Call of the Wild & White Fang
Candide
The Canterbury Tales
Catch-22
Catcher in the Rye
The Chosen
The Color Purple
Comedy of Errors…
Connecticut Yankee
The Contender
The Count of Monte Cristo
Crime and Punishment
The Crucible
Cry, the Beloved Country
Cyrano de Bergerac
Daisy Miller & Turn…Screw
David Copperfield
Death of a Salesman
The Deerslayer
Diary of Anne Frank
Divine Comedy-I. Inferno
Divine Comedy-II. Purgatorio
Divine Comedy-III. Paradiso
Doctor Faustus

Dr. Jekyll and Mr. Hyde
Don Juan
Don Quixote
Dracula
Electra & Medea
Emerson's Essays
Emily Dickinson Poems
Emma
Ethan Frome
The Faerie Queene
Fahrenheit 451
Far from the Madding Crowd
A Farewell to Arms
Farewell to Manzanar
Fathers and Sons
Faulkner's Short Stories
Faust Pt. I & Pt. II
The Federalist
Flowers for Algernon
For Whom the Bell Tolls
The Fountainhead
Frankenstein
The French Lieutenant's Woman
The Giver
Glass Menagerie & Streetcar
Go Down, Moses
The Good Earth
The Grapes of Wrath
Great Expectations
The Great Gatsby
Greek Classics
Gulliver's Travels
Hamlet
The Handmaid's Tale
Hard Times
Heart of Darkness & Secret Sharer
Hemingway's Short Stories
Henry IV Part 1
Henry IV Part 2
Henry V
House Made of Dawn
The House of the Seven Gables
Huckleberry Finn
I Know Why the Caged Bird Sings
Ibsen's Plays I
Ibsen's Plays II
The Idiot
Idylls of the King
The Iliad
Incidents in the Life of a Slave Girl
Inherit the Wind
Invisible Man
Ivanhoe
Jane Eyre
Joseph Andrews
The Joy Luck Club
Jude the Obscure
Julius Caesar
The Jungle
Kafka's Short Stories
Keats & Shelley
The Killer Angels
King Lear
The Kitchen God's Wife
The Last of the Mohicans

Le Morte d'Arthur
Leaves of Grass
Les Miserables
A Lesson Before Dying
Light in August
The Light in the Forest
Lord Jim
Lord of the Flies
The Lord of the Rings
Lost Horizon
Lysistrata & Other Comedies
Macbeth
Madame Bovary
Main Street
The Mayor of Casterbridge
Measure for Measure
The Merchant of Venice
Middlemarch
A Midsummer Night's Dream
The Mill on the Floss
Moby-Dick
Moll Flanders
Mrs. Dalloway
Much Ado About Nothing
My Ántonia
Mythology
Narr. …Frederick Douglass
Native Son
New Testament
Night
1984
Notes from the Underground
The Odyssey
Oedipus Trilogy
Of Human Bondage
Of Mice and Men
The Old Man and the Sea
Old Testament
Oliver Twist
The Once and Future King
One Day in the Life
  of Ivan Denisovich
One Flew Over the Cuckoo's Nest
100 Years of Solitude
O'Neill's Plays
Othello
Our Town
The Outsiders
The Ox Bow Incident
Paradise Lost
A Passage to India
The Pearl
The Pickwick Papers
The Picture of Dorian Gray
Pilgrim's Progress
The Plague
Plato's Euthyphro…
Plato's The Republic
Poe's Short Stories
A Portrait of the Artist…
The Portrait of a Lady
The Power and the Glory
Pride and Prejudice
The Prince
The Prince and the Pauper

A Raisin in the Sun
The Red Badge of Courage
The Red Pony
The Return of the Native
Richard II
Richard III
The Rise of Silas Lapham
Robinson Crusoe
Roman Classics
Romeo and Juliet
The Scarlet Letter
A Separate Peace
Shakespeare's Comedies
Shakespeare's Histories
Shakespeare's Minor Plays
Shakespeare's Sonnets
Shakespeare's Tragedies
Shaw's Pygmalion & Arms…
Silas Marner
Sir Gawain…Green Knight
Sister Carrie
Slaughterhouse-Five
Snow Falling on Cedars
Song of Solomon
Sons and Lovers
The Sound and the Fury
Steppenwolf & Siddhartha
The Stranger
The Sun Also Rises
T.S. Eliot's Poems & Plays
A Tale of Two Cities
The Taming of the Shrew
Tartuffe, Misanthrope…
The Tempest
Tender Is the Night
Tess of the D'Urbervilles
Their Eyes Were Watching God
Things Fall Apart
The Three Musketeers
To Kill a Mockingbird
Tom Jones
Tom Sawyer
Treasure Island & Kidnapped
The Trial
Tristram Shandy
Troilus and Cressida
Twelfth Night
Ulysses
Uncle Tom's Cabin
The Unvanquished
Utopia
Vanity Fair
Vonnegut's Works
Waiting for Godot
Walden
Walden Two
War and Peace
Who's Afraid of Virginia…
Winesburg, Ohio
The Winter's Tale
The Woman Warrior
Worldly Philosophers
Wuthering Heights
A Yellow Raft in Blue Water